ARLOTTE, BEA, VINCENT, ELENA AND ALICE, 2012

ALLEGRA AND FLOSS WITH THE SCOTTS, 1977

SYBELLA, SALLY AND GRAHAM, SARDINIA, 1987

LIZA AND HENRY, 1977

GEORGIA, JULIA AND JONATHAN, 1972

JONNY, DUNCAN AND PAULA, COLCHESTER, 1975

ANITA'S BIRTHDAY, 1975

JOHN AND NANA THORNTON, BROADSTAIRS, 1975

KAY WITH A FISH, PATTAYA, 1970

THE MANGANS & THE WOODS, MALLORCA, 1979

KAY WITH A SAUSAGE, BANGKOK, 1967

ALLEGRA AND FAMILY, DORSET, 1974

PHOTOGRAPHY BY GEORGIA GLYNN SMITH · DESIGN BY ANITA MANGAN

BOOK
4

LEON
Family & Friends

BY KAY PLUNKETT-HOGGE
& JOHN VINCENT

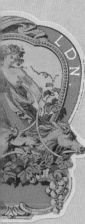

LEON

OUR FISH IS FROM SUSTAINABLE SHOALS OR FARMED ORGANICALLY

LEON

Full of Sun
35 GT. MARLBOROUGH ST.
LONDON

LEON

35 GREAT MARLBOROUGH STREET LONDON W1F 7JE   T: 020 7437 5280

LEON
LONDON
UK

FLAVOURS
FROM NATURE

LEON

35/36
Gt. Marlborough St.
London
W1F 7JE
020 7437 5280

LEON

OUR FISH IS FROM SUSTAINABLE SHOALS OR FARMED ORGANICALLY

35 GT. MARLBOROUGH ST.
LONDON

LEON   *Pure Fle*

LEON
LONDON
UK

Contents

LEON

We started Leon in order to make it easy for everybody to eat good food. And we decided that the best way to do that was to provide 'good fast food'. Food that tastes good and does you good. Food that's fun, fresh, fairly priced and swiftly served by people who smile because they want to smile.

We opened our first Leon in Soho, London, at the end of Carnaby Street just across from Liberty, the famous department store. As the queue formed outside on that very first day we had a great feeling of... you're ahead of me, aren't you... liberty.

People seemed as excited as we were about what we were doing. Of course, we made loads of mistakes but we made loads of great food, too. Enough for us to win 'Best Newcomer' at the *Observer* Food Awards.

Word got round and we got busy. So busy, in fact, that we now have thirteen branches of Leon. Our secret plan, which we've actually told lots of people, is to have Leons all over the world, making it easy for everyone everywhere to eat good food.

We have been supported by so many committed and brilliant people. Including those who come into our restaurants and eat with us. Thank you to all of you.

ABOUT KAY

Kay is a joy to work with, be with, and laugh with. Kay writes emails with 'Yippee!' and 'Yay!' Kay loves food. Not in an 'I am a foodie, you know' kind of way, but in a really loving food kind of way. She finds it tasty. She finds the people who cook it interesting. She is positive about people. Positive about cooks and chefs she loves.

Kay is really sort of Thai. Her dad worked for Ford in Dagenham and then got a job selling tractors in Thailand, so they moved to Bangkok. Kay could speak Thai before she could speak English. Which today (literally today, as we have just come back from lunch in a Thai Café) makes trips to Thai restaurants more interesting, and which as a girl helped Kay learn all the culinary tricks of the family's cook.

Kay is married to Fred, who has been rather great at managing the administration of this book. They have travelled a lot, like inquisitive people do. Kay worked as a model agent for twenty years before realizing she wanted to make her hobby her work. Kay now works with me and Henry to develop recipes for Leon, and as luck would have it she is rather good. While we have both had a hand with the concept of this book, in writing the general sections, with the identity and with pulling the team together, the bulk of the recipes are from Kay's brilliant mind and hands.

There are some people who marry loveliness and fortitude. Who live their life 'on purpose'. Kay is one.

JOHN

ABOUT JOHN

When I first met John my initial thought was … Blimey … he's loud. Big too. I still think the same thing (I'm only 5'2"), but I've learnt that the big and the loud applies to his heart, his mind and his appetite too. He's a man with big ideas. Like Leon.

John co-founded Leon with Henry and Allegra in 2004 with the simple but revolutionary idea of making fast food that's good for you. And written right through the middle of it is John's belief in better. Better meat, better veg, better nutrition.

The other big thing about John is his belief in family. Family's a big deal with Leon. That's why there are family photos all over the books, the website, you name it. John understands inherently that family's not just about blood but about community. It's about the people you like and the people you work with, too. It's broad and inclusive.

John's family are from Wembley, Edmonton and Tottenham, via Genoa, Sicily and Livorno. His wife Katie's family come from Wilmslow, Yorkshire, Holland and Brazil. Mine come from Lewisham, Ireland, Cookham and Thailand, while my husband Fred's come from Suffolk, Jamaica, Canada, Devon and Malaysia. So when we're all together, we're a bit of a United Nations of Food. UNOF. Actually – that's a pretty good idea. John's the man to make it happen. He is unbelievably creative and supportive. He has a mind like a steel beartrap. And he likes my food.

Thanks, JV.

KAY

COOKING WITH KIDS

Learning to cook is an essential part of growing up, so these are our top tips for getting your youngsters interested in cooking.

1. **Role models:** As you know, kids like to copy adults and older kids. So the more they see you or their brothers and sisters or cousins cook when they are toddlers, the more they will want to get involved.

2. **Cooking judo:** As soon as they show the first signs of interest, go with it. Don't try and force them to cook what you want them to cook. Usually it is a cake that first interests them. Make it 'their thing'. Natasha has made gluten-free pancakes her thing, and Eleanor bakes a cake that is basically a sponge cake … that is pink. And it is 'her recipe'. Last week she announced she was 'presenting it' for this cook book.

3. **Weighing with numbers:** In our experience kids like the process of weighing. Butter. Flour. Digital scales are easy and fun for them to use. A sponge cake where you have the same amount of butter and flour means they don't have to remember too many numbers.

4. **Break it down:** Teach them order from the beginning. It will help give them confidence and help them manage themselves as they get older. For example, lay out all the ingredients before you start cooking rather than rushing back and forth to the fridge.

5. **The whole routine:** Cooking, in the mind of a child, is the whole process from soup to nuts. It includes the talking about what food to make, shopping, peeling, licking the bowl, washing up, and sitting down to eat it. So let them enjoy each phase and celebrate with them as their dish is served out to everyone.

6. **Special occasions:** If you have a family gathering, let them make something that is their contribution for it. Maybe they can cook the little sausages at Christmas.

7. **Peeling can be fun:** You may be pleasantly surprised at how kids enjoy the things that you find dull. Eleanor, from the age of two, has really enjoyed peeling carrots and potatoes. It may take 20 minutes to do just a couple, but it is wonderful to watch.

8. **Find the magic:** The most fascinating dishes for kids are those that undergo the most magical transformations. Meringue. Or even popcorn.

9. **It's a gift:** Kids get most excited when what they are cooking becomes a present for a friend or member of the family.

10. **Food is relationships:** It's not really about the food is it? It is about the time you are spending with them. So make it fun. Be nice. And create some happy memories.

NUTRITION

It is easy to start an argument about nutrition. And there is a battle on in terms of who 'owns' it. Doctors? Nutritionists? Biochemists? Us, the individuals listening to our own bodies?

Here are some points of view. Our points of view:

 Eat like a scavenger with a spear. Our bodies are for the most part still made the way we lived for thousands of years. If you can't pick it or spear it, don't eat it. So, mostly eat vegetables (restrict potatoes and parsnips), berries, seeds, nuts, eggs, fresh herbs and spices, fish, chicken and a little lamb and beef. Seeds, nuts and good olive oil (or avocado oil) will give you lots of good fats, which is a GOOD THING.

 Keeping your blood sugar low is critical. A little is a lot better than a lot. Foods that raise blood sugars include glucose, table sugar, white bread and pastries, white rice (apart from basmati), beer and sugary cereals.

 Keep it varied. Eat a variety of different vegetables and proteins. You'll get a good spread of goodness, and reduce the likelihood of building up an intolerance.

 Keep your digestive system on tip-top form. By sometimes giving it a break, by chewing a lot, drinking water between meals, by doing lots of relaxing exercise, by not stressing, and only eating when you are hungry.

Never ever drink 'diet' carbonated drinks or eat 'diet' anything else. It will screw with your head and body.

Eat sea salt rather than mass-produced sodium chloride. It is full of varied minerals, unlike factory-made salt which as you know is just sodium chloride. Himalayan salt is particularly good for you.

Despite this, there is substance in the phrase 'one man's meat is another man's poison'. We are all different:

Many people would be better off without eating modern wheat and gluten. Try staying off it for a couple of weeks and see if you have more energy and more room inside your trousers. In a good way.

Many people can't digest cow's milk or cheeses made with cow's milk. Two thousand years ago, before we worked out how to milk a cow and keep it inside the village fence, almost none of us had the enzymes to break down cow's milk as adults. Many of us now do. Many of us still don't.

Your kidneys, liver, heart, intestines, pancreas are not the same as everyone else's. Your genetics, the enzymes you produce, your blood type, make you special. It is worth working out whether you need less or more of certain foods. Should you keep potassium down?

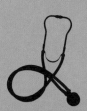

Over time, your gut may start to find it difficult to process certain foods, and you may build up an allergy. Saving up a little money to have a test to work out what makes your body respond badly may be a route to health and happiness.

Key to our recipe icons:

✓ LOW GLYCEMIC LOAD   ♥ LOW SATURATED FAT   WF WHEAT FREE

GF GLUTEN FREE   DF DAIRY FREE   V VEGETARIAN

TODAY

Welcome to today. These are recipes with one thing in mind: making it easier for you to feed your family and friends good food. Today. Dishes that taste good, do them good, and are straightforward for you to shop for and make. In between performing your varied roles.

We also hope that there are recipes here that you can teach your children. Or that your best friend Sarah, who doesn't cook, can learn. If your best friend is not called Sarah, well, we can't help you.

BREAKFAST & BRUNCH

So we know it's called the most important meal of the day. Seems a little bit harsh on the others. But we get the gist. Nutritionally, if not emotionally. The trouble is, it has become owned by companies who want to fill rectangular boxes, and our bellies, with wheat, sugar and corn.

Reclaim breakfast and make a better start to each day. And live your day as if you are the captain of your ship, just for today.

Energy Booster Smoothie

SERVES 4 • PREPARATION TIME: 5 MINUTES • COOKING TIME: NONE • ♥ WF GF DF V

The guv'nor of all smoothies. This bad boy (sorry, good boy – very good boy) is packed full of healthy omega-3 and is stuffed with all the vitamins in the alphabet. The secret weapon is avocado – one of nature's finest superfoods. As well as adding essential amino acids, it also brings a gorgeous creaminess to the smoothie.

1 **avocado**
2 handfuls EACH of any three of the following:
  hulled **strawberries, raspberries, blueberries, blackberries, bilberries, loganberries**
200ml **orange juice**
1 tablespoon **linseed**, plain or toasted
2 ripe **bananas**

1. Pop everything into the blender – it's not an exact science, just bung 'em all in – and whizz until smooth.

TIPS

* When berries are in season, use them fresh – then freeze a load to use through the winter. Just pop them straight into the blender, frozen, for a delicious chilled smoothie.

* Add soya milk instead of the orange juice if you like. If you do, add a splash of honey or agave nectar to replace the sweetness the orange juice provides.

Ralph's Mango Lassi

SERVES 2 • PREPARATION TIME: 15-20 MINUTES • COOKING TIME: NONE • ♥ WF GF V

A lovely cooling drink, especially in hot weather, this is also a great and fruity way to start the day.

300ml live **yoghurt** (low-fat if preferred), chilled
4 ripe chilled **mangoes**, peeled, stoned and chopped
30ml **clear honey**
15ml **lime juice**
2 cups of **ice cubes**
sprigs of **fresh mint**, to garnish

1. Combine the yoghurt, mangoes, honey, lime juice in a blender. Add ice and blend for 15 seconds, until smooth.

2. Serve garnished with sprigs of mint.

TIPS

* You can use buttermilk in place of the yoghurt if you prefer.

* If you can't find decent ripe mangoes, you can buy unsweetened mango pulp in cans at most large supermarkets.

* For a more savoury version, leave out the honey and add a teaspoon of salt and a couple of pinches of ground cardamom.

Lovely Ralph Monthienvichienchai is literally MADD about mangoes, so much so that he opened a dessert bar of the same name in London. If you need to know *anything* about mangoes, he's your guy. Thanks to him for this delicious recipe.

RALPH, BANGKOK, 1988

Pick 'n' Mix

SERVES 8–10 • PREPARATION TIME: 5–10 MINUTES • COOKING TIME: 15–20 MINUTES • ✓ ♥ GF DF V

Most of us of a certain age have fond memories of going with a grown-up – in Kay's case, her Grandad Valler – to Woolworth's to buy a stash of pick 'n' mix sweeties. Filling your own bag with whichever shapes and flavours you desired, sort of like a cut-price Willy Wonka...
No outing was complete without a trip to Horniman's Museum, chips and savelorys and a paper bag of Woolies Pick 'n' Mix (Kay particularly favoured the milk bottles).

So, we thought: what a great idea for breakfast. Not the sweets, obviously, but the concept. Build your own muesli or granola. With NO hidden salt, fats or sugars.

The base:
400g gluten-free **oats**
8 tablespoons **Omega seeds (pumpkin, sunflower, linseed, sesame)**
– you can buy pre-mixed at most health food stores, or create your own blend of your favourites

1. Heat the oven to 175°C/350°F/gas mark 4.

2. Put the oats and the Omega seeds on a baking tray and pop into the oven for 15–20 minutes. Stir them from time to time or until the oats and seeds are nicely toasted and golden brown – keep an eye on them, as they turn fast. Set aside to cool.

3. You now have your base. Time for the rest of it.

4. Just keep small jars of some or all of the following at hand:
   • dried goji berries • dried plums and apricots, chopped • dried blueberries and strawberries • dried strips of coconut • golden sultanas • dried unsweetened banana chips, lightly crushed • dried unsweetened mango, chopped • dates, chopped • walnuts, chopped • almonds, chopped • dried figs, chopped • raisins • soft squishy banana coins • mixed dried berries

5. Then you and the kids can add what you like. Just take a ratio of 2 handfuls of base to one handful of pick 'n' mix. And *voilà*, different cereal experience every day.

6. Serve with milk, yoghurt, fresh fruit, juice. We like a good squeeze of agave nectar or honey, too.

TIPS

* The base will keep in an airtight container, but we tend to just make up a batch every week or so.

* If you are not worried about gluten, use 400g of four-grain porridge mix instead which you can find in most supermarkets or health food stores. We like one with a mixture of barley flakes, wheat flakes, oat flakes and rice flakes, but feel free to choose your own.

* Get creative – make your own bespoke pick 'n' mix combination and store it in your own labelled jar.

Happy Cakes

(BANANA, BUCKWHEAT & BLUEBERRY HOTCAKES)

MAKES 16–20 • PREPARATION TIME: 10 MINUTES • COOKING TIME: 2–3 MINUTES PER HOTCAKE • ✓ WF GF V

Yes, eating a hotcake as good as this *is* enough to make you happy. This recipe has an added extra. And it's not illegal. Buckwheat. Rather like a sealion is not a lion, buckwheat is not a wheat at all. In fact it's more of a seed (and, strangely, it's part of the rhubarb family). There are those that say the rutin contained in buckwheat has anti-depressant qualities. We're not experts, but we feel a darn sight happier after a plate of these.

These are smallish, thickish hotcakes rather than the more traditional pancakes...

275ml **buttermilk**
2 **eggs**, lightly beaten
1 ripe **banana**, peeled and mashed
175g **buckwheat flour**
1 teaspoon **gluten-free baking powder**
100g **blueberries**
1 tablespoon **vegetable oil**
a knob of **butter**
a good pinch of **salt**

1. Put the buttermilk and the beaten eggs into a large mixing bowl and mix until combined. Add the mashed banana and mix again.

2. Sieve the buckwheat flour and the baking powder into the wet mixture and whisk in thoroughly. Stir in the salt and, very gently, the blueberries.

3. Let the batter sit for 5 minutes if you can to let it rest – it makes a fluffier cake.

4. Heat the vegetable oil and the butter in a pan over a medium heat until the butter starts to bubble slightly. Using a dessertspoon, drop dollops of batter into the pan (a 30cm frying pan can fit 4 in at once comfortably). Keep an eye on them. When you start to see them dimple on top, it's time to carefully flip them.

5. After another minute or so, flip them again and they should be ready to serve. You want them golden brown on each side, with some of the blueberries oozing purple juice. Remove from the pan on to kitchen paper, then transfer them straight on to hot plates for serving.

6. Our favourite way to serve them? Good butter, lashings of maple syrup and a side of crispy bacon.

FOOD FACT

BUTTERMILK
Traditionally the by-product of butter-making, buttermilk is the 'milk' that's left behind and is naturally low in fat. It tastes creamy and sharp, and almost yoghurt-like. It actually makes a delicious drink when you mix it in a blender with some fresh fruit.

TIPS

* If you can't find fresh blueberries, use about 50g dried blueberries.

* Try adding some ground cinnamon or grated nutmeg to the mixture, or some grated orange zest.

Kow Mun Gai
(THAI CHICKEN & RICE)

SERVES 4 • PREPARATION TIME: 15 MINUTES • COOKING TIME: 1 HOUR 55 MINUTES • ✓ ♥ DF

This is a classic Thai breakfast dish, and you'll find food stalls dedicated just to this, serving from about 4a.m. to noon, all over the country. You can spot them by the hanging chickens that adorn their stall. Kow Mun Gai tastes clean and delicious, and its zingy nam jim (dipping sauce) will wake up the most jaded palate. This is an easy version to make at home.

1 **chicken**, about 1.5kg (there will be leftovers)
1 small **onion**, peeled and chopped into chunks
4 **coriander roots**, crushed
1 clove of **garlic**, crushed
a 2cm piece of **cucumber**, chopped
1 tablespoon **fresh coriander leaves**, plus extra to garnish
275g **jasmine rice**, rinsed
peeled cucumber slices, to garnish
sea salt and **ground white pepper**

For the nam jim:
a 4cm piece of **fresh ginger**, peeled and finely sliced
2–3 **bird's-eye chillies**, sliced
a small handful of **fresh coriander**, chopped
2 tablespoons **yellow bean sauce**
2 tablespoons **rice vinegar**
2 teaspoons **sugar** (palm sugar, if you can get it)
1 tablespoon **light soy sauce**

> Whenever I go back to Bangkok, this is the first breakfast I have, usually bought on the road to the hotel from the wonderful kow mun gai guy on Soi Saladaeng. It's especially restorative after a long flight.
>
> KAY

1. Put the chicken, onion, coriander roots and garlic into a heavy-based pan, cover with water and season with the salt and white pepper. Bring to the boil, then reduce to a simmer and poach until the chicken is cooked, about 1 hour and 20 minutes or depending on the size of the chicken. (To test when it's done, jab a skewer or a fork into the thickest part of its thigh – if the juices run clear, not pinky-red, it's done.)

2. Remove the bird from the pot and set it aside. Strain and reserve all the poaching liquor and season it to taste. It should be very mild and soothing.

3. To assemble the dish, cook your rice in the usual way using 330ml of the reserved chicken liquor instead of water. Let the rice rest for 5–10 minutes before serving. In a separate pan, boil up the remaining chicken liquor.

4. Meanwhile, make the nam jim: grind the ginger to a paste using a pestle and mortar. Add the chillies and coriander. Mix together and combine well with the other nam jim ingredients, plus 2 tablespoons of the chicken liquor. Spoon out into a communal serving bowl.

5. Serve the chicken in slices beside the warm rice. Garnish with the cucumber and coriander leaves, and accompany with a small bowl of liquor and the nam jim.

CLUCK-CLUCK!

Back in the late '50s, the Egg Marketing Board spent over £12 million telling us to 'go to work on an egg', so it's hardly surprising that, for many of us, breakfast's just not breakfast without an egg or two. We couldn't agree more.

KEEPING CHICKENS

BY JOHN

Chickens provide both brilliantly fresh eggs and wonderful metaphors. Cooped-up, hen-pecked, clipping my wings, pecking order, chicken-feed, broody, ruffled feathers; they are a testament to man's close relationship with his birds.

Katie and I have been keeping chickens for three years. Here are our top tips:

The chicken or the egg?

While it is not clear which came first, I can highly recommend you buy chickens rather than eggs and hope they hatch. It's best to buy hens at 4–5 months – they will be on the cusp of laying and will be more straightforward to care for.

Some space

Your new friends will live outside in a coop, or any similar protected shack or shed. They will be happiest if you give them a perch, space to jog up and down and a cosy area with sawdust to lay eggs. (Clear this every week.)

Food & water

Keep it simple: buy chicken feed in a big sack, and some pellets. Chickens eat grit (as in very small stones) to help them digest and make good, hard eggs worthy of your breakfast table.

Out-foxing the fox. And Rambo.

I know two separate families who suddenly became fans of fox-hunting after they saw what their local foxy predators had done to their chickens. So, keep your brood safe by protecting all the sides and top of your coop with chicken wire and make sure the fox can't dig underneath by burying the wire into the ground, or have a good heavy board at the base of the wire and keep your eye out for the first sign of attempted tunnelling. At night, your chickens will naturally go inside their coop to sleep – make sure they are locked in for double security. You also need to keep your eye on some breeds of dogs. Rambo, my brother-in-law's dog (yes, he was in the army), successfully scared most of our chickens away recently. On the flipside, the little springer was very useful in sniffing them out in the hedges, while on his lead.

What chickens?

We have two bantams (one hen, one cockerel) and five farmyard hybrids whose genealogy I am too inexperienced to judge. Hybrids tend to lay well, though our neighbours are fans of Brown Leghorn and Light Sussex hens. From our six hens we get between five and eight eggs a day.

The great cockerel question

A full-size cockerel will keep you and your neighbours from waking too late. We have compromised and gone for a bantam cockerel, who manages some mild cockadoodledooing and tries to lord it over his much bigger hens.

Clipping their wings

If your hens get too good at flying, it's a good idea to get a pair of strong scissors and shorten the long feathers at the tip of their wings. You'll find diagrams on how to do this on the internet.

Loss of feathers

This winter and last winter two of our birds lost most of their feathers, to the point that they looked like they were only a few steps away from being in aisle four. They grew back, but I guess it is safest to advise that you look at proper government/Defra websites if you start to see signs of disease.

Get the children involved

I am not going to get overly sentimental here, but chickens are a great way of getting the kids interacting with animals, and understanding that eggs don't come from Sainsbury's. Ours have been named by the girls after characters from *Glee* (Rachel is a great layer). They can hold them, feed them, clean them out, lock them away at night, count and collect the eggs in the morning, and, most lovely of all, walk straight back into the kitchen and crack the eggs into a frying pan.

REGULARLY STORM YOUR CHICKEN COOP AS PART OF A '70S COP GAME

Perfect Scrambled Eggs

SERVES 2 • PREPARATION TIME: 5 MINUTES •
COOKING TIME: 5–10 MINUTES • ✓ WF GF V

In the short story *007 in New York*, Ian Fleming gives one of the definitive recipes for scrambled eggs with cream and finely chopped *fines herbes*. But let's save the full Bond for the weekend: for an everyday breakfast, we won't be quite so indulgent.

> 5 medium **eggs**
> a dash of **milk**
> a good pinch of chopped **fresh parsley**, or **basil**, or **coriander**, or **thyme** (optional)
> 1 tablespoon **butter**
> **salt** and **freshly ground black pepper**

1. Crack the eggs into a bowl, add the milk, salt and pepper (and the pinch of chopped herbs, if you're using them), and beat them all together with a fork.

2. In a heavy-based pan, melt the butter over a medium heat until it starts to foam. Pour in the eggs, and start stirring at once with a fork or a wooden spoon. Keep stirring constantly as the eggs start to come together.

3. The question now is: how runny do you like them? As the eggs begin to come together, start turning down the heat – they'll keep cooking in the residual heat. Keep stirring until you've got them just how you like them, and serve out on to plates at once. Bear in mind, the eggs at the bottom of the pan will be firmer than the eggs you serve first – just in case some people prefer them one way or the other.

4. Garnish with an extra grind of black pepper and tuck in.

Perfect Poached Eggs

SERVES 4 • PREPARATION TIME: 10 MINUTES •
COOKING TIME: 1.5 MINUTES • ✓ WF GF DF V

Kay never used to cook a lot of poached eggs until chef Bryn Williams, of Odette's in Primrose Hill, London, told her his infallible method. As he says, if you have to make fifty of the darned things a day, you want something foolproof. This is it.

> 4 **eggs**
> 1 teaspoon **salt**
> 1 tablespoon **white wine vinegar**
> 1 bowl of **iced water** – if you're not serving them at once

1. Crack the eggs into 4 individual ramekins or small dishes.

2. Fill the deepest saucepan you can find with water, add the salt and vinegar, and bring to a rolling boil. One by one, add the eggs. They will sink to the bottom of the pan, and as they do, you will see the white coming up and around the yolk. After about a minute, the eggs will start to rise up through the water. At this point, if you're making them ahead of time, scoop the eggs out with a slotted spoon and plunge them immediately into the bowl of iced water to stop them cooking. When they're cold, remove them from the water and set aside until you need them. If you're serving them now, cook them for a further 30 seconds to 1 minute in the boiling water for a firm white and a good runny yolk.

3. To reheat, bring a pan of clean water to the boil, add the cooled eggs and heat through for about 30 seconds to 1 minute.

Perfect Soft-boiled Eggs

Ease an egg into salted boiling water and cook for

3 MINUTES & 33 SECONDS

Jonny Jeffery's Fluffy Eggs

SERVES 4 • PREPARATION TIME: 10 MINUTES • COOKING TIME: 8–10 MINUTES • ✓ V

This is a fantastic Sunday breakfast recipe from Kay's friend Jonny Jeffery. It's one of those classic family recipes – something his grandmother used to cook for the kids as a treat.

4 **eggs**
4 slices of **bread**
small handful of finely grated **cheese** – **Cheddar**,
    Parmesan, **Emmental**, whichever you prefer
salt and **freshly ground black pepper**

1. Heat the oven to 190°C/375°F/gas mark 5.

2. Separate the eggs, keeping the yolks whole, and whisk the egg whites into stiff peaks.

3. Lightly toast the bread, then put the slices on a baking tray. Spread three-quarters of the egg white on to the semi-toasted bread.

4. Make a small well in the egg white on each slice of bread, and pop in a yolk – one yolk per slice. Season each yolk with salt and pepper, then cover with the remaining egg white, making sure the yolk is sealed in.

5. Sprinkle a teaspoon of grated cheese over each, then bake in the oven for 8–10 minutes, or until the top is nicely golden. This should give you a nice, runny yolk. If you prefer a firmer yolk, give it a little longer. Serve at once.

TIPS

* When Jonny cooked this for us, he served it with some delicious pan-fried chorizo, but you could try it with bacon, smoked salmon, black pudding or even some sautéed mushrooms.

* Why not, as Jonny suggests, use duck eggs instead. Then you can call it Fluffy Ducks.

* The surface area of your slice of toast is important. The smaller the slice, the higher you must pile your egg whites, which slightly affects the cooking time. We recommend slices from a large white or brown loaf.

JONNY, WITH DUNCAN AND
PAULA, COLCHESTER, 1975

When we were kids, we used to call our granny More Granny because we were always saying, 'Please can we have some more, Granny.' Her fluffy eggs were always one of my favourites.

JONNY

Deconstructed Huevos Rancheros

WITH A FRESH PEPPER & CHILLI SALSA

SERVES 4 • PREPARATION TIME: 15 MINUTES • COOKING TIME: 10 MINUTES • ✓ ♥ WF GF DF V

This Mexican breakfast dish is usually made with a fried egg, served on fried corn tortillas with refried beans and a cooked tomato and onion salsa on the side. All we've done here is pulled back on the oil by poaching the eggs, plumped for a fresh salsa, and served some simple black beans and steamed corn tortillas on the side making it brighter and lighter.

For the pepper & chilli salsa:
1 **Romano pepper**, deseeded
1 **green Serrano chilli**, deseeded
2 **tomatoes**, deseeded
1 **shallot**
2–3 cloves of **garlic**
a few leaves of **fresh basil**
a squeeze of **lime juice**
a dash of **olive oil**
salt and **freshly ground black pepper**

1 x 400g **tin of black beans**
1 teaspoon **dried oregano**
4–8 **corn tortillas**
4 **eggs**
salt and **freshly ground black pepper**

1. First make the salsa: finely chop the pepper, chilli, tomatoes, shallot and garlic, and mix them together in a bowl. Rip in the basil leaves, add the lime juice and olive oil, and season with salt and pepper. Stir together once again to make sure it's all evenly mixed. Taste for seasoning, then set aside.

2. Now empty the black beans into a pan – don't strain them, you want their liquid. Gently heat them, adding the oregano and a pinch of salt and pepper. Set aside to keep warm.

3. Wrap the corn tortillas in a clean tea towel and steam over boiling water (preferably in a tiered steamer) until they are piping hot – just only take a couple of minutes. Set aside to keep warm.

4. Finally, poach the eggs following our foolproof method on page 25. To serve, lay 1 or 2 warm corn tortillas on each plate, and top with the eggs, beans and salsa.

TIPS

* Make sure to use pure corn tortillas. We've found that a lot of the commercial tortillas available have wheat in them. To find great Mexican ingredients online, visit the Cool Chile Company at www.coolchile.co.uk.

* This is also delicious with some sliced avocado on the side, or with some of Kay's Guacamole on page 51.

Posh Poached Eggs in a Cup

WITH CHORIZO & TRUFFLED CHEESE

SERVES 4 • PREPARATION TIME: 5 MINUTES • COOKING TIME: 10–15 MINUTES

On our breakfast menu at Leon, we have what we call Egg Cups. We poach eggs in a small pot and add a few things – the don't-you-ever-take-it-off-the-menu combination is truffle, Gruyère and sliced chorizo. No chorizo to hand? It also works well with shredded ham or bacon. And once you've tried it, it'll never come off your breakfast menu either.

4–8 **eggs**
100g **chorizo**, thinly sliced
1 tablespoon **white vinegar**, for poaching
salt and **freshly ground black pepper**

For the cheese sauce:
25g **unsalted butter**
25g **gram flour**
350ml **milk**
120g **Gruyère cheese**, grated
½ teaspoon **truffle oil**

1. First make the sauce: melt the butter in a saucepan over a medium heat. Add the gram flour and whisk the two together until smooth and all the flour is incorporated in the butter and cooks out – about 2 minutes.

2. Add the milk a little at a time, whisking as you go, until you have a smooth lump-free sauce. Keep whisking until it thickens slightly, enough to coat the back of a spoon. Add the grated cheese and the truffle oil and whisk well until everything is combined and glossy, then season with salt and pepper. Set aside and keep warm.

3. In a non-stick pan, heat the olive oil over a medium heat and fry the chorizo until the slices are cooked through and crisp. Remove the chorizo from the pan and drain on kitchen paper.

4. Poach the eggs (one or two each, depending on how hungry everyone is) following the method on page 25.

5. Grind some pepper and a little sea salt on top of each egg, then pop them into their cups (I use a small teacup or similar sort of thing). Sprinkle a quarter of the chorizo on top of each egg, then pour on a quarter of the cheese sauce and grind a little more pepper on top.

6. Nummy nummy, as John's daughter Natasha used to say.

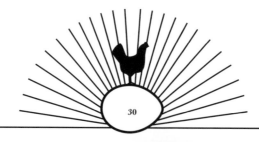

SPEEDY LUNCHES

So it turns out that I have a family motto, *festina lente*, which means 'hasten slowly'. For a long time I thought this was sillily contradictory, but now I figure it means that, just because you're in a hurry, it doesn't mean you have to cut corners. In our lunch-on-the-run times, it turns out that this is good advice. In too much haste we tend to grab something without any thought at all, forgetting that the wrong foods will make us dopey as our bodies work to digest them (it's called post-prandial torpor). But if, in the words of the wise Grail knight, we choose wisely, we can set ourselves up to face the afternoon with renewed vigour. On top of that, a good lunch helps us cut down on unnecessary snacking, which is a Good Thing.

We've worked hard to make sure that this chapter delivers on the Leon promise of fast food that's good for you. So packed herein you'll find soups, salads, wraps, dippers and, if you need that massive jolt of pasta-driven energy, a bunch of sauces to liven up any plate of spaghetti.

KAY

Roasted Pumpkin Soup with a Zing

SERVES 4 • PREPARATION TIME: 15 MINUTES • COOKING TIME: 1 HOUR 15 MINUTES • ♥ WF GF V

Creamy and comforting, this brightly coloured soup will cheer up even the darkest autumn day. To jazz it up a bit, we've added ground cumin and coriander for warmth.

1 **pumpkin**, deseeded, cut into wedges: about 1.25kg in prepared weight
3–4 sprigs of **fresh thyme**
2 tablespoons **olive oil**
725ml good **vegetable** or **chicken stock**

1–2 teaspoons **ground cumin**
1–2 teaspoons **ground coriander**
2 **limes**, cut into wedges, to serve
2 teaspoons **dried chilli flakes**, to garnish
salt and **freshly ground black pepper**

1. Heat the oven to 180°C/350°F/gas mark 4.

2. Pop the pumpkin wedges and the thyme into a large roasting tray, coat with the olive oil and season with salt and pepper. Place in the oven for 45 minutes to an hour, or until it's really soft and tender. Note, it could take even longer – every pumpkin is individual – just keep checking on it until it's done.

3. When the pumpkin is cooked, set it aside to cool, then scrape the flesh away from the skin. If it comes away in whole slices, cut it into 2cm chunks. Then put it into a pan with the stock and blitz with an immersion blender until you have a creamy consistency.

4. Add the spices and heat through for about 5 minutes. Then taste and add seasoning.

5. Serve in bowls, with the lime wedges and little piles of chilli on the side.

Leek & Potato Soup

SERVES 4 • PREPARATION TIME: 20 MINUTES • COOKING TIME: 45 MINUTES • WF GF V

This is the simplest and most soothing soup I know, and perfect for a stormy winter's day.

1 **leek**, about 350g, cleaned and sliced
350–400g floury **potatoes**, peeled and cut into chunks
2 teaspoons **sea salt**
1 litre **water**
125ml **double cream**
1 tablespoon chopped **fresh flat-leaf parsley**
freshly **ground black pepper**

TIPS

* You can also serve this cold as a vichyssoise.
* Instead of the parsley, add a couple of bunches of fresh watercress for a delicious watercress and potato soup.

1. Put the leek and potatoes into a heavy-based saucepan. Add the salt and the water and bring to the boil. Simmer until soft and cooked through, about 30–35 minutes. Then turn off the heat and, with a hand blender, whizz until smooth.

2. Add the cream and stir it into the soup, then add the parsley and a few grinds of black pepper. Taste and adjust the seasoning, and serve with crusty bread.

Kay's Minestrone Maltese

SERVES 4 • PREPARATION TIME: 20 MINUTES • COOKING TIME: 30 MINUTES

When my parents first moved to Gozo in Malta, they quickly made friends with some of the local farmers who had fields on the slopes below the house, and my mum would often buy from them directly. One of those farmers, whose name I have long since forgotten, taught her the basis of this soup. It's not a thin soup; its hearty, filling and packed with flavour.

1–2 tablespoons **olive oil**
1 **onion**, finely chopped
1 **carrot**, finely chopped
1 stick of **celery**, finely chopped
2 cloves of **garlic**, finely chopped
1 teaspoon **fresh rosemary**,
  finely chopped
1.2 litres **vegetable stock**
1 x 400g **tin of tomatoes**
1 **bay leaf**
1 piece of **Parmesan rind** (optional)

1 x 400g **tin of cannellini beans**,
  drained and rinsed
80g **little pasta shapes**
150g **peas**
1 **courgette**, cut into chunks
a good grating of **nutmeg**
70g **bacon lardons** (optional)
a few **celery leaves**, chopped
freshly grated **Parmesan cheese**,
  to garnish
salt and **freshly ground black pepper**

1. Heat the oil in a large, heavy-based pan over a low to medium heat. Add the onion, carrot, celery and garlic and soften gently for about 5 minutes. Then add the rosemary and cook for another 2 minutes or so to release its oils.

2. Now add the stock, tomatoes, bay leaf and the Parmesan rind (if you're using it), and cook for about 5 minutes. Season with salt and pepper, add the beans, and simmer for another 15 minutes or so.

3. Add the pasta, and cook, as per the instructions on the packet, until done. About 5 minutes before the end, add the remaining vegetables.

4. Finally, add a couple of gratings of fresh nutmeg and stir it into the soup, and then season to taste.

5. Serve garnished with chopped celery leaves and a good grating of Parmesan.

TIPS

* Minestrone simply means 'a big soup', so you can pretty much put into it anything you like. Instead of the peas, why not add about 400g of trimmed and sliced kale or chard?

* If I want to add some lardons, I tend to cook them in a separate pan and add them as a garnish. This means I can serve this as a completely vegetarian soup. If you prefer, you can cook the bacon right at the beginning, before the onion, to add a deep porky note to the dish.

Marion's Lentil Soup

SERVES 6 • PREPARATION TIME: 10 MINUTES • COOKING TIME: 1 HOUR • ✓ WF GF

If chicken noodle soup is Jewish penicillin, this is North London Protestant penicillin. Marion, John's mum, makes this for the family when it's cold, or when people have colds. Make lots in advance, and get it out of the freezer whenever the feeling or the need arises.

1 tablespoon **olive oil**
1 large **onion**, chopped
2 **leeks**, sliced
1 clove of **garlic**, crushed
4 rashers of **smoked streaky bacon**, chopped
2 **carrots**, sliced
3 sticks of **celery**, sliced
225g **red lentils**, washed and drained
½ teaspoon **grated nutmeg** or **turmeric**
1.25 litres **vegetable** or **chicken stock**
salt and **freshly ground black pepper**

JOHN'S MUM MARION, NICE, C.1957

1. Gently heat the oil in a large heavy-based pan. Add the onions and leeks and let them cook gently until they're transparent. Add the garlic and bacon and cook on a medium heat for another 3–4 minutes.

2. Now stir in the carrots and celery, and cook for a further 2–3 minutes. Finally, stir in the lentils, and add the nutmeg or turmeric.

3. Pour in the stock and bring the soup to the boil. Simmer with the lid on for about 30–40 minutes, or until the lentils and vegetables are tender. Season the soup with salt and pepper, then blend until smooth.

TIPS

* Marion prefers to use an immersion blender for this recipe. If you're using a stand-alone blender be very careful not to over-fill it so you don't spatter the kitchen (and yourself) with boiling soup.

* For a thicker consistency use more carrots and/or celery.

ABOVE: MARION'S LENTIL SOUP
BELOW: KATIE'S SPROUT & CARAMELIZED ONION SOUP

Katie's Sprout & Caramelized Onion Soup

SERVES 6 • PREPARATION TIME: 15 MINUTES • COOKING TIME: 1 HOUR 10 MINUTES • WF GF

Katie says: 'I love making soups. They're generally easy, and yet everyone thinks you're terribly clever. This one was the result of over-enthusiastic sprout-buying last Christmas: it was so popular it even made it on to the official Derham Boxing Day menu this year – and believe me, that hasn't changed for about three generations.'

450g **onions**, sliced
50g **butter**
1 tablespoon **sugar**
a handful of **fresh thyme**, leaves picked
450g **Brussels sprouts**, tidied up and halved
1 litre **chicken stock**
salt and **freshly ground black pepper**

1. Melt the onions in the butter. By this I mean don't brown them, just put them on the lowest possible heat in a heavy-based pan with the lid on and let them go transparent for about 40 minutes. (I found that heating them up, then putting them into the warming oven of the Aga was perfect: a low-temperature conventional oven would work, too.)

2. When they're really floppy, put them on the hob, turn the heat up a bit and add the sugar. Let them caramelize by cooking them for 5–10 minutes, stirring regularly, until they've started to colour a bit.

3. Stir in the thyme (strip the leaves off about 4 sprigs) and the sprouts, mix it all together, add a bit of salt and pepper, then add the chicken stock. (Stock cubes are naturally fine for this, though if you happen to have proper stock already made or sitting in the fridge, it will make the finished soup a notch superior.)

4. Simmer for about 10 minutes, or until the sprouts are tender. Whizz in a food processor or blender, taking care as the soup will be very hot. If you think it's looking a little thick, add a splash more stock to loosen the texture. Serve with a swirl of cream if you're feeling fancy.

KATIE, 1978

Katie is my wife and a very tremendous one. After we first met, I explained to her that she was going to marry me, and eventually the penny dropped and she did. OK, so there are some stories in between those two things, but I can tell you that in my view she would make a very good Queen of a small country. She is, in my view, pretty, interesting, interested, smart, great company, caring, a lovely Mum, good on the TV, sociable, a great team player, kind, has good posture, and I love her very much.

JOHN

The Wheel of Tomato-based Pasta Sauce

ALL DISHES SERVE 4-6 • PREPARATION TIME: 10 MINUTES • COOKING TIME: 30 MINUTES • ✓ ♥ WF GF V

The Hub of the Wheel

There's a lot you can do to change a simple tomato-based sauce into a variety of different dishes. Here's how. Two of the sauces opposite require a minor interruption to this simple process. In both cases, it comes at the onion and garlic stage.

1 tablespoon **olive oil**
1 **onion**, chopped
2 cloves of **garlic**, chopped
1 x 400g tin of **chopped tomatoes**

1 tablespoon **tomato purée**
2 teaspoons **dried basil**
1 teaspoon **dried oregano**
salt and **freshly ground black pepper**

1. In a heavy-based pan, heat the olive oil over a medium heat, then add the onion. Cook until it's soft and sweet-smelling. Add the garlic and cook for another 2 minutes or so, or until it smells like good times. Add the tomatoes, then stir in the tomato purée and the dried herbs, and season with salt and pepper…

Pomodoro è Basilico

… add a pinch of sugar to cut the acidity, and simmer the sauce for 15–20 minutes. Then rip in the leaves from a small bunch of fresh basil, and serve over the pasta of your choice. We love this with linguine or spaghetti.

All'Arrabbiata

… depending on how you like it, deseed and slice 1 or 2 red chillies and add them alongside the garlic (the second interruption). Then add the tomatoes, tomato purée, dried herbs and salt and pepper, as before.

All'Amatriciana

… the first interruption: At the very beginning, cook 70g cubed pancetta in a dry pan until it's not quite golden. Then add the onions, followed by the garlic, along with a pinch of dried chilli flakes. Then add the tomatoes, tomato purée, dried herbs and salt and pepper, as before. This is terrific with penne or rigatoni.

Papalina

… this is exactly the same as the pomodoro è basilico, except that you add 50–100ml double cream before the basil leaves, and stir it in well.

Con Tonno è Piselli

… once you've made the tomato sauce, add a drained 180g tin of tuna, ½ teaspoon dried thyme and 200g frozen peas. Reduce the sauce for about 20 minutes, and serve with conchiglie.

Zucchini

… add a pinch of sugar to cut the acidity. Then top and tail 2 courgettes and, depending on your preference, cut them into batons or rounds. After the tomatoes have simmered for about 10 minutes, chuck them in. This sauce is great with penne or fusilli.

* In all these sauces, we like to add 125ml white wine, just for that extra depth and dimension. You don't have to if you don't want to.

Wrap 'n' Roll

When we started Leon, even before we opened Carnaby Street, we made a list of all the foods that are hand-held. Burgers, sandwiches, satay sticks … you get the idea. We launched our menu with both hot wraps and cold wraps. We temporarily took cold wraps off the menu for what was meant to be a few weeks and haven't yet, seven years later, put them back on.

We have plans to fix that, because wraps and rolls make brilliant lunches.

Whether you make them in advance or let your family have the fun of preparing them real-time, they have to be one of the easiest ways of getting through a lunchtime or teatime unscathed.

As a variation on a theme, John's sister-in-law Qing (who's married to Richard in Toronto) has taught the kids to make sushi rolls. They love it, the activity, the sense of achievement and the taste. We've included her simple recipe here.

Let's wrap 'n' roll…

Fish Finger Wrap

SERVES 2 • PREPARATION TIME: 10 MINUTES • COOKING TIME: 20 MINUTES • ✓ ♥

Every kid's favourite … in a wrap.

4 **fish fingers**
2 good-quality **flatbreads**
2 tablespoons good **tartare sauce**
4–6 **gherkins**, sliced

Cos lettuce leaves, shredded
a pinch of chopped **fresh dill**
a squeeze of **lemon juice**
salt and **freshly ground black pepper**

1. Cook the fish fingers as per the instructions on the packet. If you cook them in the oven (our preferred method) you can always pop the flatbreads into the warming drawer under the oven, or just heat them up as per packet instructions.

2. Spread some tartare sauce on to the warmed flatbreads, and top with a few slices of gherkin. Add some lettuce, then the crisply cooked fish fingers. Add a little sprinkling of freshly chopped dill, season with salt and pepper, and get fancy with a squeeze of fresh lemon juice to finish. Wrap and eat.

Leon's Halloumi Wrap

SERVES 2 • PREPARATION TIME: 10 MINUTES • COOKING TIME: 6 MINUTES • ✓ V

This is based on the popular wrap we had on the menu for a while. Time to bring it back?

2 tablespoons good **mango chutney**
2 **gluten-free flatbreads**, or the **flatbread** of your choice
200g **halloumi cheese**, sliced and marinated in **olive oil**, **garlic** and **thyme**
2 **carrots**, peeled and grated
2 tablespoons **fresh flat-leaf parsley**, chopped
salt and **freshly ground black pepper**

1. Spread the mango chutney thinly on the flatbread of your choice.

2. Drain the halloumi and grill it for 3 minutes or so on each side, until golden brown.

3. Pop half the halloumi into each flatbread (heat them up if you like) and add the carrot, parsley and freshly ground pepper. And some salt if you really want it. Wrap and eat.

TIPS

* Marinate the halloumi in olive oil with a crushed clove of garlic and some fresh or dried oregano.

Natasha's Chicken Fajitas

MAKES 4 • PREPARATION TIME: 10 MINUTES • MARINATING TIME: 15 MINUTES, LONGER IF POSSIBLE
COOKING TIME: 5 MINUTES • ✓ DF

John's daughter Natasha's favourite dinner is fajitas. Saturday night, Sunday night, any night. In front of *Glee*: eleven-year-old girl heaven.

3 small **chicken breasts**, cut into strips
2 teaspoons **dried oregano**
a good pinch of **chilli powder**, or to taste
1 teaspoon **ground cumin**
1 **onion**, sliced thinly
2 **red peppers**, sliced thinly
3 tablespoons **olive oil**
4 **flatbreads** of your choice, or some **soft tortilla**
salt and **freshly ground black pepper**

1. Put the chicken, oregano, chilli, cumin, onion and peppers into a bowl with 2 tablespoons of the olive oil and mix well. Season with salt and pepper and set aside to marinate for as long as you can.

2. Heat the remaining tablespoon of olive oil in a sauté pan over a medium hob and add the chicken, onion and peppers. Cook until the onions have caught some colour, the peppers are soft and the chicken is cooked through – about 7–10 minutes. You may need to do this in 2 batches to make sure the chicken browns up nicely.

3. Serve in a flatbread or tortilla, with a bowl of the pepper and chilli salsa on the side (see page 29), or with Kay's Guacamole (see page 51).

Kay's California Rock 'n' Roll Wrap

SERVES 4 • PREPARATION TIME: 10 MINUTES • COOKING TIME: 12–15 MINUTES • ✓ ♥

This is loosely based on the idea of the California roll you get in Japanese restaurants.

300g **salmon fillet**
2 tablespoons **light soy sauce** or **tamari**
4 tablespoons **good mayonnaise**
½ teaspoon **wasabi powder** (more if you like it hot)
4 **wraps** of your choice, warmed
3 **spring onions**, shredded lengthways
1 **avocado**, sliced
1–2 tablespoons **toasted sesame seeds**
1 **lime**, quartered (optional)

1. Heat the oven to 200°C/400°F/gas mark 6 or preheat the grill.

2. Marinate the salmon in the soy sauce for a few minutes. Then either grill or bake it in the oven for about 12–15 minutes depending on its thickness, or until it's cooked (you can follow the recipe for Sweet Soy Salmon on page 116 if you like).

3. Mix the mayonnaise with the wasabi powder.

4. Put the salmon into the wrap with some shredded spring onion, sliced avocado, wasabi mayonnaise and a sprinkling of toasted sesame seeds. Serve with a wedge of lime if you like.

Prawn Satay Wrap

SERVES 4 • PREPARATION TIME: 10 MINUTES PLUS MARINATING • COOKING TIME: 10-15 MINUTES • ✓ ♥

This one should please the whole family. It's sweet, nutty, salty and a little spicy.

300g **raw peeled prawns**
2 teaspoons **Madras curry powder**
½ teaspoon **turmeric**
50ml **coconut milk**
a dash of **nam pla (fish sauce)**
4 good-quality **wraps**, warmed
Cos lettuce leaves, shredded
a good handful of **fresh coriander**, roughly chopped
½ **lime**, to serve

For the sauce:
4 tablespoons **sugar-free crunchy peanut butter**
1 tablespoon **soy sauce** or **tamari**
1 teaspoon **Madras curry powder**
a pinch of **dried chilli**
2 teaspoons **palm sugar**
a dash of **white vinegar**
1 tablespoon **coconut milk**
3–4 tablespoons **water**, to loosen

1. Put the prawns, curry powder, turmeric, coconut milk and fish sauce into a bowl and mix together. Set aside to marinate for about 30 minutes (or as long as you can.)

2. To make the sauce, put all the ingredients into a bowl and stir them until combined, adding the water a little at a time until the consistency is to your liking. If it seems a little thick, just add a little more water. Taste and adjust the seasoning.

3. Heat a grill pan and cook the drained prawns until cooked – about 8–10 minutes. Pop them straight into the warmed wraps, add a dollop or two of the sauce, and top with some shredded lettuce chopped coriander and a squeeze of lime.

Auntie Qing's Sushi Roll

MAKES 3 ROLLS, ENOUGH FOR 2 • PREPARATION TIME: 30 MINUTES PLUS COOLING
COOKING TIME: 15 MINUTES • WF GF DF

John's brother-in-law is called Richard. He's Katie's brother. He looks enough like David Cameron that we think we should start a lookey-likey agency. Richard is married to Qing. She is Chinese. With us so far? When they come over for Christmas, Qing makes sushi with the kids. It is involved enough to give them real satisfaction at having made it, it's fun to make and eat, and it's not as tricky as you might think. And at Christmas, it is an oasis of fresh exotica in amid the meaty, potato-y Yuletide carnage.

360g **Japanese rice**, rinsed thoroughly
2 tablespoons **rice vinegar**
1 tablespoon **sugar**
1 teaspoon **salt**
3 **nori** (**seaweed**) **wrappers**
2 tablespoons **mayonnaise**
½ an **avocado**, thinly sliced
½ a **cucumber**, thinly sliced
soy sauce and **wasabi**, to serve

* You will also need a bamboo mat, which you can find in most good Asian supermarkets

TIPS

* Add some cooked crabmeat to make it a California roll.
* If you want to add raw fish, make sure it's of 'sushi grade'.
* You can cool the rice with a fan to speed up the process.
* To avoid sticky fingers, keep to hand a bowl of water with a couple of drops of vinegar in it so you can rinse them when you need to.

1. Put the rice into a pan with the same volume of water and place on the heat to cook.

2. Meanwhile, mix together the rice vinegar, sugar and salt to make a rice seasoning.

3. When the rice is cooked, spread it out in a wide wooden salad bowl to cool. While it's still warm (about 40°C), sprinkle it with the rice seasoning and stir it in, spreading it through the rice, making sure it doesn't become too clumpy.

4. Lay out a sheet of nori on your bamboo mat, with its rough side facing upwards. Press a small handful of rice on to the nori and spread it evenly over the whole sheet, leaving a 2cm strip at the bottom so you can seal the wrap closed. Spread the rice with a third of the mayonnaise.

5. Mix together the avocado and cucumber, then take a third of this mixture and lay it on the mayonnaise. Try to make sure the sliced vegetables lie as closely together as possible.

6. Use the bamboo mat to roll up the sushi tightly. Keep it tight as you roll, putting pressure on all the way, otherwise it will fall apart. Chop the roll into slices – cut it in the middle first, then work out to the ends to ensure neat, elegant pieces. The rice often sticks to the knife so rinse the blade whenever you feel it's too sticky. Serve the sushi rolls with a small bowl of soy sauce and with wasabi on the side, for dipping.

④

①

SNACK PLATES

If snacks are going to be the order of the day, you really can't beat a crudité and a dip to dunk it in. Be it carrots, peppers, celery, cucumber, tomatoes or toast, homemade dips hold the key to healthy snacking. Totally transparent. What you see is what you get. And they make for a super-speedy lighter lunch, too.

① Hummus

SERVES 4-6 • PREPARATION TIME: 10 MINUTES •
COOKING TIME: NONE • ✓ ♥ WF GF V

Everybody loves hummus. Our supermarkets sell it by the tonne – literally. But have you seen what's written on the label? Try this homemade version, and cut out the additives.

> 1 x 400g tin of **chickpeas**, drained
> 1–2 cloves of **garlic**, peeled
> 2 tablespoons **tahini**
> 2 tablespoons **olive oil**
> 6 tablespoons **water**
> the juice of ½ a **lemon**
> a large pinch of **salt**
> a drizzle of **extra virgin olive oil**
> a sprinkle of **ground sumac** and/
>   or **ground cumin** (optional)

1. Just place everything except the extra virgin olive oil and the sumac/cumin in a food processor and whizz until smooth. Taste and adjust the seasoning.

2. Serve in a bowl, drizzled with a little extra virgin olive oil. Sprinkle with the sumac and/or cumin if you like.

② Lentil Masala Dip

SERVES 4-6 • PREPARATION TIME: 5 MINUTES PLUS COOLING
COOKING TIME: 10-20 MINUTES • ✓ ♥ WF GF V

Fragrant with curry and very more-ish.

> 140g **red lentils**
> 1 teaspoon **Madras curry powder**
> a pinch of **ground ginger**
> a small handful of **fresh
>   coriander**, chopped
> **salt** and **freshly ground black pepper**

1. Rinse the lentils well under running water – you want to get rid of any grit or sand. Put them into a saucepan and cover them with fresh cold water.

2. Bring to the boil and simmer for about 15 minutes, or according to the packet instructions. Drain and set aside to cool.

3. Once the lentils have cooled, whizz them in a food processor with the curry powder, ground ginger, salt and pepper. Taste and adjust the seasoning.

4. Stir in the chopped coriander and serve.

③ Tangy Cheese Dip (Cheez Whiz)

SERVES 4 • PREPARATION TIME: 10 MINUTES • COOKING TIME: NONE • ✓ ♥ WF GF V

Cottage cheese isn't just for diet fruit plates.

> 400g **cottage cheese**
> 1 clove of **garlic**, peeled and chopped
> 1 tablespoon **Worcestershire sauce**
> 1 teaspoon **tomato ketchup**
> ½ teaspoon **Tabasco sauce**
> a good squeeze of **lime** or **lemon juice**

> 1 tablespoon chopped **fresh chives**
> 4 **cherry tomatoes**, deseeded and chopped
> a small handful of **fresh coriander**, chopped
> 1 large **red chilli**, deseeded and slivered
>   (optional)
> **salt** and **freshly ground black pepper**

1. Whizz everything except the chives, tomatoes, coriander and chilli in a food processor. Taste and adjust the seasoning. You want a little spice, some sharpness and some sweetness.

2. Pour into a serving bowl and gently stir in the chives and tomatoes. Scatter some chopped coriander and the slivered chillies on top.

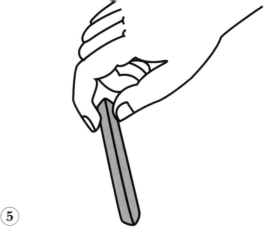

④ Kay's Guacamole

SERVES 4 • PREPARATION TIME: 10 MINUTES •
COOKING TIME: NONE • ✓ ♥ WF GF DF V

Rich, green and good for you.

> 1 clove of **garlic**, peeled
> 2 ripe **avocados**, peeled and
>   flesh scooped out
> the juice of ½ a **lime**
> 2 **spring onions**, trimmed and
>   finely chopped
> a small handful of **fresh coriander**,
>   finely chopped
> ½–1 **green serrano** or **jalapeño**
>   **chilli**, deseeded and finely
>   chopped (optional)
> 4 **cherry tomatoes**, sliced (optional)
> **sea salt**, to taste

1. Using a big pestle and mortar or a molcajete, grind the garlic to a paste. Add the avocado and pound until mashed. Add the lime juice.

2. Stir in the chopped spring onions and the chopped coriander. If using, stir in the chillies and the tomatoes. Season to taste with salt.

FOOD FACT

OH-OH-AVOCADO
Avocados are the James Bond of super-foods. They're one of nature's true wonders. Underneath that alligator-y skin lies a creamy green powerhouse of amino acids, vitamins (B, E and Kay's favourite … K) and healthy fats. They have 35% more potassium than bananas. We've even heard you can use them to wean a baby – but we're not recommending it.

FOOD FACT

SUMAC
Sumac is the fruit of a shrub that grows in the Middle East and the Mediterranean. In its dried, ground form, it's a lovely brick red and has a tart, citrusy tang.

⑤ Roasted Carrot & Cumin Dip

SERVES 4–6 • PREPARATION TIME: 10 MINUTES
COOKING TIME: 50 MINUTES • ♥ WF GF DF V

Healthy and simple. And bright orange.

> 700g **carrots**, roughly chopped
> 3 tablespoons **olive oil**
> a pinch of **cane sugar** (optional)
> 1 teaspoon **ground cumin**
> 1 clove of **garlic**, peeled
>   and roughly crushed
> 2 tablespoons **water**
> **salt** and **freshly ground**
>   **black pepper**

1. Heat the oven to 200°C/400°F/ gas mark 6.

2. Tumble the carrots in a roasting tray with 1 tablespoon of the olive oil, a pinch of sugar (if you feel like it) and a good sprinkle of salt and pepper.

3. Cover with foil and roast for 45–50 minutes, or until a knife goes through the carrots easily.

4. Remove from the oven and cool slightly.

5. Once the carrots have cooled, put them into the food processor or blender and whizz, adding the cumin, garlic and the remaining 2 tablespoons of olive oil and the water, until you have a nice creamy consistency. Serve at room temperature.

JAZZING IT UP

Every so often, I'll rummage through a kitchen cupboard for an ingredient and find cans and boxes that have been there for years. I know I'm not alone in this. So I resolved to cook more with the contents of my cupboards. The thing is, we've all been encouraged (a) to cook from fresh, and (b) to cook seasonally – both of which are Very Good Things. But we've forgotten the importance of making use of all those foods we store so we can enjoy them unseasonally. So dust off that can of sardines or beans, and let's make them new again.   KAY

Anchovies

Drain a 55g tin of anchovies. Blitz with some fresh rosemary, olive oil, lemon juice, a couple of cloves of garlic and a glug of Cognac. Serve spread on toast or use it to melt into a gravy or sauce for beef dishes.

Drain a tin of anchovies and chop them finely. Melt some unsalted butter – about 50g – in a pan. Add the anchovies and stir over a very gentle heat until melted together and smooth. Add some freshly ground black pepper and a good squeeze of lemon juice. Add a handful of halved cherry tomatoes and heat through. Toss with some cooked pasta, preferably capellini.

Tuna

Well, of course, there's the pasta sauce on page 40. But there's more we can do with the humble can of tuna.

Boil 2 or 3 large peeled potatoes. Drain and mash them well with a little butter and milk, salt and pepper. Drain a tin of tuna and mash it into the potato. Add a pinch of ground cumin and/or some finely grated lemon zest and chopped fresh parsley and/or some chopped cornichons and/or some capers and chopped spring onions – whatever you want. Form the mixture into patties and lightly coat them with a little rice flour (optional). Fry gently in a little olive oil until they're golden brown on both sides.

Toss a salad of lettuce, endive, spring onions and cucumber. Mix together a dressing of lime juice, fish sauce, a pinch of sugar, 1 chopped bird's-eye chilli and a handful of chopped fresh coriander. Drain a can of tuna and scatter over the salad. Pour over the dressing. A tasty Thai Yum Tuna.

Sardines in oil

Make a deconstructed *Sardines en Saor* – thinly slice an onion and fry it in a little olive oil until it's softened. Add a tablespoon of red wine vinegar to the pan, bubble it for a minute or two, and season with salt and pepper. Pour this over the drained sardines and garnish with raisins, toasted pine nuts and chopped parsley.

Heat some olive oil in a pan. Fry a chopped clove or two of garlic. Add a tin of drained sardines. Break them up a bit. Add a tin of tomatoes. Mix well, stirring it all together. Add a few stoned black olives, some capers and some chilli flakes or lemon zest if you like. Pour it all over pasta and top with some chopped fresh parsley.

Beans & Pulses

Beans are a treasure trove.

Bean purée – roast 2 whole bulbs of garlic by wrapping them in some foil with a dash of olive oil and a sprig or two of fresh thyme, salt and pepper. Pop into the oven at 180°C/350°F/ gas mark 4 for about 45 minutes, or until soft and cooked through. Let cool for a bit, just so you can handle them. Squeeze out the garlic into a blender or food processor. Add the drained, rinsed cannellini beans. Add 2 tablespoons good olive oil and some salt and pepper. Add some water to thin if the consistency is a little thick. Serve on toast, with a squeeze of lemon and some chopped fresh parsley, or as a side to any grilled meat – it's particularly good with the Midweek Lamb on page 130.

Kidney beans – how about a Quick 'n' Easy Jamaican Red Pea Soup? Sauté some lardons in a little olive oil with a few chopped spring onions and the leaves from a sprig of fresh thyme. Add a tin of drained, rinsed kidney beans. Add enough water to cover well. Add a small piece of Scotch bonnet chilli, with the seeds and membrane removed. Bring to the boil. When the beans are cooked, use an immersion blender or put into a food processor to blitz the soup (be careful: it will be HOT). Taste and add salt and pepper if desired. Serve with some hot sauce on the side and few chopped spring onions on top. This was Grandma Southby's (Fred's grandma's) favourite!

SALADS & BRAIN FOOD

We are what we eat, or so the saying goes. But it's only recently that scientists have begun to understand the biochemical relationships between our diet and our bodies.

Salads deliver the fibres and the raw vibrancy that cooked foods sometimes don't. That straight-from-the-earth quality that I love for both the taste, and the sheer immediacy. Pull up a beetroot. Wash it. Grate it. Squeeze over some orange juice. Sprinkle on some raisins. Eat it. Job done.

As for brain food, here we've focused on ingredients that deliver omega-3s. We're still learning how much they do for us, but all the evidence seems to point to their being key not just to the development of the growing brain, but to supporting its everyday function in adults as well. So here's to the good stuff.

KAY

Mackerel Skies Salad

SERVES: 4 AS A MAIN COURSE, OR 6 AS A STARTER • PREPARATION TIME: 15 MINUTES • COOKING TIME: NONE
✓ ♥ WF GF DF

This is FULL of omega-3 fatty acids and vitamin C, and packed with wonderful agrodolce flavour. It's quick to make, and it's colourful, too – just like a sunrise on a plate.

We've included it here as a lunch, but Kay often serves it as a starter, especially before a rich roast.

1 large **carrot**, grated into long strips
1 small **red pepper**, deseeded and sliced into strips
¼ of a small **white cabbage**, shredded
1 small **raw beetroot**, peeled and grated
½ a large **cucumber**, peeled and sliced into small cubes
200g **hot-smoked mackerel**, peeled and flaked
1 tablespoon toasted **flax seeds**

For the dressing:
3 tablespoons **olive oil**
the juice of ½ a large **orange**
3 teaspoons **red wine vinegar**
a good pinch of **sea salt**
freshly ground black pepper

1. Mix all the vegetables together in a large bowl. Mix the ingredients for the dressing together in clean jam jar, shake, and stir thoroughly into the vegetables.

2. Stir in the flaked smoked mackerel, or scatter it on the top. Up to you. Finish with the toasted flax seeds.

TIPS

* Instead of mackerel, you could use hot-smoked trout or salmon. Smoked chicken works, too.

* Sometimes Kay leaves out the fish and uses the salad as a base for leftover duck or turkey.

* Mix up the seeds – we love the crunch and flavour of toasted flax seeds, but pumpkin or sunflower would be great, too, as would walnut pieces.

A few words about mackerel

Iridescent, shiny and as fast a bullet; as fish go, it's just about as healthy as it's possible to be. It's full of omega-3 fatty acids, vitamin B12 and selenium. At the time of writing, it's one of the most sustainable fish in the sea. (Let's hope it stays that way.) And it's delicious. Smoked, grilled, steamed or roasted – and even raw – it's packed with flavour. Here are a couple of easy suggestions for mackerel-based lunchtime salads.

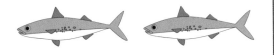

Justin Ovenden's Mackerel Ceviche

First things first: ceviche is not raw fish (that's sushi). You're cooking it chemically in the acid from the lime juice. Even so, you want *really* fresh mackerel for this, the fresher the better.

Justin says: 'This is very much a "what's in the garden, how's it looking" dish, so don't worry if you go a little over or under on the measurements.'

4 large **mackerel fillets**, skinned and boned
the juice of 1 (or 2) **limes**
1 tablespoon **olive oil** or **rapeseed oil**
1–3 **small red chillies**, finely chopped,
   depending on heat tolerance
a small handful of **fresh chives**, finely chopped
a handful of **rocket leaves**
a small handful of **fresh coriander** and/or **hyssop**
a small bunch of **baby asparagus**, lightly steamed
rock salt and **coarse ground black pepper**

1. Cut the mackerel into roughly 1cm squares or strips. Mix it with the lime juice, oil, chillies and chives, and season with salt and pepper.

2. Leave to stand for 5–10 minutes, giving it an occasional stir. Then mix it with the leaves, herbs and asparagus and serve.

FOOD FACT

HYSSOP

Hyssop is a very ancient herb with a slightly bitter, minty flavour. It's great to plant in your garden or in your windowbox because the bees absolutely love it. Be careful when you're cooking with it, though. Like sage, it has a tendency to dominate.

Mackerel is in my top three fish to eat raw. I have a wonderful memory of fishing for mackerel off the Dorset coast mid-summer with friends, when I first ventured into trying sashimi (of sorts). Since that day, I've gone fishing a hundred times, where, upon catching the first mackerel, I whip out some mustard and start sharing with whoever doesn't look at me like I'm crazy.

The love of my life, Niamh, has always expressed a distaste for this ritual, due to the fact that 'It's a bit too Boy!'. Max, our beautiful son, is a little too young for punchy mustard, so we came up with our ceviche. It's so simple, which makes it perfect to have as a quick snack, or prepare in large quantities for visiting friends and family.

JUSTIN

JUSTIN, 1975, NIAMH, 1978 AND MAXI, 2011

CONDIMENTS

Gomasio

MAKES 80G • PREPARATION TIME: NONE • COOKING TIME: 15–20 MINUTES • ✓ ♥ WF GF V

Gomasio is used a lot as a condiment in macrobiotic diets, though it originates from Japan. We use it to cut down on added salt and to add a delicious nutty flavour to soups, salads, cereals and vegetables. Sesame seeds are little treasure stores too – full of protein, iron, zinc and amino acids. You can buy gomasio in health food stores, but it's just as easy to make at home.

8 tablespoons **sesame seeds**
1 tablespoon **sea salt**

1. Heat a wide dry frying pan over a low heat and toast the sesame seeds until they are golden and fragrant – take care with this: you don't want them to burn. It should take about 10–15 minutes. Keep an eye on them and stir them occasionally.

2. Remove from the heat and let them cool.

3. Put them into a mini blender or coffee grinder with the salt and blitz until you get a coarse sprinkle – you want some texture, so don't let it get too powdery. Keep in an airtight jar and use as needed. It should keep for about 4–6 weeks.

4. Some health food stores sell ready-toasted sesame seeds, so you could just skip the toasting part. And feel free to play with the proportions.

Kay's Cajun Magic

MAKES 75G • PREPARATION TIME: 2 MINUTES • COOKING TIME: NONE • ✓ ♥ WF GF V

I used to buy Cajun spice by the case for my Dad when he lived in Gozo, Malta. He used to put it on everything, and I think we must have tried just about every brand on the market at one point or another. In the end, I realized it was much more economical (and a lot less salty) to make my own. Here it is.

2 tablespoons **ground paprika**
1–2 tablespoons good **sea salt**
½ tablespoon **ground black pepper**
2 tablespoons **cayenne pepper**

2 tablespoons **dried oregano**
2 tablespoons **dried thyme**
1 tablespoon **garlic powder**
1 teaspoon **dried roasted chilli flakes**

1. Spoon all the ingredients into a clean jam jar. Put the lid on, and shake well to combine everything thoroughly. Whizz into a powder in a mini chopper.

2. Store with your other spices until you need it.

3 Sisters Superfood Salad

SERVES 4 • PREPARATION TIME: 15–20 MINUTES • COOKING TIME: 35 MINUTES • ✓ ♥ DF V

These 3 sisters – corn, beans and squash – and their friends really pack a punch: a vibrant, delicious, colourful salad that showcases big, bold flavours influenced by the fusion of the new and old worlds.

300g **pumpkin**, peeled weight (approximately 350g before peeling), cut into 3–4cm cubes
4–6 small **purple potatoes**
a little **olive oil**
2 cobs of **corn**
4 large handfuls of **mixed leaves**
200g **sprouted beans** and **seeds**
4 **spring onions**, trimmed and sliced on the diagonal
1 **avocado**, cut into 2–3cm pieces

100g **pomegranate seeds**
a handful of **pumpkin seeds**
a good sprinkling of **gomasio** (see page 57)

For the dressing:
2 tablespoons **lemon juice**
½ tablespoon **tamari**
1 tablespoon **rice vinegar**
3 tablespoons **mild olive oil**

1. Bring 2 large pans of lightly salted water to the boil. Pop the pumpkin pieces into one and simmer until they are just tender – about 8–10 minutes. Stick a knife in to test for doneness – we want them tender but not collapsing. Drain, run under some cold water to stop them cooking, then set aside to cool.

2. In the other pan, add the whole purple potatoes and cook until just done, about 15–20 minutes depending on your spud size. Drain and set aside to cool.

3. Meanwhile, heat a griddle pan. Lightly oil the corn cobs and place them on the heated griddle. Keep turning them until they are cooked through and have some nice char-marks on the sides – about 10 minutes. Remove and set aside to cool.

4. To make the dressing, mix all the ingredients together well. Taste and adjust the seasoning if you like. We want a salty/sour/umami flavour.

5. Now take a sharp knife and, holding the corn vertically, gently slice off the kernels.

6. Divide the leaves evenly between 4 bowls and sprinkle over the sprouted seeds and beans.

7. Slice the potatoes into discs and add them, together with the pumpkin, spring onions, avocado and corn kernels, to the bowls. Scatter the pomegranate seeds over each portion.

8. Pour over the dressing and sprinkle over the pumpkin seeds and gomasio to serve.

TIPS

* This salad stands up well on its own, but you can also add grilled chicken or fish. If that's how you'd like to serve it, these proportions will serve 6.

THE 3 SISTERS

The 3 Sisters – corn, beans and squash – are central to Native American cooking and agriculture. Planting them together, in a process called companion planting, aids the growth of all three. The beans climb the corn sticks, the pumpkins' leaves shade all their roots, and the beans trap nitrogen in the soil to fertilize the corn naturally. Better yet, they're all superfoods in their own way.

P-P-PICK UP A POMEGRANATE

Ruby red and glistening, these seeds are high in anti-oxidants and full of vitamins C, E and A – more than just a pretty sprinkle…

PIMP UP YOUR PUMPKIN

We often feel for the pumpkin, dragged out just once a year to be carved into scary faces. But there is so much more to our orange friend. It's flesh is full of beta-carotene, helping to protect us from heart troubles and respiratory problems, and its seeds are bursting with zinc, iron, calcium and B–complex vitamins. So pimp up that pumpkin in as many ways as you can.

Gill's Spinach, Chorizo & Halloumi Salad

SERVES 4 • PREPARATION TIME: 15 MINUTES • COOKING TIME: 20 MINUTES • ✓

Actually, this was created by Gill's friend Jane, but it comes to us via Gill, so we're putting her name on it. It's a salad that uses up the kinds of things you find in the fridge during the summer.

> 4 large handfuls of **baby spinach leaves**, washed
> 250g **halloumi cheese**, cut into 4 pieces
> 2 fat cloves of **garlic**, crushed
> 4 tablespoons **extra virgin olive oil**
> 24 spears of **fresh asparagus**, trimmed
> 150g **chorizo**, thinly sliced
> 4 tablespoons **balsamic syrup** (see tip below)
> **salt** and **freshly ground pepper**

1. Divide the spinach between 4 large plates.

2. Lay the halloumi flat in a bowl. Mix the crushed garlic and olive oil together and pour it over the pieces of cheese leaving them for a few minutes to marinate.

3. Put a grill pan over a medium to high heat until it's very hot. Put the asparagus into a bowl and toss it in a little olive oil until it's well coated. Season with a pinch of salt, then chargrill the asparagus spears until they are nice and lined or charred. You may want to cut a few in half lengthways before putting them on the grill if they are really fat. Divide the asparagus between the bowls.

4. Now fry the slices of halloumi, pouring the marinade into the pan with them. Cook the cheese until it starts to go golden on the outside. Divide the cheese evenly between the salad bowls, laying it on top of the asparagus.

5. Finally, pan-fry the chorizo in a clean frying pan. As it cooks, it will release lots of its spicy oils. This is a good thing! When the sausage starts to get a little crispy on the outside, divide it up, along with the juices, on top of the salad bowls.

6. Drizzle over any more olive oil that you might think is needed, and finish off with a little salt, lots of pepper, and a tablespoon of balsamic syrup per serving.

TIPS

* You can buy balsamic syrup in the shops, but it's very easy to make your own. Pour 250ml of balsamic vinegar into a small saucepan, bring to the boil over a medium heat and reduce it by at least half. Set aside to cool. Then behold your syrup.

A WALK IN THE PARK

Growing up in North London suburbia, I came to value the pockets of green one could escape to on a Sunday. If Saturdays were about sport and parties, Sundays were about homework. Around the time I couldn't take any more maths or my head was too full of French, my mum would suggest an outing to Grovelands, or if we were feeling adventurous, to Forty Hall or Whitewebs or Trent Park. All of them were pockets of preserved greenery that had escaped urbanization. We would come back to the house with colour in our cheeks, clear heads and with clarity about how to tackle that equation.

Then when I was older, Katie and I would escape to Hyde Park on a Sunday afternoon. And later we'd do the same with the girls.

These recipes are, by their description, meant to be easy ways of putting things in the oven so they'll be ready to greet you with an aromatic hello when you get back.

JOHN

Chicken & Tarragon Casserole

SERVES 4–6 • PREPARATION TIME: 20 MINUTES • COOKING TIME: I HOUR 20 MINUTES • ✓

Tarragon is a perfect foil for chicken, adding sweetness and bags of flavour. No wonder it's become such a classic combination. Here, we've used it to add a big herby accent to a one-pot supper. Bundle everything in, pop to the pub or the gym for an hour (or have that walk in the park), then come home to dinner.

> 6–8 **chicken thighs**, depending on their size
> 1 tablespoon **olive oil**
> 1 **onion**, chopped
> 1 stick of **celery**, chopped
> 1 **carrot**, chopped
> 1 clove of **garlic**, crushed
> 750ml **chicken stock**
> 1 **bay leaf**
> 1 small bunch of **fresh tarragon** or 1 teaspoon **dried tarragon**
> 1 **red pepper**, deseeded and cut into squares
> 1 small **cabbage**, trimmed and cut into quarters through the root
> 1 tablespoon **crème fraîche**
> 1 tablespoon **Dijon mustard**
> **salt** and **freshly ground black pepper**

1. Heat the oven to 180°C/350°F/gas mark 4.

2. Trim any excess fat off the chicken thighs. In a heavy-based casserole, heat the olive oil on a medium heat. Brown the chicken thighs in batches on both sides, then remove and set aside.

3. Now turn down the heat and cook the onion, celery and carrot until soft. Add the garlic and cook for a further 2 minutes before adding a dash of the stock. As it bubbles up, scrape up any sticky cooking residues off the bottom of the casserole.

4. Return the chicken to the pan, along with the herbs, red pepper and cabbage. Pour in enough stock to cover the chicken, season with salt and pepper, then put the lid on the casserole and bake in the oven for about an hour.

5. Take the casserole out of the oven and place it on the hob. Remove the chicken, the cabbage and the red peppers to a plate and reduce the cooking liquor by half, boiling hard for about 3–4 minutes. Then turn down the heat and stir in the crème fraîche and the mustard.

6. Finally, whizz the sauce with a immersion blender for an extra silky finish. Taste and add more salt and pepper if necessary. Return the chicken, cabbage and peppers to the pan to coat them with the sauce and serve at once.

* You could serve this with new potatoes or some wide flat noodles.

TIPS

Chilli Game Hot Pot

SERVES 4–6 • PREPARATION TIME: 15 MINUTES • COOKING TIME: 1 HOUR 15 MINUTES • ✓

This was the product of indecision: chilli or Lancashire hot pot. Our solution – why not combine the two?

340g **stewing venison**
340g boned **pheasant breasts**
120g **pigeon breasts**
2 tablespoons **olive oil**
4 cloves of **garlic**, chopped
1 large **jalapeño chilli**, chopped
125ml **red wine**
1 x 400g tin of **chopped tomatoes**
4 teaspoons **ground cumin**
1 teaspoon **chilli powder** (or to taste)
1 teaspoon **ground cinnamon**
2 teaspoons **dried oregano**
20g **dark chocolate**
2–4 **potatoes**, depending on size, peeled and thinly sliced
50g **Cheddar cheese**, grated
a little **melted butter**, to glaze
salt and **freshly ground black pepper**

1. Heat the oven to 180°C/350°F/gas mark 4.

2. Chop the venison, pheasant breast and pigeon breast into small pieces or pulse in the blender. Be careful here: we don't want a mush. Set aside.

3. Heat the oil in a heavy-based casserole and gently cook the garlic and chilli until softened. Add the game and cook until it's browned. Add the red wine and let it all bubble, then add the tinned tomatoes, cumin, chilli powder, cinnamon, oregano, chocolate and salt and pepper. Stir and bring to a simmer. Let it simmer for about 20 minutes, then taste and more salt and pepper if necessary. Set aside to cool slightly.

4. Layer the potatoes on top of the game chilli in overlapping circles. Brush with a little melted butter and scatter half the grated cheese over the top. Pop into the oven for about 40 minutes, then add the rest of the cheese and cook for a further 5–10 minutes, or until bubbly and golden brown.

5. Serve with some simply cooked or sautéd green vegetables.

TIPS | * Feel free to make your own combination of game, or do without the game altogether and make this with lamb or stewing beef.

Joyce-Ann's Jamaican Curried Lamb Shanks

SERVES 6 • PREPARATION TIME: 15 MINUTES • COOKING TIME: 3 HOURS 30 MINUTES • ✓

When we first started talking about this book, we initially thought of writing recipes to mark events across the year. Well, the inspiration for this dish comes from a Jamaican party that Fred's mum, who moved to London in the early 60s to become a stewardess for BOAC, cooked with her flatmate Maureen to celebrate the leap year in 1964.

Back then, they were trying to make curried goat, but had to make do with mutton from the North End Road market, just around the corner from their flat on Talgarth Road. We're using lamb shanks here, simply because you'll find them easier to source than goat, kid or mutton. But if you can track some down, goat will make this dish more authentic.

4 tablespoons **vegetable oil**
6 **lamb shanks**
2–3 cloves of **garlic**, peeled but left whole
2 **onions**, chopped
4 tablespoons **Jamaican curry powder** (see opposite)
2 **spring onions**, trimmed and cut into chunks
2 **carrots**, sliced
2 large **potatoes**, peeled and cubed
1 **bay leaf**
2 sprigs of **fresh thyme**
1 **Scotch Bonnet chilli**, deseeded and finely chopped
500ml **stock**, any flavour (or 400ml if using coconut milk)
150ml **coconut milk** (optional)
the juice of ½ a **lime**
salt and **freshly ground black pepper**

JOYCE, HEATHROW AIRPORT, 1962

1. Heat the oven to 160°C/325°F/gas mark 3.

2. In a heavy-based frying pan, heat 2 tablespoons of the vegetable oil and brown the lamb shanks thoroughly over a medium heat. When they're done, pop them into a large casserole with a well-fitting lid.

3. Add the garlic cloves to the frying pan and cook until they're nutty brown, then add them to the lamb. Now add the remaining vegetable oil to the frying pan and, when it's hot, add the onions. Stir them through the oil, then add the curry powder. Cook, stirring, for about 5–7 minutes.

4. While the onions are cooking, add the carrot, potatoes, spring onions, herbs and the Scotch bonnet to the casserole.

5. When the onions are soft and deliciously fragrant, add a ladleful of the stock to the frying pan, stirring everything together into a sauce, and scraping up any cooking residues from the base of the pan. Pour over the lamb and vegetables.

6. Add the rest of the stock and the coconut milk, and season with salt and pepper. If the vegetables are not covered with the liquid, top it up with water. Bring to the boil on the hob, cover, then transfer the casserole to the oven and cook until the lamb shanks are tender – about 3 hours. Remove from the oven, skim off the excess fat, then stir in the lime juice.

7. Serve piping hot, with rice (or rice and peas). Joyce-Ann recommends serving with some good mango chutney, too.

JOYCE-ANN & MAUREEN'S MENU
29TH FEBRUARY 1964

Curried goat, made with mutton
•
Rice & peas
•
Boiled green banana
•
Steamed cho-cho
•
Pineapple with rum & nutmeg
•
Lashings of Stripe & Appletons

TIPS

* Scotch bonnets are super-fiery, so to tone down the heat just use half the chilli or put it in whole. (However, it does carry the inherent risk of the chilli exploding in the sauce, defeating the purpose.) If you want it hotter, leave the seeds in. And if you want it hotter still, add a generous slug of Grace's Hot Pepper Sauce.

* Some people wash the lamb shanks in the lime juice before they brown them. This changes the flavour of the curry, giving it a caramelized limey base note instead.

Jamaican Curry Powder

MAKES ABOUT 150G • PREPARATION TIME: 5 MINUTES • COOKING TIME: 10 MINUTES • ✓ ♥ WF GF DF V

As a general rule, you don't find any chilli in a Jamaican curry powder – they use fresh Scotch bonnets to add the heat.

2 tablespoons whole **coriander seed**
2 tablespoons whole **cumin seed**
2 tablespoons whole **fennel seed**
1 tablespoon **black mustard seed**
1 tablespoon whole **fenugreek**
1–2 tablespoons **allspice berries**
1 teaspoon **ground cinnamon**

1 teaspoon **freshly grated nutmeg**
1 teaspoon **ground ginger**
1 teaspoon **garlic powder**
½ teaspoon **mustard powder**
3 tablespoons **turmeric**
1 tablespoon **dried thyme**

1. In a dry frying pan, toast the whole seeds, fenugreek and allspice over a low heat, stirring all the time to prevent them burning, until they're really fragrant. Then grind them in a pestle and mortar or with an immersion blender and pour them into a clean, dry, jam-jar.

2. Add the remaining ingredients, screw the lid on, and shake well to combine everything together. This will keep for 4–6 weeks in a sealed container.

Storecupboard Daube

SERVES 4 • PREPARATION TIME: 30 MINUTES • COOKING TIME: 2 HOURS 30 MINUTES • ✓ DF

Our version of the Provençal classic. As the title suggests, this was born from Kay's storecupboard, the fridge and the little patch of herbs on the roof.

450g **stewing beef,** cubed
1 tablespoon **flour seasoned with salt and pepper**
1 tablespoon **olive oil**
70g **lardons**
1 large **carrot**, roughly chopped
1 large **onion**, roughly chopped
4 cloves of **garlic**, roughly chopped
1 x 55g tin of **anchovies in olive oil**, drained and chopped
4 tablespoons **brandy**

1 bottle of **red wine**
2 big sprigs of **fresh rosemary** or 1 teaspoon **dried rosemary**
a few sprigs of **fresh thyme** or 2 teaspoons **dried thyme**
2 strips of **fresh or dried orange peel**
1 x 400g tin of **chopped tomatoes**
55g stoned **black olives**
small handful of **chopped flat-leaf parsley**, to garnish
salt and **freshly ground black pepper**

1. Toss the beef in the seasoned flour and shake off the excess (see tip, below).

2. Heat the olive oil in a casserole over a medium heat and brown the meat on all sides. Remove and set aside. (You may have to do this in batches – don't overcrowd the pan, otherwise the meat will turn a nasty grey colour and you won't get the flavour.)

3. Add the lardons, carrot and onion to the oil and cook to soften slightly. After a couple of minutes add the garlic and continue to cook for a further 2–3 minutes. Then scoop everything out and set it all aside with the beef.

4. Add a splash more oil if needed, then add the anchovies, stirring and crushing them into the oil until you get a sort of emulsion. Add the brandy and let it bubble furiously for a couple of minutes, scraping up any cooking residues on the bottom of the casserole with a wooden spoon.

5. Now return the meat, lardons, and vegetables to the casserole and add the red wine, rosemary, thyme, orange peel and chopped tomatoes. Season with salt and pepper, and bring the whole lot to the boil. Then put the lid on the casserole and pop it into the oven for about 2 hours.

6. About half an hour before it's due to be ready, open it up and throw in the olives.

7. When it's ready, taste the sauce and adjust the seasoning if necessary. Serve sprinkled with chopped flat-leaf parsley, and accompanied by a bitter leaf salad and some crusty bread or boiled new potatoes.

TIPS

* Kay tosses the beef in the seasoned flour to thicken the finished sauce. If you want to use a gluten-free alternative, you can replace the flour with buckwheat.

TEA TIME & HIGH TEA

Each meal we eat together has a meaning and a particular role. Tea time is an especially interesting one to me.

At Leon, we often hear snippets of conversation from people who leave their offices or escape from shopping at around 4p.m. The occasions are ritualistic, the conversations often a little conspiratorial. This is the time of day, it seems, to talk about people you fancy, bosses who are frustrating you, and jobs you would prefer.

At home, Katie and I have recently encouraged anyone in our house at 4p.m. (even if we're not there) to sit down and spend time together, have a cup of tea and a small treat in nice cups and on nice plates. This has been partly inspired by our finding the records of a lady who lived in our house before us: back around 1910, Mary insisted on doing the same thing.

But that is not what tea time with kids is mostly like. It's about kicked-off shoes, mud on the carpet, bags slung across the sofa, and children who are hyper one day and tired the next.

Whether your tea time is Edwardian or Elizabethan (the current one), we hope you find some rituals here.

JOHN

Things on Spuds

Sometimes there's nothing better than a hot baked potato, crusty on the outside and steaming and soft within, just begging to be buttered. But what else can we do with them? Here are some suggestions from family and friends to making the best baked spuds ever...

1. Pick your potato – this is very important. Buy a variety that bakes well – floury types are best. We recommend King Edwards.

2. Heat the oven to 220°C/425°F/gas mark 7.

3. Wash the spuds under cold, running water. Shake them a little to remove the excess water, but don't dry them completely.

4. Roll them in some sea salt.

5. Pop them straight into the oven, directly on to the shelf. Bake them for about an hour – it depends on the size of your potato. Just poke them with a skewer to test for 'give' and doneness.

6. Take them out and let everyone admire their crispy exterior and wow at their fluffy insides.

Some ideas for toppings, from left to right:

Georgia's Eggy Potato

This comes from our photographer Georgia. Scoop out the insides of the cooked potato. Mash it in a bowl with a lightly beaten egg, then season with salt and pepper. Add some crisply fried bacon bits (or leftover ham or bacon from breakfast), and some cheese if you like… or any bits of cooked veggies you have to hand. Scoop it all back into the potato skin, top with a little nut of butter, and pop back in the oven for 15 minutes, or until it's puffy and crispy on top.

Cheesy Spinach & Mushrooms

This is for Abi and Issy, the vegetarian element of our team. Sauté some sliced mushrooms in a little olive oil and butter with a sprinkle of garlic and parsley, and set aside. Then wilt down a handful or two of spinach in the same pan. Season with salt and pepper. Pile it on to the potato with the mushrooms and top with some cubes of Gruyère cheese.

GEORGIA'S EGGY POTATO   CHEESY SPINACH & MUSHROOMS   ELEANOR'S TOP TABLE POTATOES

Eleanor's Top Table Potatoes

Eleanor is John's younger daughter. One day at school in year 1 she was allowed to sit on Top Table with Mr and Mrs Heinrich, and to have baked potatoes with her favourite topping: lashings of butter and EXTRA grated Cheddar cheese, salt and pepper. Now that's what we call TOP marks.

Beetroot, Crème Fraîche & Chives

Simply chop some cooked (not pickled) beetroot into cubes. Spoon a splodge of crème fraîche on to the buttered potato. Scatter over the beetroot and finish with chopped fresh chives, salt and pepper.

Herb Butter

Very retro, but very good. Make the herb butter of your choice – we use finely chopped fresh parsley, garlic, fresh thyme and salt and pepper mashed into some softened unsalted butter. If you have time, using some clingfilm or foil, roll the soft butter into a sausage shape and refrigerate it. Then just slice off a few discs and place them artfully in a steaming, split potato.

The Leftovers Spud

Baked potatoes take to leftovers like ducks to water (actually, left-over duck would be fantastic). There are plenty of recipes in this book which will provide suitable chums for your spud: the Pepper & Chilli Salsa on page 29, Natasha's Chicken Fajitas on page 44, Hummus and the Lentil Masala Dip on page 50, the Ragù alla Toscana on page 134, Salsa Verde on page 170, Diamond Jubilee Chicken on page 186, not to mention the Quick Cornerstore Curry on page 267, and many, many more. So use 'em up.

BEETROOT, CRÈME FRAÎCHE & CHIVES

HERB BUTTER

THE LEFTOVERS SPUD

Things on Toast

Toast, glorious toast. Sometimes we just need to jazz it up a bit. Here are some suggestions from the Leon team:

Brown Crab, Lemon & Dill

Spread some thick brown crabmeat on your toast. Squeeze over some lemon juice. Finish with freshly ground black pepper and a scattering of chopped fresh dill.

Marmite, Avocado, Tomato, Basil & Gomasio

Kay's favourite: spread a smear of good unsalted butter on the toast. Then a smear of Marmite. Follow this with sliced avocados and halved cherry tomatoes. Scatter a few fresh basil leaves on top and finish with a good grinding of black pepper and a sprinkle of our Gomasio (see page 57).

Graig Farm's All Meat Sausage on Fig Jam

Grill or oven-roast some sausages until cooked. Spread the toast with a thick layer of fig jam. Slice the sausages in half lengthways and lay them on the toast.

Poached Egg & Sautéd Mushrooms

Slice some mushrooms and sauté them with some garlic in a little olive oil. Sprinkle in a few leaves of fresh thyme or some chopped fresh parsley. Set aside to keep warm. Meanwhile, poach an egg (see page 25), then pile the mushrooms on the toast with the poached egg on top.

Goat's Cheese, Honey, Thyme & Walnuts

Cut a goat's cheese log (the type with rind) into slices. Place 2 or 3 slices overlapping on each slice of toast. Pop under a hot grill for 1 minute or so, just to get the cheese slightly melt-y. Drizzle with honey and scatter with chopped walnuts and fresh thyme.

Cinnamon Butter with Sliced Apples

Mix some softened butter with a good pinch of ground cinnamon and a squeeze of agave nectar. Spread on the toast. Place slices of raw apple on top. Sprinkle with a final dusting of cinnamon.

Miss Morton's Lemon Cake

SERVES 10 • PREPARATION TIME: 15 MINUTES PLUS COOLING • COOKING TIME: 50 MINUTES • V

This is a Hogge family institution, and one of those very rare occasions when Kay uses imperial measures. For some reason, it never works when she tries to make it metric. We think that's because the ghost of Miss Morton disapproves …

4oz **butter**, softened
6oz **caster sugar**
6oz **self-raising flour**
2 **eggs**
1 teaspoon **gluten-free baking powder**
4 tablespoons **milk**
grated zest of 1 **lemon**

For the icing:
juice of 1 **lemon**
12 tablespoons **icing sugar**, sieved

1. Heat the oven to 180°C/350°F/gas mark 4. Grease and line a 20 x 10cm loaf tin with baking parchment.

2. Put the cake ingredients into a food processor and whoosh it together until you have a smooth batter.

3. Pour into the cake tin and bake in the oven for about 50 minutes. To test if it's cooked, stab the cake with a skewer. If it comes out clean, it's done.

4. Remove from the oven and leave in the tin for 10 minutes. Then turn out of the tin and prick the cake all over with a fork.

5. To make the icing: mix the lemon juice and icing sugar together to make a thick white paste. Spoon and pour it over the top of the cake, smoothing it on with a palate knife. Leave to set, then devour.

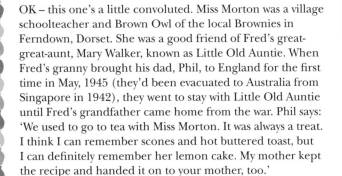

OK – this one's a little convoluted. Miss Morton was a village schoolteacher and Brown Owl of the local Brownies in Ferndown, Dorset. She was a good friend of Fred's great-great-aunt, Mary Walker, known as Little Old Auntie. When Fred's granny brought his dad, Phil, to England for the first time in May, 1945 (they'd been evacuated to Australia from Singapore in 1942), they went to stay with Little Old Auntie until Fred's grandfather came home from the war. Phil says: 'We used to go to tea with Miss Morton. It was always a treat. I think I can remember scones and hot buttered toast, but I can definitely remember her lemon cake. My mother kept the recipe and handed it on to your mother, too.'

FRED'S GRANDFATHER, ARTHUR,
HOLDING PHILIP, PENANG, 1941

Flatplanet Brownies

MAKES: 12–16 SLICES • PREPARATION TIME: 10 MINUTES PLUS COOLING
• COOKING TIME: 1 HOUR 25 MINUTES • WF GF V

Although Leon is his first love, John has also spent some time on a little concept called Flatplanet. It's his attempt at creating a little café that recreates what was best about the original coffee shops, where people experience positivity, energy, good food and good ideas.

He's not the biggest fan of modern wheat. So at Flatplanet, they cook spelt flatbreads and wheat-free and gluten-free cakes. The most popular of which is this brownie.

Originally developed by Sarah Jenkins, these brownies are now made for Flatplanet by Sarah Hale and served with amazing energy instore by Ot.

450g **butter**, chopped
450g **chocolate** (minimum 50% cocoa solids), chopped
400g **caster sugar**
6 **eggs**
300g **ground almonds**

1. Heat the oven to 120°C/250°F/gas mark ½.

2. Over a very low heat, melt the butter in a large saucepan. When almost melted, add the chocolate and stir until smooth. Remove the pan from the heat and stir in the sugar.

3. In a separate bowl, beat the eggs lightly together with a balloon whisk. Then use the balloon whisk to beat them into the pan of chocolate mixture. Add the ground almonds, again mixing them in with the balloon whisk until there are no large pockets of almonds remaining.

4. Grease and line a 26 x 36cm baking tray. Pour the mixture into the tray and bake in the oven for 1 hour 10 minutes, or until starting to crack on the surface.

5. Allow the brownies to cool in the tray for about an hour, as they will still be very soft.

6. When cool, slice, then remove from the tin and enjoy.

Courgette Fairy Cakes

MAKES: 12 • PREPARATION TIME: 20 MINUTES PLUS COOLING • COOKING TIME: 30 MINUTES • ✓ GF V

There is a small deli in John's nearest village and the thing John likes most about it is the gluten-free courgette cupcakes. This is our version of the little beauties.

125g **butter**, softened
125g **light brown sugar**
2 **eggs**
175g Bob's Red Mill or similar **gluten-free
    self-raising flour**
1 teaspoon **ground cinnamon**
½ teaspoon **ground mixed spice**
juice and zest of 1 **orange** or 1 **lemon**
175g **courgettes**, grated
25g **walnuts**, roughly chopped (optional)

For the lemon or orange cream cheese icing:
25g **unsalted butter**, softened
65g **cream cheese**
150g **icing sugar**
the juice and zest of ¼ of a **lemon** or **orange**

1. Heat the oven to 180°C/350°F/gas mark 4.
    Line a cupcake tin with paper cake cases.

2. Beat the butter and sugar together in a mixing bowl so it goes all creamy.
    Add an egg and stir it in. Do the same with the second egg.

3. Sift the flour, cinnamon and mixed spice into a bowl. Fold the flour mixture into
    the butter, sugar and eggs, stopping halfway through to add the orange or lemon
    juice and zest. Then stir in the courgettes, and the walnuts (if using).

4. Scoop a large tablespoonful of the mixture into each cake thingy and stand the
    tin on a baking tray. Put it all into the oven for 30 minutes.

5. Listen to John's wife's show on BBC Radio 3 while you're waiting.

6. Then take the cakes out of the oven and cool them on a rack if you have one, or
    anywhere clean if you don't.

7. To make the icing, beat the butter and cream cheese together, and gradually add
    the icing sugar and the lemon or orange juice and zest. Spread over the cakes
    once they have cooled down.

TIPS

* Why not make these with less sugar
and have them for breakfast?

Susanna Mattana's Amaretti Macaroons

MAKES: 24 • PREPARATION TIME: 20 MINUTES PLUS COOLING • COOKING TIME: ABOUT 40 MINUTES • WF GF V

Our friend Susanna can *really* cook. This macaroon recipe has been handed down to her from her grandma via her mother. No saint's day, wedding or feast in her native Sardinia would be complete without these glorious almond clouds …

500g **ground almonds**
300g **caster sugar**
the zest of 1 **lemon**
6 **egg whites**
24 **whole blanched almonds**

1. Heat the oven to 170°C/325°F/gas mark 3½. Line a large baking sheet with baking parchment.

2. In a large bowl, thoroughly mix the ground almonds, sugar and lemon zest using your hands.

3. In a separate bowl, beat the egg whites into stiff peaks – really give them a good seeing to! Then gently fold them into the almond mixture, a spoonful at a time, mixing carefully but thoroughly.

4. Now form them into 24 'meatballs' (as Susanna says). Place them on the baking sheet, push a blanched almond gently into the top of each one and pop them into the oven for about 40 minutes. They should be golden brown and smell gorgeous. Cool before serving.

SUSANNA, COSTA SMERELDA,
SARDINIA, 1982

Susanna Mattana and Massimo Usai run a wonderful, warm Sardinian restaurant in Putney, southwest London, called Isola del Sole. Their handmade pastas are to die for. Susanna's pumpkin or artichoke raviolis are sigh-inducing, like angels' pillows.

Massimo supports Arsenal.

CRUNCH!

SQUISH!

SLURP!

Food's not just about the look and the taste of it. Eating employs every one of our five senses. Sight, taste and smell are a big part of the process, but let's not forget hearing and touch. Mouth-feel matters. And so does sound. Half the joy of eating crackling is that glorious sound it makes as you bite into it. And think of how the perfect sauce can feel silky on your tongue.

So the following recipes are here to explore a little more of the tactility of food.

KAY

Ot's Chicken Ton-katsu

SERVES: 4 • PREPARATION TIME: 20 MINUTES • COOKING TIME: 20 MINUTES • ✓ ♥

Traditionally, ton-katsu is a breaded, deep-fried piece of pork cutlet or fillet, served sliced, with shredded cabbage and rice. But, as Ot says: 'It doesn't have to be pork. And it doesn't need to be covered in breadcrumbs or deep fried.' Here are her secrets.

4 **chicken fillets**, about 500g in total
1 good handful of **rice flour**
2 **eggs**, beaten
1 good handful and a little bit extra of **porridge oats**
   (if the oats are too big they fall off easily, so you may
   want to whoosh them quickly in a blender)
3 tablespoons **olive oil**
salt

OT & HER DAD (TAKEN BY HER MUM),
HOKKAIDO, JAPAN, 1983

1. Cut the chicken fillets into strips no more than 1cm thick and season with salt.

2. Prepare 3 shallow plates. Put the rice flour in one, the beaten eggs in the next, and the oats in the third.

3. One by one, dust the chicken pieces in the rice flour, making sure they're thoroughly covered, but shaking off any excess. Then, again one by one, dip them into the egg. Then finally dredge them through the oats. When all the pieces are well coated, shake off the excess oats. (This is a good opportunity to put the kids to work: you want a little factory assembly line, with one person in charge of dunking the chicken into each plate!)

4. Heat the olive oil in a frying pan over a medium heat and fry the chicken in batches until each piece is cooked through and golden brown. Try not to move them around the pan too much so that the crumbs stay intact.

5. Serve with lettuce and 'bulldog sauce' (see tip below).

TIPS

* Bulldog sauce can be very expensive outside Japan. So here's Ot's legendary, patented cheat's version: mix equal parts of tomato ketchup and Worcestershire sauce. Job done.

* Why not add some dried basil or parsley to the oats? You can also flavour the cooking oil by frying a little garlic, then removing it when it's golden brown, before cooking the chicken. Serve with a little salad of baby tomatoes and basil.

* YOU MUST MAKE EXTRA PIECES AND PUT THEM IN THE FRIDGE FOR TOMORROW. Ot has a point. The katsu sandwich is something else. In fact, they sell more katsu sandwiches in Japan than actual ton-katsu.

Ot is a ball of fire – she's our go-to fix-it girl, and she's John's right-hand woman. Frankly, without Ot, the wheels would've come off the bicycle long ago. She's from Hokkaido, an island in the north of Japan. And she has such a great palate, I think she's a super-taster. But she won't say if this is true. Or not.

OPPOSITE: PAPER CHICKEN BY ABI

CRUNCH!

Chef Ann's Malaysian Prawns

SERVES: 4 • PREPARATION TIME: 10 MINUTES • COOKING TIME: 20 MINUTES

Spicy-creamy prawns with a crunch.

600g big **raw peeled prawns**
2 **eggs**
cornflour, for coating (or plain flour is fine)
500ml **sunflower oil** or **vegetable oil**, plus extra to cook the egg
10 **curry leaves**
1 whole **bird's-eye chilli**
300ml **whipping cream** or **double cream**
chicken stock cube, to taste
a handful of **gluten-free oats** (optional)
salt and **freshly ground black pepper**

1. Season the prawns with salt and pepper. Beat one of the eggs in a bowl and coat the prawns, then roll them in the cornflour (or plain flour – I've used both).

2. Heat the oil in a wok or deep frying pan – when a dribble of egg dropped in sizzles then it's hot enough. Deep-fry the prawns until golden brown. (This part of the recipe can be done well in advance.) Drain the prawns on kitchen paper.

3. Heat up a frying pan with a small drizzle of oil and fry the curry leaves and the chilli for a minute. Add the cream, a sprinkle of crumbled chicken stock cube (or bouillon powder) and a pinch of salt.

4. When the cream has thickened, add the prawns and toss everything together so that they are all covered in cream and are utterly self-indulgent.

5. This dish can easily be eaten now (and believe me, it will be scoffed very quickly), but a bit of crunch is an excellent addition, so here comes the really clever bit. Separate the second egg, beat the yolk (you can freeze the white for meringues). Clean your wok, then heat 2cm of oil until very hot. Deep-fry the yolk by dribbling it very slowly into the very hot oil. Swirl it around until it looks like a kind of crispy egg bird's nest. Golden, crispy egg is what you're after. If you can get it in a single strand, you win a prize. If not, it'll taste good anyway – serve it with the prawns. If that seems a bit complicated, try quickly frying some oats (this only takes a minute at most – you want them golden, not dark!).

6. You can serve this as a starter or as part of a real feast, with maybe a meat dish and a noodle dish as well as a big bowl of rice.

> We spent last New Year in Malaysia at the rather ritzy and incredibly friendly resort of Tanjong Jara. The monsoon was late – either that or we'd misread the weather section of our travel guide – and it rained. A lot. To keep the whole family entertained, we learned to cook some local dishes. The resort's head chef, Chef Ann, taught us how to make this simple but incredibly delicious dish.
>
> KATIE

Bo-That's Bananas

SERVES: 4–6 • PREPARATION TIME: 10 MINUTES • COOKING TIME: 8–10 MINUTES • V

This is a simple version of a Thai dish called *gluay buat chee*, which means 'bananas that have been ordained as nuns'. We guess it's because they are clothed in white milk, the same colour as the robes of Thai Buddhist nuns. It's really delicious, and very simple to make.
This version is named after Kay's elephant Bo-That, because he *loves* bananas.

4–6 **bananas**
200ml **coconut milk**
a 5cm piece of **pandan (screwpine) leaf**
    or a drop of **pandan essence**
2 tablespoons **palm sugar**
a large pinch of **salt**
150ml **coconut cream**

1. Peel the bananas and slice them in half lengthways, then chop them into 3 so that each banana gives you 6 pieces.

2. Heat the coconut milk with the pandan leaf and, when it comes to the boil, add the banana pieces, sugar and salt. Bring back to the boil and add the coconut cream.

3. Gently bring back to a simmer and let the bananas cook for 3–4 minutes. Remove the pandan leaf and serve warm or at room temperature.

TIPS

* Kay eats this dish for breakfast, hot on a cold morning or chilled on a hot morning.

* You can find pandan leaves or pandan essence in most Asian stores. If you can't find them, don't worry. It's just as good without.

OPERATION DUMBO DROP, MAE HONG SON, 1993

I was in Thailand working on a Disney movie in the early 90s when I met Bo-That. We'd flown in a movie star elephant from Hollywood (yes, really), but we used Thai elephants as extras. At the end the shoot, we found a rather poorly orphaned elephant. The company bought him and put him into the safe hands of the Thai Elephant Conservation Centre in Lampang. He was just 5 at the time. He's now a strapping though rather stroppy bull elephant of 22. If I can say this about a chap who's 10 feet tall, he's still my baby boy.
KAY

Jenny's Sago Gula Melaka

SERVES: 4–6 • PREPARATION TIME: 10 MINUTES PLUS RESTING / CHILLING
COOKING TIME: 30 MINUTES • WF GF DF V

This cool, soothing Far Eastern classic comes to us from Kay's friend, the food writer Jenny Linford. It's their childhoods in a nutshell. Don't be put off by the fact that it resembles frog spawn – just focus on the fact that it tastes like nectar.

> 200g fine **sago** or **tapioca pearls**
> 200g **palm sugar (gula melaka)**
> 200ml **water**
> 2 **pandan leaves** (see tip on page 89)
> 1 x 400ml **tin of coconut milk**
> a pinch of **salt**

1. Bring a large pan of water to the boil. Add the sago pearls and return the water to the boil, stirring. Cook for 10 minutes, stirring. Then remove from the heat, cover and set aside for 10 minutes.

2. After 10 minutes the sago should be translucent. Uncover the pan and drain it in a sieve. Rinse the sago under cold running water, then leave it in the sieve to drain thoroughly.

3. Transfer the sago to 4 or 6 individual small bowls rinsed with cold water, allow to cool, then chill until ready to serve.

4. Place the palm sugar in a heavy-based pan with the 200ml of water. Tie a pandan leaf in a knot and add to the pan. Bring to the boil and simmer until the palm sugar has melted into a syrup. Strain into a jug and set aside to cool.

5. Pour the coconut milk into a pan. Tie the other pandan leaf in a knot and add to the coconut milk with the salt. Bring to the boil, then simmer, stirring, until slightly reduced. Strain into a jug, cool and chill.

6. To serve, slide a knife around each portion of sago and transfer on to serving dishes. Pour over some coconut milk and a little of the palm sugar syrup and enjoy!

Although Jenny was born in London, she spent much of her childhood living in the tropics, especially in Singapore. She says: 'My memories of it are very vivid – particularly of the food. I remember going with my cousins down to the harbour, which in those days was filled with boats, on velvety warm tropical nights. In the humid tropical heat, a serving of sago gula melaka was a treat to be savoured – the cool, jelly-like sago combined with rich creamy coconut milk and dark, bitter, caramel-flavoured palm sugar syrup. Comfort food for the tropics.'

JENNY & HER MUM LYDIA, SINGAPORE, 1970

Watermelon Slurpie

SLURP!

SERVES 2–4 • PREPARATION TIME: 10 MINUTES • COOKING TIME: NONE • ♥ WF GF V

All over Thailand, you see carts advertising *ponlamai puun* or 'spun fruit'. These icy cool fruit drinks come in myriad flavours – perfect for the tropical heat. Our favourite is the watermelon – pink, refreshing and sweet.

1 smallish ripe **watermelon** (2–3kg), peeled, deseeded
  and diced, preferably chilled
½ teaspoon **salt**
a few **ice cubes**
2 tablespoons **simple syrup** (see page 229)

TIPS

* To be Very Thai you could finish the slurpie off with a spoonful or two of sweetened condensed milk or some coconut milk.
* Add a few fresh mint leaves and a squeeze of lime.

1. Whizz up the watermelon in a blender with the salt and ice cubes. Only add the simple syrup if the watermelon is not sweet enough.

Date Shake

SERVES 2–4 • PREPARATION TIME: 5 MINUTES • COOKING TIME: NONE • WF GF V

15 whole **dates**, pitted and roughly chopped
250ml unsweetened **soya milk**
1 ripe **banana**, peeled and chopped
2–4 **ice cubes**
a pinch of **ground cinnamon**
  or **ground cardamom**

TIPS

* You could use whole milk or skimmed milk or rice milk – it's up to you.
* Try replacing the banana with a scoop of good vanilla ice cream or another handful of pitted dates.

1. Put everything into a blender and whizz on high power until it's really well blended: thick and creamy. Pour and serve immediately.

Toph's Strawberryade

SERVES 2 • PREPARATION TIME: 5 MINUTES • COOKING TIME: NONE • WF GF V

180ml **water** or **sparkling water**
1–2 tablespoons **agave nectar** (depending how sweet
  you like it – I like it tart, so I just use 1 tablespoon)
50ml **lemon juice** (about 2 lemons)
5–6 fresh **strawberries**, hulled and chopped

1. Blend all of the above together (add a little ice if you wish, but if you do, then drop the water).

LEFT TO RIGHT: DATE SHAKE; WATERMELON SLURPIE; TOPH'S STRAWBERRYADE

OOH HONEY HONEY!

THE BENEFITS OF HONEY BY JOHN

OK, so I like it when Katie dresses up. What can I tell you. But that is not why I bought Katie a beehive for her birthday last year. Apart from doing what we can to protect the bee population, and apart from the joy of being so connected with one's surroundings, honey is rich in vital life-giving nutrients.

There's a lot of research going on, and views will continue to develop. Here's what I know so far:

Honeys are not created equal
The honeys at the top of their game are the raw, unheated, unprocessed ones. They are darker in colour and, unless you have your own hive, more expensive. Unfortunately, when mass-produced honey is made it's heated and processed, and this means that the vitamins and enzymes and other good things are pretty much destroyed.

The best of the best
Apart from locally made honey, the honey with the best reputation today is Manuka honey, a natural honey from New Zealand which scores highly for its antibacterial and antiseptic properties. Vying for the top spot is eucalyptus honey, aka stringy bark honey, which is made by adding eucalyptus oil to natural honey, and this has become popular as an antibacterial and anti-inflammatory and even as an anti-depressant.

Honey & blood sugar
Let's start with the bad news. Mass-produced honey is no better for you than sugar or syrup. Honey comprises 40% fructose (low GI), 30% glucose (very high GI) and 1% sucrose and 9% other sugars. Which means it has a similar make-up to inverted sugar syrup, and around a net GI of 60, which is the same as sucrose (table sugar). The good news: some natural honeys have low GIs because of the balance of sugars. Look for locust honey (not made from locusts) with a GI of 32, yellow box honey with a GI of 35 and stringy bark honey with a GI of 44. So these are the best honeys to either cook with or use as a sweetener.

The treasure chest
Beyond the sugars, however, honey provides a small but rich treasure chest.

It's not so much about depth as breadth. Whereas table sugar has no nutritional benefit, a good honey has over 600 natural ingredients – principally vitamins, minerals, enzymes and anti-oxidants. Vitamins B1, B2, B3, B5, B6 and B9 (I have matured enough to resist any bee jokes) and vitamin C. Minerals include iron, zinc, manganese, copper, calcium, potassium, sodium, magnesium and phosphorus. Honey also contains eighteen of the twenty-two amino acids humans need – but admittedly only in small quantities. Manuka honey, almost uniquely, has wound-healing powers inside the body. Take a look at the work of Professor Peter Molan at the University of Waikato in New Zealand.

Local honey & prevention of allergies
When Katie came back from her first bee-keeping lesson (she only got stung once), one of the things that struck me were the claims about the anti-allergenic effects of eating natural honey that has been produced locally. The theory is that the bees have used pollen from all the local flowers and provide you with a small, almost vaccine-like, amount of local pollen that protects you from developing allergic reactions. There is some research to support this, and anecdotal evidence, but more would be welcome.

Topical antiseptic
There are now many people (scientists with white coats and normal people with jeans and trainers) who use the raw Manuka and eucalyptus honeys for cleaning wounds and cuts and sores. There is now consensus that it has good, practical antiseptic, anti-fungal, anti-inflammatory and anti-microbial properties. In Australia and other countries it is used to heal burns. But I suggest you do your own research.

Tiger's Milk

SERVES: 1 • PREPARATION TIME: 3 MINUTES • COOKING TIME: 2–3 MINUTES • WF GF V

Tiger, Tiger, burning bright … No, no — not THAT kind of tiger! You think we're mad enough to try to milk one? No, this was the only way anyone could get the small Kay to drink milk. The tale went that it was 'tiger's milk' because it was stripy … Kay can't for the life of her believe that she fell for that one! The honey 'stripes' disappear after about three seconds, so she must have been an extraordinarily gullible child!

She says: 'It wasn't until I was recreating this that I discovered that the mixture of cinnamon, honey and warm milk has a mildly soporific effect, perfect for pre-bedtime imbibing. It has been firmly reinstated here, stripes or no stripes…'

Adults could add a tot of something fortifying …

1 mug of **milk**
1 small **stick of cinnamon**
1 tablespoon **honey**
an extra pinch of **ground cinnamon** (optional)

1. Heat the milk in a pan until it's just warm – you don't want it too hot. Then use an immersion blender to froth the milk. This guarantees you will get stripes.

2. Pop the cinnamon stick into the mug and pour the warmed milk over it. Now – watch for it – drizzle the spoonful of honey into the milk, from a height, in concentric circles. See those stripes? Stir it in with the cinnamon stick and add an extra pinch of cinnamon, if you like.

3. Sweet dreams.

LUNE & KAY, 1965

Lune was a huge part of our family, and was my nanny when I was growing up. She was also the manufacturer of this particular tall tale. We adored each other. Except for when she tried to comb the tangles out of my perpetually wayward hair. Then I wasn't so keen.
KAY

Spiced Honey & Orange Cake

MAKES: 18-24 PIECES • PREPARATION TIME: 15 MINUTES • COOKING TIME: 2 HOURS • V

Kay's husband Fred is obsessed with those gooey, sticky but oh-so-good honey cakes sold in Middle Eastern bakeries. He often reminisces, misty-eyed, about the ones he had when travelling through Lebanon and Syria… This one has the taste he remembers, but without the flour. It's a moist, dense cake, drenched in honey and orange flower syrup. Best served in small squares with mint tea or strong coffee. Or eaten straight out of the tin, as seems to be the habit with our friends …

1 large **orange**
3 **eggs**
200g **golden caster sugar**
1 tablespoon **orange blossom honey**
150g **ground almonds**
50g **walnuts**, ground
2 tablespoons **buckwheat flour**
1 teaspoon **gluten-free baking powder**
¼ teaspoon **ground cinnamon**
¼ teaspoon **ground ginger**
the seeds from 8–10 **cardamom pods**,
   lightly crushed
a pinch of **salt**

For the syrup:
4 tablespoons **orange blossom honey**
2 tablespoons **orange flower water**

1. Pop the orange into a large pan of boiling water. Bring back to the boil and simmer for 50 minutes to 1 hour, until tender. Drain and set aside to cool slightly. Cut the orange into quarters, remove any seeds and place in a food processor. Blend until smooth.

2. Heat the oven to 180°C/350°F/gas mark 4. Grease a 23 x 23cm cake tin and line with greaseproof paper.

3. Put the eggs and sugar into a bowl and beat together. Add the tablespoon of honey and beat again. Add the ground almonds and walnuts, the buckwheat flour and the spices. Add the puréed orange and stir well to combine.

4. Scrape the mixture into the prepared tin, then pop it into the oven for 50–60 minutes, or until a little springy and deep golden-brown. Cool completely in its tin.

5. To make the syrup, heat the honey and orange flower water in a saucepan over a gentle heat until combined.

6. When the cake has cooled, lift it out of the tin keeping it on its greaseproof paper, then drizzle the syrup over it with a spoon (if you try to pour it directly from the pan, it tends to gloumph – technical term – out in a big splodge.) Leave to soak in, then cut into squares and serve.

John's Ultimate Cold-Buster

SERVES 1 • PREPARATION TIME: 5 MINUTES • COOKING TIME: NONE • WF GF V

There aren't many upsides to being ill, but this is one of them. In fact, I often have one of these just in case I might be going to get ill. The posher the glass, the better it tastes. Try it in one of those bulbous-y, tallish brandy type glasses. For kids, leave out the brandy, I guess.

> 1 teaspoon **Manuka honey**
> a mug of **hot water** (i.e. boiled water that has cooled a little)
> ½ a slice of **orange** with 8–12 **cloves** spiked into it
>   (where the segments meet the rind)
> 1 stick of **cinnamon**
> a slug of **brandy** or **your favourite sticky alcohol**
>   (Cointreau or Glayva perhaps)

1. Stir the honey into the hot water. Then pop in the slice of orange with its cloves on.

2. Add the cinnamon stick and then the brandy to taste. Not hard. Very good.

Kay's Hard Core Cold-Buster

SERVES 1 • PREPARATION TIME: 5 MINUTES • COOKING TIME: 10 MINUTES • ♥ WF GF V

This sounds so horrible, but truly, it's not. I got it from a naturopath when I was in college, and it's never failed me. Just take it before bed when you have a stinker of a cold. Yes, you may sweat garlic through the night, but you'll wake up feeling tons better.

> 2 mugs of **water**
> 20 cloves of **garlic**, peeled
> 2 teaspoons **dried sage**
> 1 tablespoon **raw honey**

1. Bring the water to the boil in a pan. Add the garlic and simmer for about 8 minutes, or until the water has reduced to about a mugful. Take off the heat and stir in the sage and honey.

2. Strain through a sieve into a mug and drink immediately. Sleep.

TIPS

* You can use any honey, but raw untreated honey seems to work better, and Manuka honey seem to work best.

Honey & Rose Baklava

MAKES: 18-24 PIECES • PREPARATION TIME: 35 MINUTES PLUS COOLING • COOKING TIME: 1 HOUR • V

These are just one of the most beautiful things going – thin, crispy sheets of filigree-like pastry, delicate rosewater and fragrant honey.

12 sheets of **filo pastry** (have a few more on standby if you're clumsy)
200g **unsalted butter**, melted
an extra tablespoon of **orange blossom honey**, to finish (optional)

For the syrup:
75ml **orange blossom honey**
55ml **water**
55g **caster sugar**
2 tablespoons **rosewater**
a pinch of **ground cinnamon**
2 **star anise**

For the filling:
225g **soft brown sugar**
100g shelled **pistachios**
125g **walnut pieces**
100g **ground almonds**
50g **flax seeds**, toasted
1 teaspoon **ground cinnamon**
the seeds from 10 **cardamom pods**
1 tablespoon **dried rose petals** (optional)

1. Heat the oven to 180°C/350°F/gas mark 4. Grease a 30 x 22cm baking tin.

2. Put all the filling ingredients into a food processor and whizz until broken down. You want some texture so don't grind it to a paste. Tip into a bowl and set aside.

3. Unroll the filo pastry and cut the sheets in half – they should be about 30 x 20cm when cut. (Keep the sheets covered with a damp tea towel, as they dry out quickly.)

4. Layer the pastry sheets in the tin, one at a time, brushing each sheet with melted butter until you have stacked 10 sheets. On top of the tenth sheet, spoon over a nice layer of filling. Then place another sheet on top and butter again. Add another layer of filling and repeat the layers until the filling is used up – it will probably take 2 more layers. Finish with 10 sheets of filo layered on top, remembering to butter every sheet as you go and give the top sheet a final buttering.

5. Cut the baklava diagonally into diamond shapes.

6. Place in the oven for 45 minutes to 1 hour. (Check them after 45 minutes: you want a golden-brown crisp exterior.)

7. Meanwhile, make the syrup. Gently heat the syrup ingredients in a pan over a medium heat and simmer for 5–10 minutes, or until thick and fragrant. Take off the heat and leave to cool.

8. As soon as the baklava comes out of the oven, pour the cool syrup evenly over the surface. Finish by drizzling the extra tablespoon of honey over the top if you want to and sprinkle over any left-over filling. Leave the baklava to cool in the tin before gently removing and putting on a serving plate. If you're feeling fancy, decorate the cooled baklava with some dried rose petals.

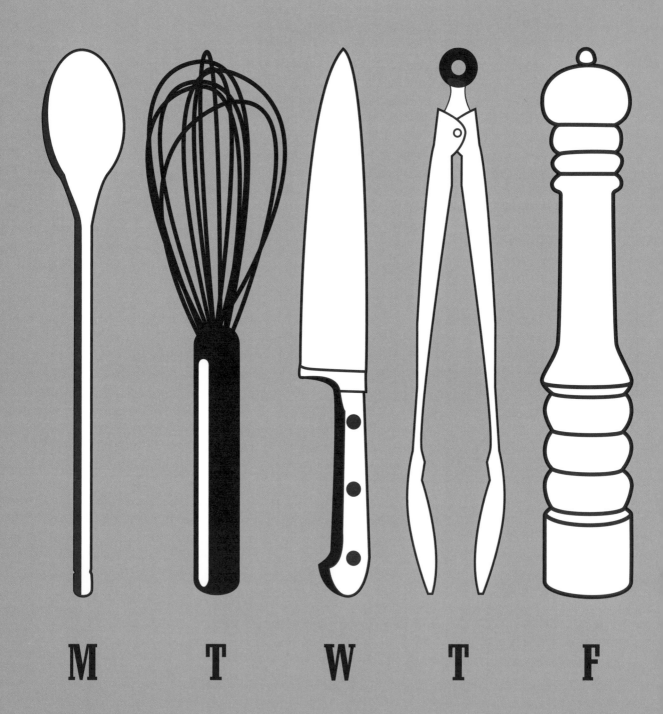

M   T   W   T   F

SUPER WEEKDAY SUPPERS

I never saw the point of a ready-meal. Takeaways, yes (you can't always be bothered to cook and, besides, with Bangkok's food stalls, I grew up in a takeaway culture), and restaurants, of course. But ready-meals? They're neither one thing nor the other, neither freshly made nor especially good for you. So ever since I left home, I've cooked. It's more about habit than anything else. But is it really any harder to put some chicken thighs in a pan than to prick holes in the top of some foil? They both take forty minutes in the oven.

Most of these recipes are quick and convenient. A couple take a little effort, but that's a good thing. And I've always found, after a not-so-great day at the office, that there's something very soothing and karmically restorative about taking your wrath out on the onion you're chopping.

KAY

FOUR
RISOTTOS

Sometimes, there's nothing more comforting than a bowl of piping hot risotto. It's healthy, soothing, and much easier to make than some people think. So if you haven't made one before, give it a go.

Here we give you one basic method with four variations. And we are departing a little from tradition. Risotto is usually made with butter. But to be that little bit healthier, we're using olive oil with just a dash of butter so you should get that creamy flavour with less risk of a coronary.

Basic Risotto Bianco

SERVES 4 • PREPARATION TIME: 5–10 MINUTES • COOKING TIME: 25–30 MINUTES • WF GF

1 litre **chicken** or **vegetable stock**
2 tablespoons **olive oil**
1 teaspoon **butter**
1 **onion**, finely chopped
375g **risotto rice**

125ml **white wine**
2 tablespoons freshly grated
   Parmesan cheese
salt and **freshly ground**
   black pepper

1. Pour the stock into a large saucepan and bring it to a gentle simmer. Keep it there, quivering away.

2. In a separate pan, heat the oil and then the butter over a medium heat. When the butter begins to foam, add the onion and cook gently until it's soft and translucent, about 5 minutes. Now add the rice and stir until all the rice is evenly coated with butter and oil, about 2 minutes.

3. Now add the wine, stir it into the rice and, when it's almost completely absorbed, add the first ladle of hot stock – just enough to cover the rice. Turn down the heat to low-to-medium, and keep stirring so that the rice doesn't stick. (When you've done this a few times, you don't have to stir it religiously, but you have to pay it appropriate attention.)

4. As the rice absorbs the liquid, keep adding stock in smaller and smaller quantities, even if you have to do so quite frequently, until the rice is cooked: you don't want a soupy, runny risotto, the rice should be *al dente*. It should be creamy, and not-exactly-dry. This can take up to 20 minutes and sometimes longer.

5. Season with salt, pepper and Parmesan and there you have a simple *risotto bianco*.

TIPS

* Rice likes to rest. So when cooked, cover with a lid and leave it to stand for 5 minutes to let it relax.
* With risotto, the cooking temperature is crucial. If it's too high, the rice won't cook evenly and the grains will be chalky inside. Too low, and the rice will be claggy. You'll get the hang of it.

OPPOSITE ABOVE: TRAFFIC LIGHT RISOTTO,
BELOW: PEA & HAM RISOTTO

Pea & Ham Risotto

WF GF

Peas and ham – just made to go together.

> 1 x **basic risotto bianco** (see page 103)
> 100g shredded **ham**
> 200g **peas** (we often use thawed frozen peas for this)
> 1 teaspoon **fresh thyme leaves**

1. Make the basic risotto bianco as per the method on page 103. When the rice is cooked, stir in the ham, peas and thyme before you season with salt, pepper and Parmesan, then serve.

2. You could use a ham stock when making the risotto. Just make sure it's not too salty.

Grilled Asparagus & Lemon Risotto

WF GF

These are fresh and sunny flavours. Grilling the asparagus adds an extra smokey dimension.

Variations to the basic risotto bianco:
change the wine for 75ml **white vermouth**
add 1 clove of **garlic**, finely chopped, when you fry the onion

Then add:
400g **asparagus**, washed and trimmed
1 tablespoon **olive oil**
2 sprigs of **fresh thyme**, leaves picked
the juice of ½ a **lemon**
the zest of 1 **lemon**
1 tablespoon finely chopped **fresh parsley**, plus extra to garnish
salt and **freshly ground black pepper**

1. Heat a griddle pan until you can *really* feel the heat rising off it when you hold your hand about 6cm above it.

2. Dry the asparagus thoroughly, then toss it in the olive oil. Season it with salt and pepper, and sprinkle it with the thyme leaves.

3. Grill the asparagus, turning occasionally, for about 5 minutes, or until it's nicely soft, with elegant black char-lines on it. Remove from the heat and set aside. When it's cooled a bit, cut it into bite-sized pieces.

4. Now for the risotto: make the risotto as per the method above, substituting the vermouth for the wine, and adding the garlic when the onion is halfway there.

5. When the rice is cooked, add the grilled asparagus, lemon juice, lemon zest and parsley. Stir everything together, and finish with salt, pepper and Parmesan as usual. Serve garnished with a little extra parsley.

Traffic Light Risotto

♥ WF GF

Peppery and sweet – this is a colourful favourite.

1 x recipe **basic risotto bianco** (see page 103)
2 tablespoons **olive oil**
3 cloves of **garlic**, peeled and thinly sliced
1 mild **red chilli**, sliced (seeds are optional, depending on how spicy you like it)

1 **red pepper**, cut into 1–2cm chunks
1 **yellow pepper**, cut into 1–2cm chunks
1 **green pepper**, cut into 1–2cm chunks
2 tablespoons **fresh flat-leaf parsley**, finely chopped

1. Make the basic risotto bianco as per the method on page 103.

2. While you're cooking the rice, heat the olive oil in a frying pan over a medium heat. Add the garlic, and sauté until it begins to colour. Then add the chilli and the peppers and stir. Season with a pinch of salt and cook, stirring occasionally, until the peppers are soft and hot. Set them aside until the risotto's ready.

3. When the rice is cooked, take it off the heat and stir in the peppers, then taste, adjust the seasoning as required, and serve.

Summer Squash & Nasturtium Risotto

WF GF

By squash, we mean what the Americans like to call summer squash: pattypans, yellow crooknecks and so on. If you can't find them in the shops, you can substitute courgettes. The nasturtium flowers add a shock of colour, as well as a sweet-peppery bite.

1 x recipe **basic risotto bianco** (see page 103)
2 tablespoons **olive oil**
2 cloves of **garlic**, finely chopped
2 tablespoons chopped **fresh thyme**

250g mixed **summer squash**, roughly chopped into 2cm cubes
a few **fresh basil leaves**, torn
8 **nasturtium flowers**

1. Make the basic risotto bianco as per the method on page 103.

2. While the rice is cooking, heat the olive oil in a separate frying pan over a medium heat. When it's hot, add the garlic and fry until it just begins to colour. Add the thyme, stir for another minute, then add the squash. Allow it to colour and the garlic to turn a nutty-brown. Then take the pan off the heat and set aside.

3. When the risotto is cooked, add the squash and the basil leaves, then stir everything together. Serve, garnishing each bowl with a pair of nasturtium flowers.

Tasty Herby Chicken Thighs & Salad

SERVES 4 • PREPARATION TIME: 10 MINUTES • COOKING TIME: 50 MINUTES • ✓ WF GF

An old standby in the Plunkett-Hogge household.

> 8 **chicken thighs**
> 3–4 cloves of **garlic**
> 1–2 tablespoons **olive oil**
> a small bunch of **fresh lemon thyme**
> 4 **Little Gem lettuces**
>   or 4 large handfuls of **baby leaves**
> 100g **watercress**
> 200ml **white wine**
> 20g **butter**
> **salt** and **freshly ground black pepper**

1. Heat the oven to 200°C/400°F/gas mark 6.

2. Trim the excess fat off the chicken thighs and place them skin side up in a roasting tray. Throw in the garlic cloves, then drizzle everything with the olive oil – try to make sure everything's well covered.

3. Now strip the leaves off the lemon thyme stalks, and scatter them into the tray. Season the chicken thighs with salt and pepper and pop them into the oven for 45 minutes, or until they're cooked through.

4. While the chicken's in the oven, trim the lettuces and slice them into 1cm strips. Put them into a bowl and toss them with the watercress, then divide the salad equally between your plates.

5. When the chicken's ready, remove it from the oven and place on top of the salad. Deglaze the roasting tray with the wine, scraping up all the cooking residues from the bottom of the tray and squashing the roasted garlic into the sauce.

6. Finally, whisk in the butter for a nice glossy finish. Pour the sauce over the chicken and salad, and serve.

TIPS

* If you fancy a change from chicken thighs, this will work perfectly well with drumsticks or with entire thigh/leg sections. We don't make it with chicken breast because it tends to dry out.

* Try using different herbs – you can make this with pretty much any herb you like, though go easy on the sage.

* For a sweeter, less peppery salad, why not substitute pea shoots for the watercress?

* If you don't want to use wine, just use a good chicken stock to deglaze the roasting tray.

Grilled Chicken Angelus

SERVES 4 • PREPARATION TIME: 30 MINUTES PLUS MARINATING • COOKING TIME: 40 MINUTES • ✓ ♥ WF GF DF

Herby and spicy, this features a dry-rub that's halfway to Cajun. Try it on the barbecue.

1 heaped tablespoon **allspice berries**
1 teaspoon **cayenne pepper**
1 teaspoon **ground paprika**
a good pinch of **ground cumin**
1 teaspoon **dried oregano**
1 teaspoon **dried thyme**
a good pinch of **salt**
2 cloves of **garlic**, chopped
2 **spring onions**, trimmed and chopped
a couple of grinds of **black pepper**
1 tablespoon **olive oil**
1 **chicken**, spatchcocked
the juice of ½ a **lemon**

1. Grind the allspice berries with a pestle and mortar. Add the other ground spices and the dried herbs and grind together a little more. Now add the salt, the garlic and the spring onions and grind to a paste. Add the black pepper and the olive oil and mix together. You should have a loose, fragrant putty to smear over the bird.

2. Slash the back and thighs of the chicken with a sharp knife. Rub the putty well into the bird, especially into the slashes, then leave to marinate in the fridge for up to 4 hours. (But, of course, if you only have 20 minutes, that'll do.)

3. Grill the chicken over a medium heat until it's completely cooked through, about 30–40 minutes in all.

4. When it's done, squeeze over the lemon juice. Serve with a salad and some extra lemon wedges on the side.

This is named for the street where we often stay in Los Angeles, at my great friend Sue McNamara's house. Sue has a wonderful indoor/ outdoor kitchen which inspires me to grill whenever we're there.

KAY

Pesto Chicken

SERVES 4 • PREPARATION TIME: 20 MINUTES • COOKING TIME: 25 MINUTES • ✓ WF GF

We also like to make this with fresh pesto when we have a little extra time (see tip below).

750g boneless, skinless **chicken breasts**,
   sliced 1cm thick
2 tablespoons **olive oil**
20g **butter**
2 cloves of **garlic**, peeled and finely chopped
225ml **white wine or chicken stock**
2 tablespoons **pesto sauce**
a squeeze of **lemon juice**
sea salt and **freshly ground black pepper**

1. Season the chicken breast slices with a little salt and pepper.

2. In a heavy-based frying pan, melt the oil and butter over a medium heat and, in batches, sauté the chicken until it's cooked through. Each batch should take about 5–7 minutes to cook and the chicken will be golden in colour. Set aside.

3. Turn down the heat and add the garlic to the residual oil in the pan. Cook, stirring gently from time to time, until it begins to colour for about another 2 minutes. Now turn the heat back up and add the wine or stock. Bubble until reduced by about half its volume, scraping up any cooking residues from the pan.

4. Stir in the pesto and the lemon juice, and season with salt and pepper to taste. Return the chicken to the pan, toss it through the sauce, and serve.

TIPS

* If you have time, this homemade pesto will make it taste all the fresher:

1 tablespoon **pine nuts**, toasted
1 clove of **garlic**
a pinch of **sea salt**
a large handful of picked **fresh basil leaves**
25g **Parmesan cheese**, freshly grated
150ml **olive oil**

1. In a small immersion blender, blitz the pine nuts and garlic together with a pinch of salt. Add the basil, the cheese and 100ml of the oil and blitz again until you have a rough paste.

2. If you don't want to use it immediately, spoon it into a jar, top with the remaining oil, and store in the fridge. It should keep for a couple of days.

Back in the 80s, a jar of pesto was the height of sophistication, so this quick, simple storecupboard supper was something of a weekly favourite when I was growing up. Pesto is still something I keep in the fridge – you never know when it will come in handy.
FRED

Deb Henley's Chicken Enchiladas Verdes

SERVES 4–6 • PREPARATION TIME: 20 MINUTES • COOKING TIME: 50 MINUTES • WF GF

Our friend Deb always roasts a chicken especially for her enchiladas. She devised this particular recipe when she moved back to London from Mexico City in the summer of 2000, after all her Mexican friends kept asking her: 'Please cook us something from home'.

> 1 x 790g **tin of tomatillos**
> 2 **serrano** or other **medium-hot green chillies**,
>   or 1 **jalapeño chilli**
> 1 clove of **garlic**
> 1 small **onion**, chopped
> 1 tablespoon of **fat** from roasting your
>   chicken (optional)
> a bunch of **fresh coriander**, finely chopped
> 100ml **chicken stock**
> 8–12 **soft, pure corn tortillas** (see tips opposite)
> 325g **cooked chicken**, shredded
> 150ml **double cream**
> 50g young **Manchego cheese**, grated
> **sea salt**

1. Heat the oven to 180°C/350°F/gas mark 4.

2. Drain the tomatillos and set them aside in a bowl.

3. Pop the chillies into a small pan and add 125ml of water. Bring to the boil, simmer for 5 minutes, then remove from the heat. Put the chillies and their cooking water, the tomatillos, garlic and onion into a blender or food processor, and blitz until smooth.

4. If you're using the chicken fat, put it into a deep pan and heat gently. Add the blitzed salsa verde (the tomatillo mixture) and 2 tablespoons of the chopped coriander and cook for about 5 minutes over a medium heat. Add the chicken stock, season with salt and cook until it thickens up a little – about 4 more minutes. Keep the salsa warm while you prepare the enchiladas.

5. Wrap the tortillas in a clean tea towel and steam them, preferably in a tiered steamer, over boiling water for 1–2 minutes. You may want to do this in batches of 4–6 to avoid them sticking together.

6. Put a good portion of the shredded chicken on to each tortilla, roll them up like fat cigars and lay them side by side in a baking dish about 32 x 22cm and 6cm deep. Pour over the green salsa, then the cream, and finally sprinkle with the grated cheese. Bake in the oven for about 30 minutes.

7. Serve sprinkled with the rest of the chopped coriander.

TIPS

* You can buy tins of tomatillos online from the Cool Chile Co.

* Traditional corn tortillas are 100% corn, making them gluten free, and about 15cm in diameter. However, in supermarkets outside the Americas, I've found many that are a mix of wheat and corn and a whopping 22cm, so just bear that in mind.

* Deb roasts a small chicken and uses its meat for this but, if you prefer, you could just poach what you need. You can also use roast chicken leftovers.

* If you are lucky enough to find fresh tomatillos, you'll need 750g. Just simmer them in enough boiling water to cover them for 5–10 minutes, or until their colour changes from a bright to a drab green. Drain the tomatillos and the chilli, reserving 125ml of the water. Continue with the recipe as normal, taking extra care when you blitz the sauce, so that you don't burn yourself.

DEB, SYDNEY, 1970

Deb Henley is from Sydney, Australia. She is Kay's Pilates teacher and a great friend. She first moved to Mexico City in the mid-1990s to work as a ballet dancer and soon fell in love with the culture. Luckily for us, she then moved to London.

Kim's Spanish-style Chicken

SERVES 4–6 • PREPARATION TIME: 10 MINUTES • COOKING TIME: 1 HOUR 35 MINUTES • ✓ DF

Kay's sister Kim has two strapping teenage sons who can look at a fridge the way that locusts look at a farm. So she specializes in big, chunky recipes that go the distance. This one does just that.

8 **chicken thighs**
1 tablespoon **olive oil**
100g **chorizo**, sliced ½–1cm thick
1 **onion**, finely chopped
1 x 400g **tin of cannellini beans** or **butter beans**,
　drained and rinsed
a couple of sprigs of **fresh oregano**
a couple of sprigs of **fresh tarragon**
a pinch of **cayenne pepper**
1 bulb of **garlic**, halved horizontally
　through the middle
a strip of **orange zest**
a glass of **white wine** or **dry sherry**
1 teaspoon ground **paprika**
12 **cherry tomatoes**
400ml **chicken stock**
1 tablespoon chopped **fresh parsley**, to garnish
salt and **freshly ground black pepper**

My big sister Kim (who's actually really rather small) is everything I'm not: organized, efficient, green-fingered … and a parent. When we were little, she used to order me to fetch her lemonades and snacks, since she was so exhausted from school back in England. Once again, I fell for it. I have forgiven her. She's a bundle of energy, and a real inspiration.

KAY

KIM, JOMTIEN, 1963

1. Heat the oven to 180°C/350°F/gas mark 4.

2. Clean and dry the chicken thighs, cutting away any excess fat. Put a heavy-based, non-stick frying pan over a medium heat, then add the olive oil. Thoroughly brown the chicken thighs all over, then set them aside in a large casserole.

3. When you've browned all the chicken, fry the chorizo slices until they release their oil into the frying pan and are cooked through, about 3 minutes each side. Add them to the casserole.

4. Turn down the heat under the frying pan, add the onion and fry until soft. While it's cooking, add the beans, herbs, cayenne, garlic and orange zest to the casserole.

5. When the onions are cooked, pour the wine or sherry into the frying pan and bubble it up hard, scraping all the cooking residues off the bottom of the pan with a wooden spoon. Add the paprika and stir it in. Pour everything into the casserole, add the cherry tomatoes, then top it up with enough chicken stock to cover the thighs.

6. Season with salt and pepper, pop on the lid and put the casserole into the oven for about 1 hour and 10 minutes. Serve in big bowls with lots of bread for dunking, with sautéd greens or a simple green salad.

Sweet Soy Salmon with Mushrooms & Pea Shoots

SERVES 4 • PREPARATION TIME: 15 MINUTES • COOKING TIME: 8–10 MINUTES • ♥ DF

A Japanese-inflected salmon. The wasabi provides a punch that salmon takes really well. For an extra kick try adding a pinch of dried chilli flakes.

4 **salmon steaks**, about 125–150g each
4 tablespoons **tamari**
1–2 teaspoons **wasabi paste**, or to taste
2 teaspoons **sugar**
4 teaspoons **rice vinegar**
1 tablespoon **olive oil**, plus 1 teaspoon
a 2cm piece of **fresh ginger**, peeled
   and finely slivered
4 **spring onions**, trimmed and sliced
   on the diagonal
3 cloves of **garlic**, chopped
100g **fresh shiitake** and/or **girolles**
   mushrooms, trimmed and sliced
a pinch of **dried chilli** (optional)
a squeeze of **lemon juice**
50g **pea shoots**
salt and **freshly ground black pepper**

TIPS

* When pea shoots are out of season, use watercress or rocket leaves.

* You could also mix in 100g of frozen peas or some edamame beans when cooking the mushrooms.

* Experiment with different mushrooms – chestnut mushrooms work just as well, as do enoki.

1. Heat the oven to 200°C/400°F/gas mark 6.

2. Put the salmon into a small roasting tray. Mix the tamari, wasabi, sugar, vinegar and the teaspoon of oil together in a bowl, and pour over the fish, coating it well.

3. Divide up the slivers of ginger and half the sliced spring onions into 4 little piles, and sprinkle one evenly over each piece of salmon. Season with a pinch of pepper, and roast for about 8 minutes, or until the salmon is just cooked through.

4. While the salmon is in the oven, heat the tablespoon of olive oil in a frying pan over a medium hob. When it's hot, add the garlic and cook until soft but not browned. Now add the mushrooms and cook for a few minutes, making sure that all the water evaporates out of them, otherwise they'll be soggy (mushrooms are 90% water). Add the pinch of chilli (if you like), a squeeze of lemon and the rest of the spring onions and continue cooking for a few minutes. Remove from the heat, and season with a little salt and pepper.

5. Remove the salmon from the oven and pop it on to 4 plates. Top with the mushroom mixture and finish with an even scattering of the pea shoots.

Salmon in a Bag Three Ways

SERVES 4 • PREPARATION TIME: 10–15 MINUTES • COOKING TIME: 15–20 MINUTES

Even people who say they don't really like fish seem to like salmon. Pink and juicy, it's packed with all sorts of good-for-you goodies. It's high in protein, in vitamins D and B12, and don't forget those omega-3 fatty acids – good for the heart, limbs and the old brain. Top food.

This method of cooking salmon (*en papillote*) is super quick and easy. Essentially, you're steaming the fish in a 'bag' so you lose none of its goodness. Here are three of our favourites.

Provençal Salmon

✓ ♥ WF GF DF

These flavours always remind us of summers in France.

4 **salmon fillets,**
    about 140g each
8 **cherry tomatoes,**
    or 4 **larger tomatoes,**
    halved
16 **black olives**
2 cloves of **garlic,**
    peeled and chopped
a handful of **fresh basil**
    leaves, plus a little
    extra to garnish
a drizzle of **olive oil**
a splash of **dry white**
    vermouth
salt and **freshly ground**
    black pepper

St Clement's Salmon

✓ ♥ WF GF DF

Oranges and lemons, say the bells of St. Clement's …

4 **salmon fillets,**
    about 140g each
4 thin slices of **lemon**
4 thin slices of **orange**
2–3 sprigs of **fresh dill,**
    finely chopped
2 cloves of **garlic,** peeled
    and chopped
the juice of ½ a **lemon**
the juice of ½ an **orange**
    (you should have about
    4 tablespoons of liquid
    from the two halved fruits)
a drizzle of **olive oil**
a few sprigs of **fresh dill,**
    to garnish
salt and **freshly ground**
    black pepper

Thai Salmon

✓ ♥ WF GF DF

Exotic and warming, with some fiery red chilli …

4 **salmon fillets,**
    about 140g each
1 **red bird's-eye chilli,**
    deseeded and
    finely chopped
2 **coriander roots,**
    chopped
2 cloves of **garlic,**
    chopped
1 tablespoon **nam pla**
    (fish sauce)
2 **spring onions,**
    trimmed and chopped
2 tablespoons **lime juice**
a good grinding of
    white pepper
a bunch of **fresh**
    coriander, to garnish

1. Heat the oven to 180°C/350°F/gas mark 4.

2. Pop each salmon fillet on to a square of either greaseproof paper or foil measuring about 35 x 35cm. Then add the flavourings and the liquids, depending on which version you're making. Seal the 'bag' or parcel with tight folds, making sure there's room inside for the salmon to steam. If you're using greaseproof paper, don't scrunch instead of folding as this may unravel, spilling all those precious juices.

3. Place the parcels on a baking tray and cook them in the oven for 15 minutes, or until the salmon is just cooked through.

4. Remove from the oven and place carefully on to plates. Then rush them to the table so that everyone can open their own bag and add their own garnish.

Easy Pad Thai

SERVES 2 · PREPARATION TIME: 10 MINUTES PLUS SOAKING · COOKING TIME: 5–10 MINUTES · WF GF DF

This has nothing on the Pad Thai at Pratu Pee (the Ghost's Gate) in Bangkok, but it's pretty darn good, and streamlined for speed.

It's better to make this in small batches, so the recipe here feeds two.

150g **rice noodles**
1 tablespoon **vegetable oil**
3 cloves of **garlic**, chopped
150–200g **raw peeled prawns**
2 **eggs**, lightly beaten
2 handfuls of **bean sprouts**
2 **spring onions**, trimmed and chopped
2 tablespoons **dried prawns**
2 tablespoons **unsalted, roasted peanuts**,
 roughly chopped
3 tablespoons **nam pla** (fish sauce)
2 tablespoons **lime juice**
2 tablespoons **sugar**
½ teaspoon **tamarind purée**
¼ teaspoon **chilli powder**

For the garnish:
2 **spring onions**, trimmed and chopped
1 tablespoon **fresh coriander**, leaves picked
a few slices of **cucumber** (optional)
½ tablespoon **unsalted, roasted peanuts**,
 roughly chopped
2 **lime wedges**

1. Soak the rice noodles in warm water for 5–10 minutes, or until they're just malleable. (The instructions on the packet will probably say to soak them for 15–20 minutes, but this will make them too soggy for the finished dish.) Drain, rinse and set aside.

2. Heat the oil in a wok over a high flame. Add the garlic and stir-fry quickly until just turning golden. Add the fresh prawns and stir-fry for a minute or two. Then add the noodles and stir through before adding the eggs, bean sprouts, spring onions, dried prawns and peanuts, stirring after each addition.

3. When everything is well combined, add the *nam pla*, lime juice, sugar, chilli powder and tamarind purée. Stir thoroughly, then serve at once, garnished with spring onion, coriander, cucumber and peanuts, with lime wedges on the side.

TIPS

* If you prefer, you can change the prawns for the same amount of chicken or pork.

West Indian Seafood Curry

SERVES 2 • PREPARATION TIME: 15 MINUTES • COOKING TIME: 15 MINUTES • ✓ ♥ WF GF

This is based on a dish Kay had when she went to visit Fred's rather extended family in Montego Bay, Jamaica. It sort of sums up all the ethnic influences on the island. It's a melting pot of a dish.

1 teaspoon **coriander seeds**
1 teaspoon **black mustard seeds**
1 teaspoon **cumin seeds**
2 **allspice berries**
¼ teaspoon **chilli flakes**
1 tablespoon **vegetable oil**
1 **shallot**, peeled and chopped
1 clove of **garlic**, peeled and chopped
1 x 400g tin of **chopped tomatoes**
½ teaspoon **tamarind purée**
the juice of ½ a **lime**
2 **fresh kaffir lime leaves**
1–2 teaspoons **caster sugar**
a couple of drops of **hot pepper sauce** (optional)
   (we like to use Grace's Hot Pepper Sauce)
½ teaspoon **sea salt**
350g **white fish fillets** – anything firm and
   sustainable: haddock, pollock,
   farmed cod – cut into chunks
2 tablespoons **coconut cream** or **yoghurt** (optional)
¼ **red pepper**, thinly sliced, to garnish
freshly ground black pepper

1. Heat a dry frying pan and toast the spices over a low heat for 3–4 minutes, or until fragrant. Grind them in a pestle and mortar or a coffee grinder and set aside.

2. Heat the vegetable oil in a wide heavy-based pan, and soften the shallot and the garlic. Add the spices and stir for 30 seconds more. Add the tinned tomatoes, tamarind purée, lime juice, one of the kaffir lime leaves, sugar, hot pepper sauce (if using), the sea salt and a grinding of black pepper. Simmer for 1 minute.

3. Add the fish and simmer for a further 3–5 minutes, or until the fish looks white and is falling apart.

4. Taste for seasoning. If you want, swirl through some coconut cream or yoghurt. Serve with rice and garnish with the other lime leaf, slivered into ribbons, and strips of red pepper.

TIPS

* If your sauce seems a little thick, add a splash of water to loosen it up.

Linguine with Crab & Tomato

SERVES 4 • PREPARATION TIME: 10 MINUTES • COOKING TIME: 10–12 MINUTES • DF

This is Kay's absolute favourite pasta sauce.

400g **linguine**
3 tablespoons **olive oil**
2 cloves of **garlic**, finely chopped
1 **red serrano** or other **medium-hot chilli**,
 deseeded and sliced into small pieces
8–12 **cherry tomatoes**
250g **white crabmeat** or 2 x 170g **tins of crab**
2 tablespoons **dry white vermouth** or **white wine**
2 tablespoons **dark crabmeat**
1 tablespoon **fresh flat-leaf parsley**, chopped
salt and **freshly ground black pepper**

1. Bring a large pan of salted water up to a rolling boil. Check the cooking time on your pasta pack – we find, normally, for *al dente* pasta, that it takes a little less time than advertised – and pop in the linguine.

2. Meanwhile, heat 2 tablespoons of olive oil in a large sauté pan over a medium heat. Add the garlic and stir until you can just smell it. Now add the chilli and the tomatoes. Stir until the garlic just begins to colour, then add the white crabmeat or tinned crab. Stir for a moment or two, then add the vermouth or wine, the dark crabmeat and a good pinch of the parsley. Season with salt and pepper and stir together well. All in, this should take no more than 5 minutes.

3. If the pasta isn't quite cooked, set the sauce aside to keep warm. When the linguine's done, drain it and toss in the remaining tablespoon of olive oil. Stir the crabmeat sauce through the pasta and serve with a sprinkling of parsley and a good grind of black pepper. Oh, and with a good glass of crisp Italian white.

TIPS

* We often make this with tinned crab and without the dark crabmeat – it's a quick and easy storecupboard staple. But if you really want to go for it, buy ready-prepared crab meat – we like the white and dark crabmeat pots from Seafood and Eat It.

* The wine or vermouth adds an important dimension to this dish, but you can substitute water if you'd prefer.

* To make the sauce a little spicier, why not use a pinch of dried peperoncino or some rinsed green peppercorns instead of the chilli.

* Sometimes, for an extra seaside flavour, Kay replaces the tomatoes with 150g of samphire.

Henry's Meatballs with Herb Salad

MAKES 12 • PREPARATION TIME: 20 MINUTES • COOKING TIME: 20 MINUTES • ✓ WF GF

These lightly spiced meatballs contain a surprise within. Make sure there are no holes or the cheese will ooze out.

For the meatballs:
8 **cardamom pods**
2 teaspoons **coriander seeds**
4 **cloves**
4 large cloves of **garlic**
a large pinch of **salt**
300g lean **minced beef**
200g **minced pork**
½ teaspoon **turmeric**
chilli powder, to taste
1 free-range **egg**, beaten
1–2 tablespoons **groundnut oil**
115g **cream cheese**

200g **baby plum tomatoes**, cut in half lengthways
1 tablespoon **plain yoghurt**

To serve:
2–3 tablespoons chopped **fresh coriander leaves**
2 tablespoons **flaked almonds**, toasted
4 **shallots**, finely sliced and deep-fried

For the salad:
150g mixed **salad leaves**
2 tablespoons finely chopped **fresh mint leaves**
2 tablespoons finely chopped **fresh chives**
2 tablespoons finely chopped **fresh flat-leaf parsley**
2 tablespoons finely chopped **fresh oregano**
1 teaspoon **white wine vinegar**
1 teaspoon **English mustard**
3 tablespoons **olive oil**

1. Take the seeds out of the cardamom pods, place them in a coffee grinder or pestle and mortar with the coriander seeds and cloves, then grind to a fine powder. Chop the garlic with the salt until it forms a paste, or add it to the pestle and mortar.

2. Put the beef and pork into a large bowl and mix together vigorously to soften the texture – this will help stop the cheese escaping.

3. Add the ground spices, turmeric, chilli powder and garlic to the meat and mix really well with your hands, then add the beaten egg and combine well.

4. Wet your hands, then take pieces of the mixture and roll into balls the size of ping-pong balls. You should have about 12 meatballs.

5. Lightly oil a clean work surface with a little of the groundnut oil and gently press the meatballs into flattened circles.

6. Put a teaspoon of cream cheese in the centre of each meat circle and carefully bring the meat up round it to enclose the cheese completely, making rather larger meatballs. Roll gently and make sure there are no holes.

7. Heat a large frying pan until hot, then add the remaining oil and fry the meatballs for 10 minutes over a medium-high heat, turning regularly, until nicely coloured and cooked through. Put the meatballs into a serving dish and keep warm.

8. Turn the heat up under the frying pan, then add the tomatoes and flash-fry them quickly. Remove the pan from the heat and stir in the yoghurt.

9. For the salad, toss together the leaves and herbs in a large bowl. Whisk the vinegar, mustard and olive oil together and season with salt and black pepper. Toss together with the salad leaves.

10. To serve, arrange the salad around the edge of a serving platter and place the meatballs in the centre. Pour the tomato mixture over the meatballs and garnish with the chopped coriander, almonds and fried shallots.

THE DIMBLEBY FAMILY IN THE DORDOGNE, 1976

'My mum used to love making us dishes with surprises in them: ice cream bombes which spilled grated chocolate, puddings with hidden custards, and stuffed meatballs. This recipe is my take on a dish that appeared in her alliteratively named *Marvellous Meals with Mince* in the 80s – a book of its time.'

HENRY

Quick Guay Tiew Nam Moo

(PORK MEATBALL NOODLE SOUP)

A super-quick short cut to a tasty Thai pork noodle soup. You can find variations on this theme on practically every street corner in Thailand. To be honest, it's perfect at any time of day. And it's great for the morning after the night before …

For the meatballs:
1 teaspoon **white peppercorns**
2 fresh **coriander roots**
2 cloves of **garlic**
a pinch of **salt**
200g **minced pork**
a dash of **nam pla** (fish sauce)

For the soup:
100g medium-width **rice noodles**
1 tablespoon **vegetable oil**
1 clove of **garlic**, smashed
1.2 litres **stock**, any flavour
2 tablespoons **light soy sauce**
2 tablespoons **nam pla** (fish sauce)
100g **bean sprouts**
100g **pak choi** (about 1 head), roughly chopped
3 **spring onions**, trimmed and finely chopped
a handful of **fresh coriander leaves**, chopped

TIPS

* In Thailand, you get this served with a selection of condiments called *kruang prung*. These could be some ground, roasted dried chillies, rice vinegar with mild chillies sliced into it, nam pla with finely sliced bird's-eye chillies; lime juice; sugar; plain nam pla and crushed peanuts.

1. Fill a large bowl with water and pop in your rice noodles; this just softens them and gets rid of a lot of the starch, which would otherwise make your soup 'gummy'.

2. In a pestle and mortar, pound the peppercorns, coriander roots, garlic and the salt to a paste. Then, in a clean bowl, mix the paste with the minced pork and *nam pla,* mushing it thoroughly with your hands. Form the mixture into 16 meatballs and set them aside.

3. Now for the soup. Heat the oil in a large saucepan and, once it's hot, add the smashed clove of garlic. Cook for a minute or so until it's really fragrant – but don't let it colour. Pour in the stock and bring to the boil. Add the soy sauce and the nam pla, bring it back to the boil, then add the meatballs. When they're cooked through – in about a minute or two – add your drained noodles.

4. Bring it all back to the boil and add your bean sprouts and pak choi. Bring back to the boil again and cook for 3 minutes. Check that the noodles are cooked – by this time your vegetables will be ready. You want them with a little bite.

5. Divide between bowls and top each bowl with a few spring onion bits and some chopped coriander.

Midweek Lamb

SERVES 4 • PREPARATION TIME: 15 MINUTES • COOKING TIME: 40 MINUTES • ✓ WF GF DF

This is an incredibly easy dish that tastes as though you've spent loads of time on it.

> a small bunch of **fresh rosemary**
> 1 boned **leg of lamb**, about 1.25kg in weight
> 6 **anchovies** – about half a 55g tin
> 2 large cloves of **garlic**, peeled
> the zest of ½ a **lemon**
> 2 **dried chillies**
> 1 tablespoon **olive oil**
> **salt** and **freshly ground black pepper**

1. Heat the oven to 220°C/425°F/gas mark 7.

2. Strip the leaves off the rosemary and set aside. Scatter the twigs in a roasting tray. Open out the lamb, pat it dry and lay it on top of the rosemary twigs.

3. Now put all the remaining ingredients into a food processor with the rosemary leaves and blitz to a paste. Spread the paste over the lamb.

4. Roast in the oven for 40 minutes, or until the lamb is still nicely pink inside. Set it aside to rest for at least 15 minutes before serving.

TIPS

* Deglaze the roasting tray with 200ml of wine, stock or water to make a luscious yet simple gravy.

* Feel free to substitute black olives for the anchovies – say about 18 large ones.

* If you want more of an all-in-one supper dish, chop up some red peppers and a bulb or two of fennel and scatter them in the base of the roasting tray. Drizzle with a little olive oil and moisten with a splash of stock, wine or water, then lay the lamb on top and roast as above.

John's Big Bowl of Sunday Night Lamb

SERVES AS MANY AS YOU LIKE • PREPARATION TIME: 20 MINUTES PLUS MARINATING
COOKING TIME: 20–25 MINUTES • WF GF DF

This is a simple dish I used to cook, normally on a Sunday night, when we lived off the Edgware Road in Kilburn come Maida Vale.

These are all ingredients that I bought from the Middle Eastern shop behind the bus stop opposite the Islamic Centre. In a nutshell, it ends up as a big bowl of basmati rice with dried fried onion, lots of grilled marinated lamb chops and a little chopped coriander. I used to serve it with broad beans.

Kids will eat two chops each, and you will eat as many as you fancy, don't let me decide.

1. Marinate the **lamb chops** in whatever you fancy: **olive oil**, **lemon juice**, **salt and pepper**, **garlic**. Try **rosemary**. Try anything once. Leave for 15 minutes at least, longer if possible.

2. Cook ½ a cup of **white basmati rice** per person with double the amount of **water**. Add a little **salt** and **olive oil** because that seems to be the done thing.

3. Grill the lamb chops under a medium heat. To keep them a little pink, turn them after a couple of minutes. Longer if you want them to, but they won't taste as good. Cook on the other side for the same time.

4. Fill a high-sided serving bowl with the drained, cooked rice, and pop open a pack of **fried onions**. Sprinkle them over the rice, maybe folding some in, but leaving a lot on top as if they are savoury hundreds and thousands.

5. Place the lamb chops on top, then sprinkle with some roughly chopped **fresh coriander** or **flat-leaf parsley**.

6. Serve with some **green beans** or **broad beans** to make you feel good and look good.

7. Ta daaaa. You can now put it on the table and feast, either elegantly or carnivorously – you choose.

JOHN AT BROADSTAIRS, AGED 3

TIPS

* I buy my onions ready-fried for this. You can find them in most Asian supermarkets in plastic jars or packets. Alternatively, you can heat a couple of tablespoons of vegetable oil in a wok until it's very hot, then throw in a couple of finely sliced shallots or one finely sliced onion, stir-frying for a couple of minutes until they're golden brown. Remove immediately with a slotted spoon and drain on kitchen paper. When they're cool, store them in a Tupperware container or a food bag.

Fred's Ragù alla Toscana

MAKES ENOUGH SAUCE TO SERVE 8 EASILY
PREPARATION TIME: 30 MINUTES • COOKING TIME: 1 HOUR 30 MINUTES • ✓ DF

This is rich, meaty, and well worth the effort. Fred was taught it in Florence from his landlady, Signora Capelli. Apparently, she used to say that some things can cook fast, and some things can't. And to deny time to the things that can't is to cook without love.

So why is this in a Weekday Suppers chapter? Because it makes twice as much as you need, and tastes just as good when reheated.

3 tablespoons **olive oil**
1 **onion**, finely diced
1 stick of **celery**, finely diced
1 **carrot**, finely diced
1 clove of **garlic**, sliced as thinly as you can
300g good-quality **minced beef**
100g **chicken livers**, cleaned and chopped
150ml **red wine**
700g **passata** (sieved tomatoes)
a 10cm sprig of **fresh rosemary**
salt and **freshly ground black pepper**

FRED, FAWLEY, 1975

I met Fred over a sponsorship deal. It involved many martinis. A proposal of marriage wasn't meant to be one of his deliverables, but somehow it turned out like that after a flirtation involving the copious swapping of … recipes. He's an amazing cook, a great barman and, with a crazy Jamaican background and a love of travel, has broadened my food horizons more than I can say. (He's also *really* annoying!)

KAY

1. Heat 2 tablespoons of the oil in a large, heavy-based pan. Add the onion, celery and carrot and cook over a low heat for 10 minutes, stirring occasionally – you don't want the vegetables to catch or burn.

2. Add the garlic and cook for another 5 minutes or so, then remove from the pan and set aside. They should be warm and golden and sweet-smelling.

3. Add another tablespoon of oil to the pan and brown the minced beef and liver in batches. Remove the meat from the pan and set aside. We want sticky, rich, meaty bits left on the bottom of the pan.

4. Deglaze the pan with the wine, scraping up all the yumminess on the bottom with a wooden spoon. Now return the vegetables and meat to the pan. Add the passata, rosemary and season with salt and pepper.

5. Bring to the boil, then simmer over the lowest heat possible for at least an hour, stirring occasionally. The sauce is done when it's thick and rich.

6. Serve with the pasta of your choice – we prefer fettucini or tagliatelle for this, but hey, sometimes you want shells, sometimes spaghetti …

TIPS

* For an extra special kick, substitute rabbit livers for the chicken livers. It gives the sauce a game-y topspin which is irresistible.

Kay's Pad Krapow Neua

(STIR-FRIED BEEF WITH HOLY BASIL)

SERVES 2 AS A MAIN COURSE OR 4 AS PART OF A LARGER THAI MEAL
PREPARATION TIME: 10 MINUTES • COOKING TIME: 5 MINUTES • ✓ DF

This is one of my favourites, a real Bangkok staple, and my ultimate comfort food whenever I find I'm missing Thailand. I like to serve it as a single meal over a plate of plain rice, with a Thai-style fried egg on top, just waiting to ooze out its yellowy goodness. It provides a creamy counter-balance to the salty-spiciness of the dish.

4–6 **bird's-eye chillies**
1 medium–large red **chilli**, cut into chunks
6 cloves of **garlic**, peeled
a pinch of **salt**
2 tablespoons **dark soy sauce**
1 tablespoon **light soy sauce**
1 tablespoon **nam pla** (fish sauce)
2 tablespoons **water**
a pinch of **sugar**
1–2 tablespoons **vegetable oil**
200–300g **beef**, minced or finely chopped
a large handful of picked **bai krapow,**
    or **Thai holy basil leaves** – the more the
    merrier – plus a few to scatter at the end
100g **green beans**, topped, tailed and
    cut into 1cm pieces

TIPS

* You can really use anything you like in this: prawns, duck, tofu, chicken, finely sliced beef, and so on.

* If you can't find Thai holy basil, you can substitute it with *bai horapha* (sweet basil), or regular basil.

* Traditionally, this is served with some *nam pla prik* on the side. To make this, chop up a few bird's-eye chillies and cover with 2–3 tablespoons of *nam pla*.

1. In a pestle and mortar, pound the chillies, garlic and salt together into a rough paste, then set aside.

2. Now mix the soy sauces, *nam pla* and water together in a small bowl, and stir in the sugar. (This is a short cut to speed things up at the wok. Properly, you should add them individually.)

3. Heat the oil in a wok until it's really hot. Throw in the chilli-garlic paste and stir-fry for a few seconds – until you can really smell everything in the pan, but not long enough to colour the garlic. Add the beef and stir-fry until it's almost cooked through. Then add the green beans and keep stir-frying until the beef is done.

4. Finally, add the soy sauce mixture and stir, keeping it moving in the wok and allowing it to bubble up before adding the basil and wilting it into the dish.

5. Serve over steamed Thai jasmine rice, and finish with a scattering of a few extra basil leaves.

6. For a very Thai touch, heat about a 2–3cm depth of vegetable oil in another wok and, when it's super-hot, crack in an egg. Fry until the white is crispy on the outside, and the yolk runny within – it should take about a minute. Drain, and serve on top of your *pad krapow* and rice. Everyone should have their own egg, or there'll be fighting.

Cabbage, Peas & Pancetta

SERVES 4 • PREPARATION TIME: 10 MINUTES • COOKING TIME: 15 MINUTES • ✓ WF GF

This is a great combo, and the pancetta brings out everything that's glorious about cabbage.

75g **pancetta**, cubed
½ a **January King cabbage**, sliced
a couple of sprigs of **fresh flat-leaf parsley**
25g **butter**
200g **frozen peas**, thawed
salt and **freshly ground black pepper**

1. In a small, non-stick frying pan, cook the pancetta until golden. Set aside.

2. Put the cabbage into a large pan with a good-fitting lid. Add a splash of water, no more than 1cm deep. Add the parsley, the butter and some salt and pepper, put the lid on and place the whole thing over a medium heat.

3. When you see steam starting to escape, throw in the peas, give the pan a good shake and cook for 3–5 minutes, or until the cabbage is soft but still retains some bite.

4. Strain off the buttery water leaving a little to coat the leaves. Then toss the pancetta through the cabbage and serve at once.

Fragrant Cardamom Basmati Rice

SERVES 4 • PREPARATION TIME: 5–10 MINUTES • COOKING TIME: 15–20 MINUTES • WF GF V

The smell of this turns our kitchen into an exotic, faraway land … at least, with our eyes closed.

1 tablespoon **vegetable oil** or **butter**
1 tablespoon finely chopped **onion**
200g **basmati rice**, rinsed and drained
5–6 **cardamom pods**, lightly crushed
a pinch of **saffron**
300ml **water**
a pinch of **salt**

1. Heat the oil in a pan with a tight-fitting lid. Add the onions and sauté gently for a few minutes, or until they're just softening.

2. Stir in the rice. Add the crushed cardamom pods and the saffron and stir again. Add the water and a pinch of salt, then bring to the boil. As soon as it comes to the boil, turn down to the lowest heat, cover and cook for 10–12 minutes.

3. Check to see that the rice is cooked and all the water has been absorbed, then turn off the heat and let the rice sit with a lid on for 5 minutes before serving.

Stuffed Tomatoes

SERVES 4 • PREPARATION TIME: 10 MINUTES
COOKING TIME: 25 MINUTES • DF V

We love these tomatoes so much that we'll
sometimes have them for lunch on their own,
with some sliced fennel. This is also a useful
recipe if you have leftover baguettes.

> 4 large firm **tomatoes**
> 150g **breadcrumbs**
> 3 tablespoons good **olive oil**
> 2–4 cloves of **garlic**, chopped
>   (we like it really garlicky)
> a handful of **fresh flat-leaf parsley**,
>   chopped
> **salt** and **freshly ground black pepper**

1. Heat the oven to 180°C/350°F/gas mark 4.

2. Halve the tomatoes and carefully scoop
   out and discard the insides. In a separate
   bowl, mix together the breadcrumbs, olive
   oil, garlic, parsley, salt and pepper.

3. Pack the breadcrumb mixture into the
   tomato halves making a nice little mound
   on top. Put the tomatoes in a roasting tin
   and bake in the oven for 20–25 minutes.

4. Serve at once. But do be careful – they can
   be nuclear-hot inside.

TIPS

* Whizz up any leftover bread in
  the blender and stick it in the
  freezer in bags until you need it.

* This often makes too much
  filling, depending on the size
  of your tomatoes. Toast off any
  leftovers in a dry frying pan
  for a few minutes until golden
  brown, then serve it with the
  tomatoes (or sprinkled over
  a salad) for extra crunch.

Sautéd Summer Vegetables

SERVES 4 • PREPARATION TIME: 10 MINUTES • COOKING TIME: 15 MINUTES • ♥ WF GF DF V

Perfect as an accompaniment to so many summer dishes, or just on its own as a light lunch.

2 tablespoons **olive oil**
2 cloves of **garlic**, chopped
½ a large **red chilli**, deseeded and chopped
200g **peas**
3 small **courgettes**, sliced

12–16 **cherry tomatoes**, or 10–12 **small tomatoes**, halved
a few sprigs of **fresh thyme**
a good dash of **white wine**
salt and **freshly ground black pepper**

1. Heat 1 tablespoon of olive oil in a heavy-bottomed pan over a medium heat. Add the garlic and chilli and cook for two minutes, just until the garlic takes colour.

2. Now add the vegetables, tomatoes, thyme, salt and pepper. Cook for a couple of minutes, then add the wine. Bubble it up, stirring everything together in its steam, then turn down the heat and add the rest of the oil. Cook for a further 7 minutes or so, stirring occasionally. Serve at once.

Sautéd Radishes with Their Tops & Peas

SERVES 4 • PREPARATION TIME: 10 MINUTES • COOKING TIME: 10 MINUTES • ♥ WF GF DF V

There's something about the lovely peppery-ness of French radishes with the sweetness of English peas, so we suppose that this is the *entente cordiale* in a side dish. It tastes fresh and it uses everything.

400g **radishes,** with their tops on
2 tablespoons good-quality **olive oil**
3 cloves of **garlic**, thickly sliced

250g **frozen peas**, thawed
a couple of big handfuls of **pea shoots**
salt and **freshly ground black pepper**

1. Remove the tops from the radishes and wash them thoroughly. Slice the radishes into fat ovals, about 0.5cm thick. Set aside.

2. Heat 1 tablespoon of the olive oil in a non-stick frying pan over a medium heat. Add the garlic and cook until it starts to colour.

3. Now add the radish tops. Cook until they start to wilt, then add the sliced radishes and the peas. Cook for a further minute or so, then add the pea shoots. Keep everything moving around the pan until the pea shoots are just wilting. Add the remaining olive oil and salt and pepper to dress. Serve promptly.

TIPS

* We think it's best to use frozen peas for this, unless you're growing your own, in which case you can pick them at their perfect sweetness. Sometimes those fresh peas in the supermarket are so old that they'd be better used as buckshot.

* You can whip up this dish quickly while a chop or a steak is resting. By the time you're done, the meat should be perfect.

Will's Onion Rice

SERVES 6–8 • PREPARATION TIME: 5–10 MINUTES •
COOKING TIME: 15 MINUTES • WF GF DF V

Well, this recipe has become Will's, but it started out as Katie and Pop's. However, because Will doesn't have the largest of repertoires, and he cooks it so well, we are happy for him to claim it.

It is a simple way of making a tasty, oniony rice. But we invite you to add your own flourishes.

> 1 tablespoon **olive oil**
> 1 **onion**, chopped
> 4 mugs of **water**
> 2 mugs of **white basmati rice**
> 1 tablespoon **bouillon, chicken**
>   or **vegetable stock**
> **freshly ground black pepper**

1. Heat the olive oil in a large saucepan. Add the chopped onion and fry until it's translucent. Add the water and bring to the boil. Then add the rice.

2. Simmer with a lid on over a low heat until it's cooked, around 10–12 minutes. The water should all be absorbed.

3. Add the bouillon or stock and stir it in. Season with a good grinding of freshly ground black pepper, then serve.

TIPS

* Try adding other things to the rice such as peas, broad beans, asparagus or mushrooms.

* You can substitute brown or wild or Camargue rice, but you'll need to double the cooking time.

HOW MANY SHEPHERDS DOES IT TAKE TO MAKE A PIE?

Hats off to Mrs Freeman, Eleanor's teacher. This year we went to Christmas Eve carols and Eleanor was able to answer all the questions about the angel and the shepherds that the vicar could throw at us.

Now, the fact that shepherd's pie is made of lamb is like zoo-keeper's pie being made of lion: I mean, aren't they meant to be looking after them? Either way, shepherd's pie and all related pies in the pie genus are about goodness, comfort and love. Something we explore a little in our Pie Fest video on our website, see www.leonrestaurants.co.uk.

JOHN

Alice's Vegetarian Shepherd's Pie

SERVES 4–6 • PREPARATION TIME: 20 MINUTES • COOKING TIME: 1 HOUR • V

This is based on a simple pumpkin gratin, the idea being to cook all those ingredients you might like to eat *with* your gratin *in* your gratin. It's a perfect autumn dish.

1 small **pumpkin/butternut squash**, weighing about 1.2kg
3 cloves of **garlic**
25g **butter**
1 tablespoon **olive oil**
1 **onion**, finely sliced
300g **mushrooms**, chopped (chestnut, oyster, shiitake, are more flavoursome than button ones)
2 sprigs of **fresh thyme**
200ml **sherry** (an amontillado or an oloroso)
2 x 400g **tins of haricot beans** or **cannellini beans**, drained and rinsed
250g **spinach leaves**
25g **strong cheese** (e.g. Cheddar, Gruyère), grated
25g **breadcrumbs**
salt and **freshly ground black pepper**

ALICE, OXFORDSHIRE, 1971

Alice is Kay's sister-in-law. She writes books. She lives in the country. If we say any more about her, she'll hunt us down.

1. Heat the oven to 200°C/400°F/gas mark 6.

2. Peel and deseed the pumpkin/squash, then cut it into chunks. Place in a pan with salted water to cover and cook over a low heat until the pumpkin is soft and mashable (about 15 minutes). Drain, then mash with a fork. Crush 1 clove of garlic and stir it in, then season with salt and pepper. Set aside to cool.

3. Meanwhile, heat the butter and oil in a frying pan, then add the onion and fry slowly until it's coloured as brown as you like it. Chop the remaining cloves of garlic and add to the pan with the mushrooms, thyme, sherry and beans. Season well with salt and pepper and let the mixture simmer away until the sherry has reduced – about 10 minutes or so (you don't want the filling to be too sloppy). At the last moment stir in the spinach leaves to wilt.

4. Place the filling in a casserole dish and spoon the pumpkin mash on top. Mix the cheese with the breadcrumbs and sprinkle on top, then give it a light drizzle of olive oil. Bake in the oven for 35–45 minutes, or until the topping is golden brown.

A SHORT PHOTO STORY

REAL SHEEP

A REAL VEGETARIAN (NOT A REAL SHEPHERD)

TIME TO GO HOME

THE BUS IS LATE

SHEPHERD'S PIE FOR THE LOCAL?

Mrs V's Shepherd's Pie

Perfect English comfort food.

1kg **potatoes**, peeled and cut into chunks
30g **butter**, plus extra for glazing the top
2 tablespoons **milk**
1 large **onion**, finely chopped
2 tablespoons **vegetable oil**
500g **minced lamb**
1 large or 2 medium **carrots**, grated
1 stick of **celery**, finely chopped
570ml **stock** (water and 1 tablespoon
   Marigold bouillon granules)
½ teaspoon **dried mixed herbs**
1 teaspoon **Worcestershire sauce**
2 teaspoons **tomato purée**
salt and **freshly ground black pepper**

1. Boil the potatoes and when they're cooked, mash together with the butter and the milk. Season with salt and pepper, then set aside and leave to cool.

2. Meanwhile, heat 1 tablespoon of the oil in a large, deep frying pan. Add the onions and fry gently until transparent and beginning to brown. Remove the onions with a slotted spoon and set aside.

3. Add the rest of the oil to the pan and add the lamb, using a wooden spoon to break it up. Once browned, add the carrot, celery and fried onion and season with salt and pepper.

4. In a separate pan slowly bring the stock to the boil. Add the herbs, Worcestershire sauce and tomato purée, then pour it into the frying pan, mixing it well with the mince and vegetables.

5. Cover the pan and simmer gently over a low heat for 45 minutes, stirring occasionally. If the mixture seems rather runny, raise the temperature to reduce it a little.

6. Heat the oven to 200°C/400°F/gas mark 6. Tip the mince mixture into a deep enough oven dish and spread the mashed potato over the mince. Brush the surface with a little melted butter and cook in the oven for 30 minutes, or until the top is brown and crispy.

JOHN AND HIS MUM MARION, 1973

My mum is sort of a shepherd. She is one of the best and most committed teachers I know, and there are many former pupils who will tell you so. She has spent many years tending her many flocks, while taking time to understand each one. This is the recipe I grew up with, and it saw me through many years of late-night homework and sports matches. Mum has always been very good at getting the potato nice and crispy.
Thank you Mrs V aka Mum.
JOHN

Fisherman's Pie at 91a

SERVES 4–6 • PREPARATION TIME: 15 MINUTES • COOKING TIME: 1 HOUR 5 MINUTES •

Kay is not a great lover of fish pie. Too many memories of dry, egg-ridden school dinners. We however, are big fans of a proper fishy fish pie. So she created one for us. Here it is.

350g **whiting or cod fillets**, skinned and cut into chunks
350g **undyed smoked haddock**
600ml **whole milk**
50ml **double cream**
1 **bay leaf**
½ a small **onion**
10 **peppercorns**
1 clove of **garlic**
1 stick of **celery**
a pinch of **saffron**
160g **hot-smoked salmon**, cut into chunks

1 heaped tablespoon **capers**, rinsed
1 tablespoon rinsed and chopped **cornichons**
a small bunch of **chervil** or **fresh flat-leaf parsley**, chopped
1kg floury **potatoes** (King Edwards are Kay's preference), peeled and cut into chunks
100g **butter**, plus extra to dot on top
1 heaped tablespoon **flour**
sea salt and **freshly ground black pepper**

1. Put the whiting and haddock into a shallow pan and pour over the milk and cream. Add the bay leaf, the onion half, peppercorns, garlic clove, celery and saffron. Bring slowly to the boil, then simmer for 5 minutes, or until the fish is cooked.

2. Remove the fish from the pan, reserving the milk, and flake into a lightly buttered casserole or pie dish, peeling away any skin and checking for bones. Flake in the hot-smoked salmon now too and mix in well, along with the capers and cornichons and some chervil or parsley. Set aside to cool completely.

3. Strain the reserved poaching milk into a jug and leave to cool.

4. Meanwhile, boil the potatoes in plenty of salted water until very tender and mashable. Drain them and put them back into the pan. Add 3 tablespoons of the poaching milk, 50g of the butter, some salt and pepper and mash well. Set aside.

5. Heat the oven to 200°C/400°F/gas mark 6.

6. Now make the creamy sauce. Melt the remaining butter in a pan, then add the flour and cook for a minute or two. Add the remaining poaching milk and whisk well until combined and smooth. Put the pan back on the heat, bring to the boil and stir until the sauce has thickened.

7. Remove the sauce from the heat and pour over the fish. Spread the mashed potatoes over the fish and sauce mixture and dot a little butter on top.

8. Pop into the oven for 35–40 minutes, or until golden brown on top.

Cottage Pie

SERVES 4–6 • PREPARATION TIME: 15 MINUTES PLUS COOLING • COOKING TIME: 1 HOUR 10 MINUTES

When is a shepherd's pie not a shepherd's pie? When it's made of beef – and it's a cottage pie! We don't care what you call it.

1kg **potatoes**, peeled and cut into chunks
50ml **milk**
50g **butter**
2 tablespoons **olive oil** or **vegetable oil**
1 **onion**, finely chopped
1 **carrot**, finely chopped
1 stick of **celery**, finely chopped
1 clove of **garlic**, finely chopped
1½ tablespoons finely chopped **fresh flat-leaf parsley**
500g **minced beef**
125ml **red wine**
1 **beef stock cube**
300ml **water**
1 tablespoon **tomato purée**
a few good dashes of **Worcestershire sauce**
salt and **freshly ground black pepper**

1. Bring a large pan of salted water to a rolling boil, add the potatoes and cook until tender. When they're done, drain them and mash them with the milk, butter and some salt and pepper to taste. Set aside to cool.

2. In a sauté pan, heat 1 tablespoon of the oil over a low to medium heat and gently cook the onion, carrot and celery until they're soft and the onion has a golden, almost translucent quality. Add the garlic and parsley and cook for 2 minutes, until really fragrant. Then spoon all the vegetables out of the sauté pan into a bowl.

3. Turn up the heat, return the sauté pan to the hob and add the remaining oil. Now brown the beef. When it's done, pour in the wine. Bubble it up hard to cook out the alcohol, then crumble in the stock cube, add the water, tomato purée and Worcestershire sauce and stir them in well. Season with salt and pepper.

4. Add the vegetable mixture to the meat, stir it in well and cook on the hob for 5–7 minutes to reduce and to amalgamate all the flavours.

5. Heat the oven to 200°C/400°F/gas mark 6. Tip the meat and vegetable mixture into your pie dish, then cover with the mashed potato and score it with a fork. Dot with a extra butter and bake in the oven for 45 minutes, or until brown and crispy on top.

TIPS

* Feel free to change the herbs – rosemary is lovely, as is marjoram.

* Cut the potato with some boiled mashed carrot or celeriac to ring the changes.

(PIE IT YOURSELF)

The (humble) pie: it's the ultimate all-in-one meal. Even in Thailand, we had pies. What's a classic curry puff if not a tiny, perfect pie? My mum, Betty, used to make a cracker of a steak and kidney, with golden shortcrust pastry and a rich, meaty gravy. You can make a pie with just about anything, and I started early, by trying to sell mud-pies to passers-by. I thought they'd be particularly good with worms and extra baby mud crabs. There's no mud in these pies, but there's a good cross-section, running from the simplest tomato and thyme to the richest tartiflette. All here to give you some *pie-deas*. Just leave out the mud.

KAY

Chard & Bacon Tart

SERVES 6–8 • PREPARATION TIME: 25 MINUTES • COOKING TIME: 40–50 MINUTES

The marriage of cream, bacon, chard and cheese sits happily-ever-after in a crisp pastry shell. One of our more indulgent favourites. And you don't need to roll out the pastry either …

70g **lardons** or chopped **bacon**
1 tablespoon **olive oil**
1 clove of **garlic**, peeled and finely sliced
100g **chard leaves** or **kale**, shredded
2 **eggs**, lightly beaten
1 **egg yolk**
200ml **double cream**
1–2 sprigs of **fresh thyme**, leaves picked

100g **Gruyère cheese**
salt and **freshly ground black pepper**

For the pastry:
250g **plain flour**
125g **unsalted butter**, straight from the fridge, diced
a good pinch of **sea salt**
a small glass of **iced water**

1. Heat the oven to 200°C/400°F/gas mark 6. Butter a 23cm round, non-stick tart tin with a removable base.

2. First make your pastry. Measure out the flour into a large bowl and add the butter. Start rubbing the flour and butter together with your fingertips, lifting it and gently working it until you have what looks like fine breadcrumbs.

3. Add the salt. Then add the iced water a teaspoonful at a time, until the pastry just comes together. Don't add too much water or you'll get a hard pastry.

4. Roll it into a loose ball and using your fingertips gently push the dough into the prepared tart tin, easing it around until it evenly covers the base and sides. Cover the whole thing with a sheet of greaseproof paper and weight it down with some baking beans. Then bake it in the oven for 10 minutes.

5. Over a medium heat, cook the lardons or chopped bacon in a frying pan until cooked through, about 5 minutes. Remove with a slotted spoon and set aside.

6. Wipe out the pan, then return it to the heat and add the olive oil. Add the garlic. Fry for a minute or so – don't let it colour too much – then add the chard and a pinch of salt, and cook until it is just wilted. Remove from the heat, set aside and leave to drain in a colander. Then, when it's cool, squeeze out any excess liquid.

7. Take the tart shell out of the oven. Carefully remove the greaseproof paper and the baking beans, and pop it back into the oven for another 5 minutes to crisp up.

8. In a clean bowl, beat the eggs, egg yolk, cream, salt and pepper with an electric whisk. Stir in the Gruyère and the thyme leaves and season with salt and pepper.

9. Remove the tart shell from the oven. Scatter the chard across the base. Sprinkle the bacon bits in, then pour in the cream and egg mixture.

10. Bake the tart in the oven for about 30–40 minutes, until the filling has puffed up and the pastry is a lovely golden brown.

Tomato, Thyme & Goat's Cheese Tart

SERVES 4–6 • PREPARATION TIME: 15 MINUTES • COOKING TIME: 20–25 MINUTES • V

You can whip this up in minutes, making it the perfect quick lunch or supper dish.

1 sheet of **ready-rolled puff pastry**
2 tablespoons **extra virgin olive oil**
400g **cherry tomatoes**, halved, or **small tomatoes**, quartered
4 sprigs of **fresh thyme**, leaves picked
1 clove of **garlic**, peeled and chopped
80g **soft goat's cheese**
salt and **freshly ground black pepper**

1. Heat the oven to 220°C/425°F/gas mark 7.

2. Lay out the puff pastry on a baking tray lined with baking paper. Then, using a sharp knife, score a line – not all the way through – down and across each side of the pastry, about 2cm in from the edges. This will give the tart a nice crusty raised edge.

3. Put the olive oil, cherry tomatoes, thyme leaves and garlic into a bowl and mix until they are well coated. Season with salt and pepper and mix again.

4. Tumble the tomato mixture evenly over the pastry, keeping it within the lines.

5. Crumble the goat's cheese over the top among the bits of tomato.

6. Add another quick dash of freshly ground pepper and pop it into the oven for about 20 minutes, or until it's golden brown and puffy on the outside and the tomatoes are collapsing slightly and the cheese is melt-y, then serve.

TIPS

* For something a little sweeter, you could replace the tomatoes with sliced fresh figs. Keep everything else the same – just add a good drizzle of runny honey before serving.

Katie's Tartiflette

SERVES 8 • PREPARATION TIME: 20 MINUTES • COOKING TIME: 30 MINUTES • WF GF

Tartiflette is one of those skiing dishes that you shouldn't need to be above 3,000 metres to eat. It's completely indulgent and works well with a salad, or just on its own for lunch.

This recipe is inspired by our friend Charlie Tomlinson (a lady, and wife of lovely Patrick) who made this for us at the end of a long week of work, with a gorgeous steak. Can you think of a better way of reviving the spirits?

> 1kg **potatoes**, peeled and thickly sliced
> 1 tablespoon **olive oil**
> 2 **onions**, chopped
> 6 rashers of **smoked streaky bacon**, cut into strips
> 1 whole **Reblochon cheese**, cut into cubes
> 400ml **double cream** or **full-fat crème fraîche**
> 125ml **white wine**
> **salt** and **freshly ground black pepper**

1. Steam or parboil the potatoes until they're tender but not overcooked, about 10 minutes.

2. Heat the oven to 180°C/350°F/gas mark 4.

3. Meanwhile, heat the olive oil in a frying pan and cook the onions until they're translucent. Add the bacon to the onion and fry until the bacon is cooked – you don't want the onion to burn.

4. Put a fat layer of potato into an ovenproof dish, season with salt and pepper, add half the onion and bacon mix and spread over half the cheese. Layer the rest of the sliced potato on top, with the rest of the bacon and onion, and top with the remaining cheese. Season a bit more.

5. Mix the double cream with the white wine and pour over the whole shooting match. If you're using crème fraîche, warm it through in a pan with the wine to loosen it up for pouring.

6. Put the dish into the oven for 20 minutes or so, or until it's golden and bubbling. Check the potatoes really are cooked through. Then dive in.

FOOD FACT

Reblochon is a cows' cheese from the Haute-Savoie region of France. Its name apparently comes from a fourteenth-century tax dodge. Back then, landowners would tax farmers according to the amount of milk their herds produced. So these canny chaps would not fully milk their cows until the landowners had measured their output. Hence 'reblocher' – to pinch the cow's udder again. This retained milk is richer, creamier and sinfully delicious. When it comes to a cheese for tartiflette, accept no substitute.

My best snowy memory is the message I got from John when I was struggling home in the snow one evening. 'We're going to pretend we're on a skiing holiday,' he said. 'When you get home, get into your ski kit, our neighbours are coming over, we're going to walk around the garden in the snow and then come indoors and drink glühwein and eat tartiflette.' And we did. It was a very silly evening and the tartiflette was just as delicious eaten at home as it is in the Alps.   KATIE

MAKE IT BURGER NIGHT

A good burger is so easy to make. You can cook them just how you like them, and everyone can pick their own favourite garnishes. Hell, if you want to, you can even bake your own bun. At our place, they're just the thing for a live footie match on the telly (though, at the ground, I think you've got to have a pie.). So here're our burgers. Go on … you know you want to.

KAY

FRED'S CLASSIC BEEF BURGER

Fred's Classic Beef Burger

MAKES 4 • PREPARATION TIME: 10 MINUTES • COOKING TIME: 10–15 MINUTES • ✓ WF GF

This is about as simple as it gets: just beef, onion, salt and pepper. Fred says he used to mess around with it a lot more, but he made so many burgers for his chums during Euro 96, and this was the version everyone preferred.

> 1 **onion**, peeled and cut into chunks
> 450g good-quality **minced beef**
> 1 tablespoon **olive oil** or **vegetable oil**
> **salt** and **freshly ground pepper**

1. In a food processor, blitz the onion into tiny pieces. Add the minced beef and pulse just enough to mix the onion into it. You don't want to be too over-zealous here, or you'll end up with a meat paste. We want it well blended, but with texture.

2. Turn the meat mixture out into a bowl and season well with salt and pepper, mixing it together thoroughly with your hands. Now divide it into 4 equal-sized patties.

3. Heat a non-stick frying pan over a medium to high heat. Rub both sides of the patties with olive oil and season them again with salt and pepper. Then pop them into the pan. Fry for 10–15 minutes, turning once or twice, until they're cooked how you like them. Serve on a bun, with lettuce, cheese, ketchup and mustard.

Kay's Hollywood Turkey Burger

SERVES 4 • PREPARATION TIME: 15 MINUTES • COOKING TIME: 15–20 MINUTES • ✓ ♥

A favourite amongst all our LA pals. Low in fat, big on flavour. Just the thing before you squeeze into your Oscar frock.

500g **minced turkey**
2 cloves of **garlic**, finely chopped
2 **spring onions**, finely chopped
a large handful of **fresh coriander**, finely chopped

½ a **serrano** or other **medium-hot chilli**, finely chopped
1 tablespoon **olive oil**
salt and **freshly ground black pepper**

1. In a food processor, mix the turkey, garlic, spring onions, coriander and chilli together in a series of short pulses. Turn the mixture out on to a board, and work it into 4 equal-sized patties.

2. Heat the olive oil in a non-stick frying pan over a medium heat. Season the burgers on both sides with salt and pepper, then fry until cooked through, about 8–10 minutes each side.

3. Serve in a wholemeal or gluten-free bun with a slice of tomato, lettuce and a little chipotle mayonnaise.

'Ciao Bella' Italian Burger

SERVES 4 • PREPARATION TIME: 10 MINUTES • COOKING TIME: 15–20 MINUTES • ✓

Think Sophia Loren on a bun.

1 **onion**, cut into chunks
1 clove of **garlic**
1 sprig of **fresh rosemary**, leaves picked
3 sprigs of **fresh flat-leaf parsley**
170g **minced veal**

170g **minced pork**
170g **minced beef**
1 tablespoon **olive oil**
salt and **freshly ground black pepper**

1. In a food processor, blitz the onion, garlic and herb leaves. Add the meat and pulse to blend it together.

2. Turn the mixture out into a bowl and season with salt and pepper, working the seasonings in thoroughly with your hands. Now divide it into 4 equal-sized patties.

3. Heat a non-stick frying pan over a medium high heat. Rub the patties on both sides with the olive oil and season with salt and pepper. Fry them for 15–20 minutes, turning once or twice, or until they're cooked to your liking.

4. Serve on ciabatta rolls, with lettuce, tomato and maybe some *mostarda di frutta* or a spiky onion relish.

The Veggie Burger

SERVES 4 • PREPARATION TIME: 10 MINUTES • COOKING TIME: 15 MINUTES • ✓ ♥ V

This is not your usual veggie burger bulked up with beans, this is just veggies pure and simple.

2 tablespoons **olive oil** (more if you are cooking in 2 batches)
4 large **Portabello mushrooms**, about 150g each, trimmed and wiped
1 **red pepper**, deseeded and cut into 8 rings
3–4 cloves of **garlic**, peeled and chopped
a good handful of fresh **parsley**, chopped
1 **avocado**, sliced
4 **wholemeal rolls** (or rolls of your choice), to serve
salt and **freshly ground black pepper**

1. Heat 1 tablespoon of the olive oil in a wide frying pan. Pop in the mushrooms and gently fry them, turning occasionally until they are just done – about 5–7 minutes in all. Remove the mushrooms from the pan with a slotted spoon and set aside.

2. Heat the remaining tablespoon of olive oil. Sauté the red pepper rings until they start to colour, but are still crisp. Remove them from the pan and set aside. Pop in the garlic and parsley and sauté until softened and fragrant – just a couple of minutes.

3. Reintroduce the mushrooms to the pan, along with any juices that have come from them. Stir to mix everything thoroughly and season with salt and pepper.

4. Place the mushrooms on the halved buns. Pop two red pepper rings on top of each, a few slices of avocado and top with mayo.

KAY'S HOLLYWOOD TURKEY BURGER   'CIAO BELLA' ITALIAN BURGER

Spicy Thai Pork Burger

MAKES: 4 • PREPARATION TIME: 10 MINUTES • COOKING TIME: 15–20 MINUTES • ✓

We saw something similar to this served rather innovatively between two discs of sticky rice in northern Thailand. So we decided to create our own.

1½ tablespoons **white peppercorns**
2cm **fresh ginger**, peeled and chopped
3 **coriander roots**
3 cloves of **garlic**, peeled
a pinch of **salt**

500g **minced pork**
1 tablespoon **nam pla** (fish sauce)
1 tablespoon chopped **fresh coriander**
2 tablespoons **vegetable oil**

1. Grind the peppercorns in a pestle and mortar. Then add the chopped ginger, coriander roots, garlic and a pinch of salt, and grind them into the pepper until you have a dry paste.

2. Put the paste into a bowl, add the pork mince, along with the nam pla and the fresh coriander, and work all the ingredients together. (You can do this in a food processor, just don't blitz it too hard.) Form into 4 evenly-sized patties.

3. Heat the oil in a non-stick frying pan and fry the patties for about 15–20 minutes, turning them from time to time until they're cooked through. Serve in a soft white bap, with mayonnaise, sriracha sauce, crisp lettuce and a slice of cucumber or tomato.

TIPS

* White pepper is a key ingredient in Thai food. By all means, cut down the pepperiness if you like, but leave in at least half a tablespoonful or the burger will be very bland.

VEGGIE BURGER

SPICY THAI PORK BURGER

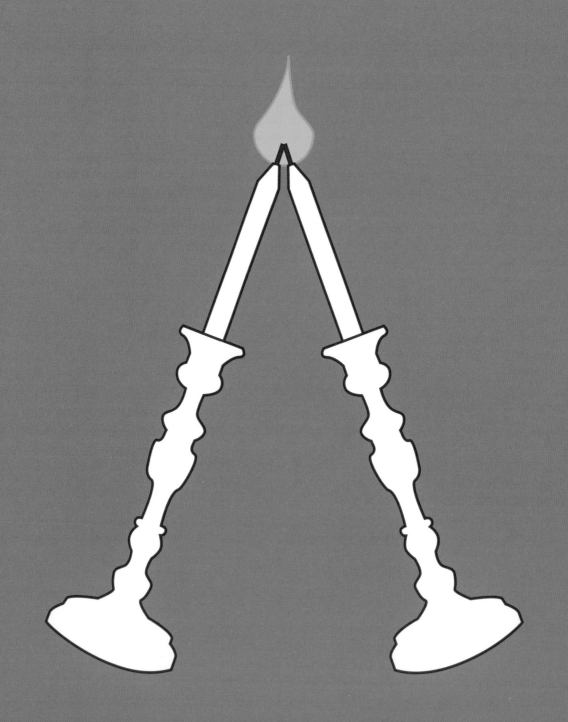

AFTER LIGHTS OUT

There is something magical about putting your kids to bed. Occasionally. At other times it is a nightmare. You end up at 10.30p.m. having finally got them to sleep. You are exhausted, in need of caffeine, and you have to start on your work that needs to be done the next day.

These recipes are for those almost fairytale evenings where the kids say at 7.30p.m. that they're tired and will go to bed. Where they get into their pyjamas themselves, clean their teeth, pack everything for the next day, where the bedroom is tidy and smells of lavender, where they read one chapter of an enriching book, ask you a few life-enhancing questions to which you have good and pertinent and loving answers, and where the lights go out and you glide downstairs to enjoy a romantic dinner just like on TV.

If it ever happens, or if you ever get close, these recipes are for you.

Betty's Quick Prawn Red Curry

SERVES 2 • PREPARATION TIME: 10–15 MINUTES • COOKING TIME: 10 MINUTES • ✓ WF GF DF

Here's a quick trip to Thailand in one very simple curry.

> 1 tablespoon **vegetable oil**
> 2 cloves of **garlic**, peeled and finely chopped
> 1 tablespoon **Thai red curry paste**
> 200ml **coconut milk**
> 100ml **water**
> a 2cm square of **fresh ginger**, peeled and slivered
> 12 **fresh basil leaves**, plus a few for garnish
> 3 **kaffir lime leaves**, slivered
> 1 tablespoon **roasted peanuts**, crushed
> 300g large **prawns** or **prawn tails**
> a squeeze of **lime juice**
> 2 teaspoons **sugar**
> 2 teaspoons **nam pla** (fish sauce)
> 1 large **red chilli**, finely slivered

BETTY, BANGKOK, 1963

1. In a wok or a pan heat the oil and fry the garlic until it just begins to brown. Add the curry paste and stir in well, until you can really smell it.

2. Add 100ml of the coconut milk and bring to the boil. Add the water and bring back to the boil, then add the rest of the coconut milk and bring to the boil again. Add the sugar and nam pla and stir in well.

3. Add the ginger, basil, 2 of the lime leaves and the peanuts, one ingredient at a time, stirring well after each addition. Then stir in the prawns. They will turn pink when they are cooked through – in no more than a minute or two.

4. Add a squeeze of lime, then turn out on to a serving dish. Garnish with the slivered chilli, the last lime leaf and a few leaves of basil. Serve with jasmine rice (see page 272).

TIPS

* When you buy your curry paste, make sure you get a good one. Kay recommends the Mae Ploy brand.

* Remember that chillies freeze really well, so don't worry if you have to buy a whole pack. Just freeze them for next time. The same goes for lime leaves – pop them into a plastic bag and freeze them too, and coconut milk: freeze it in an ice cube tray.

* Serve some of the *nam pla prik* on the side for extra punch (see tip on page 137).

My mum, Betty, had big blue eyes, dangerous curves and cool pastry hands. She and my dad were childhood sweethearts. Engaged at sixteen, married at twenty-two, they embarked on a grand adventure together, a few years later, when they left south London for the bright lights of 1960s Bangkok. She immediately fell in love with the food and the country.

I found this recipe written on a scrap of paper in Mum's handwriting when I was going through some bits in the kitchen. She was an amazing cook. She only ever had a handful of cookbooks – the classics: Marguerite Patten, Delia, Josceline Dimbleby, and a stack of *Aussie Women's Weekly*. And she would come up with incredibly delicious dishes that never failed.

I have a lot to thank her for. And I miss her terribly.

KAY

Perfect Pepper Steak

SERVES 2 • PREPARATION TIME: 10 MINUTES • COOKING TIME: 10–15 MINUTES • WF

Pepper steak, or steak au poivre, is a bistro classic that we all take for granted. And it's one which, because it's so simple, is all too often made really badly. We think this recipe gets it just about right, all the way down to the retro 70s whisky cream sauce.

> 2 **steaks** of your choice
> 1 clove of **garlic**, halved
> 1 teaspoon **olive oil**
> 1 tablespoon **whole white peppercorns**, coarsely crushed
> 1 tablespoon **whole black peppercorns**, coarsely crushed
> 1 tablespoon **coarse sea salt**
> 100ml **whisky** (optional)
> 125ml **double cream** (optional)
> 1 tablespoon **green peppercorns**, rinsed (optional)

1. Pat the steaks dry and rub the cut side of the garlic liberally over both sides of each steak, then rub with the olive oil.

2. Pat the crushed pepper on to the steaks and leave to macerate for an hour. (If you're in a hurry, don't worry – the steaks just won't be as peppery.)

3. Heat a wide frying pan as hot as you dare. Season the steaks with the sea salt then slap the meat in the pan. Now, here's the thing – every steak has its own time scale. We swear by the following test: Hold out your left hand. With your right hand, feel that fleshy bit of palm under your thumb. You'll see it goes from soft and squishy to hard by your wrist. Keep touching the steaks with your finger. Soft and squishy = rare: medium = medium; hard = well done. It really is the best way.

4. When the steaks are cooked just how you like them, set them aside on a warm plate to rest for at least 5 minutes. This is very important. It lets the fibres of the meat relax and the flavours develop.

5. While the steaks are resting, deglaze the pan with the whisky, then pour in the cream. Bubble it up so the cream thickens for about a minute, then add the green peppercorns. Pour the sauce over the steaks, and serve with a green salad, or a baked potato and spinach.

A SHORT PHOTO STORY...

PERFECT PEPPER STEAKS

OR SOME WILD MUSHROOMS...

READY TO PLAY 70S COP SHOW

KEEP YOUR EYE ON THE TARGE

John's Wild Mushroom Sauté

(A THEME AND VARIATIONS)

SERVES 4 • PREPARATION TIME: 15 MINUTES • COOKING TIME: 15–20 MINUTES • ✓ ♥ WF GF DF V

Genghis Khan was, apparently, so prolific in his 'travels' that most of us are in some way related to him. In that spirit, I have tried here to give you a dish that can provide the grand-daddy from which many variations and related dishes can come.

6 tablespoons **olive oil** – judge for yourself how much
700g **mushrooms**, sliced – ideally lots of different varieties,
   but if you only have button mushrooms then that's cool
4 cloves of **garlic**, chopped
some **fresh herbs** you like (such as **thyme, tarragon**), chopped
a couple of tablespoons finely chopped **fresh parsley**
salt and **freshly ground black pepper**

1. Heat 2 tablespoons of the oil to quite a high temperature (you know, until the steamy effect occurs). Cook the mushrooms until they're just sealed. You'll need to do this in batches: the idea here is to flash-cook the mushrooms and to keep the moisture in, so set each batch aside on a warm plate as you go. And add a little more oil, as needed, for each batch, too.

2. If your mushrooms throw a little moisture into the pan, spoon it out and keep cooking.

3. When all the mushrooms are cooked and set aside, add the chopped garlic, the thyme and the tarragon to the pan. When the garlic is lightly golden, return the mushrooms to the pan, season with salt and pepper and stir in the parsley. Serve at once.

TIPS

Once you have mastered the basic dish, try:

* Adding blue cheese and melting it into the mushrooms.
* Popping on a poached egg.
* Adding strips of bacon.
* Cooking with dried porcini mushrooms (you'll need to soak these for half an hour before cooking).
* Adding truffle oil.

Or try your very own variation:

My variation is:

THE CHASE HAS BEGUN

COVER ME

QUICK SNACK

AND A SIT DOWN. TIME FOR TEA.

Spatchcocked Poussins with Rosemary & Garlic

SERVES 2 • PREPARATION TIME: 15 MINUTES • COOKING TIME: 30 MINUTES • ✓ ♥ WF GF DF

At Leon, we love to spatchcock. And with a poussin it really speeds up the cooking time, so this quick and healthy dish won't take too long to make after a hard day.

2 **poussins**, spatchcocked
a bunch of **fresh rosemary**
2 cloves of **garlic**, chopped
the zest of 1 **lemon**
2 tablespoons **olive oil**
salt and **freshly ground black pepper**

1. Heat the oven to 220°C/425°F/gas mark 7.

2. Clean and dry the poussins. Then scatter all but one sprig of rosemary across the bottom of a roasting tray and lay the birds, skin side up, on top.

3. Strip the leaves off the remaining sprig of rosemary and chop them as finely as possible. You should end up with about a teaspoonful. Mix with the garlic, lemon zest, olive oil and some salt and pepper, then spread the mixture evenly over the poussins.

4. Roast in the oven for 25–30 minutes, or until cooked through, then serve with a green salad.

TIPS

* If you like it spicy, why not turn these into Devilled Poussins by adding a teaspoon of mustard powder and plenty of black pepper to the olive oil mixture.

Moules Marinières

SERVES 2 • PREPARATION TIME: 25 MINUTES • COOKING TIME: 20 MINUTES • WF GF DF

If you think 2kg of mussels seems a lot – don't! By the time you have lost the bad ones in the process then picked them out of the shell it's a perfect amount. Just serve with a salad and some bread for dunking, or some boiled new potatoes.

2kg **mussels**
50g **butter**
2 tablespoons **olive oil**
2 **banana shallots**, finely chopped
2 sticks of **celery**, finely chopped

2 cloves of **garlic**, finely chopped
a large handful of **fresh flat-leaf parsley**, finely chopped
300ml **dry white wine**
salt and **freshly ground black pepper**

1. Wash and scrub the mussels under running water, de-bearding them as you go. The beard is, well, a beard-y thing sticking out the side of the shell. Just rip it off, discarding any mussels that won't close up.

2. Heat the butter and olive oil in a deep saucepan over a medium heat. Add the shallots, celery, garlic and half the parsley and cook for about 5–7 minutes, or until they are soft and fragrant, adding salt and pepper to taste. Be careful with the salt at this stage – the mussels will bring some salt of their own.

3. Once the vegetables are soft and fragrant, add the wine and bring to the boil. Add the mussels and immediately put a lid on. Cook them for about 4–5 minutes, shaking the pot every minute or so. The mussels at the bottom will cook faster than the ones at the top, so make sure you shift them around.

4. Give it all a stir, adding the rest of the parsley. They're done when all the mussels are nicely open. Any that remain closed were dead before you started – so don't even try opening those. Serve immediately.

Aioli

SERVES 2 • PREPARATION TIME: 5 MINUTES • COOKING TIME: NONE • DF V

3 cloves of **garlic**
3 **egg yolks**
1 level tablespoon **Dijon mustard**

150ml **vegetable oil**
a squeeze of **lemon juice**
salt and **freshly ground black pepper**

1. Peel and roughly chop the garlic and place in a food processor with the egg yolks, mustard, salt and pepper.

2. Whizz together, then slowly drizzle in the oil while the processor is still running.

3. Check the seasoning and add a squeeze of lemon juice.

Roast Cod with Salsa Verde

SERVES 2 • PREPARATION TIME: 10 MINUTES • COOKING TIME: 10-15 MINUTES • ✓ ♥ WF GF DF

There's plenty of garlic in this one, so share it with the one you love/have to kiss.

½–1 tablespoon **olive oil**
2 skinless, boneless **cod steaks**,
about 150–180g each
salt and **freshly ground black pepper**

1. Heat the oven to 220°C/425°F/gas mark 7.

2. Rub the oil over both sides of the fish and season with salt and pepper. Place in a roasting tray and cook in the oven for 10–15 minutes, or until the fish is white and flaky.

3. Take the roasting tray out of the oven and transfer the fish to serving plates. Serve with Salsa Verde (see below), some new potatoes and your favourite vegetable.

Salsa Verde

SERVES 4 • PREPARATION TIME: 6 MINUTES • COOKING TIME: NONE • ✓ ♥ WF GF DF

6–8 cloves of **garlic**,
peeled and roughly chopped
1 x 55g **tin of anchovies**,
drained and chopped
1 tablespoon **capers**,
rinsed and chopped
a large handful of **fresh flat-leaf
parsley**, chopped
a large handful of **fresh mint**,
chopped

a large handful of **fresh basil**,
chopped
the juice of ½ a **lemon**
2 tablespoons **olive oil**
2 tablespoons **extra virgin olive oil**
salt and **freshly ground
black pepper**

1. Mix together the garlic, anchovies, capers, parsley, mint and basil. Then, using your pestle and mortar, pound them all gently together. If you have a small pestle and mortar, do this in batches. Add the lemon juice and both olive oils. Season to taste and set aside. It may look like a lot – but this is very MOREISH!

TIPS

* Salsa verde also goes well with steaks, the Midweek Lamb on page 130, and the Roast Chicken on page 265.
* If you have cod with the skin still on, roast it skin side down, then serve it skin side up.
* If you don't want to eat cod, or can't find any that has been caught sustainably, pollock, coley or pouting will serve you well.

FOOD FACT

COD
Our fish stocks are in crisis and we need to do our bit to preserve our oceans' biodiversity. Please buy cod from sustainable fisheries. There are numerous websites which will help, if in doubt, or ask your fishmonger.

SOMETHING SWEET

Most of us cannot resist a tiny, or sometimes large, treat of sweetness. At the end of a dinner. For elevenses. For high tea.

The terrible thing is, when it comes to sugar, our evolution works against us. Back when we were hunter-gatherers, most of our sugar came from the fruits and vegetables we foraged. For that super-sweet hit that, even then, we craved, we had to find honey. Which, before beekeeping, came with the inherent risk of stings. Early humans evolved to cope with scarcity. When we found sweet, our bodies were programmed to gorge on it, storing the energy for the hard times that undoubtedly lay ahead. In our plentiful times, this evolutionary need to stuff our faces has become something of a problem.

Here at Leon, we're not preachers and we're not hypocrites: we love dessert as much as the next restaurant. But we say all things in moderation. We try to avoid processed sugars wherever possible. And we go easy on the cream.

That said… who's for pud?

Lychees with Fresh Ginger & Sherry

SERVES 2–4 • PREPARATION TIME: 10 MINUTES • COOKING TIME: 5 MINUTES • WF GF DF V

We know – it's very simple. But how does that saying go again? Sometimes it's the simplest things that give the most pleasure. Here we have sweet, honey-ish lychees, spiky fresh ginger and mellow sherry.

Try to make sure all three elements are well chilled …

> 1 x 567g **tin of lychees**, drained save for 12 tablespoon of liquid
> 100ml **medium sherry**
> a 1cm piece of **fresh ginger**, peeled and julienned finely
> 4 **ice cubes**, crushed

1. Put the drained lychee liquid into a small bowl, cover and refrigerate until needed. Pour the reserved lychee liquid, sherry and the ginger into a small pan. Bring to the boil, then turn down the heat and simmer for a few minutes, or until slightly reduced and thickened. Remove from the heat and leave to cool. When completely cold, cover and place in the fridge to chill.

2. Divide the chilled lychees between 4 glasses. Pop a spoonful of crushed ice into each glass and stir quickly. Pour over the sherry/ginger mixture. Stir again. Serve.

TIPS

* Tins of lychee vary in size as do the size of the lychee within. Our 567g tin yielded 14 large lychees.

Prosecco & Nectarines

SERVES 4 • PREPARATION TIME: 5-10 MINUTES • COOKING TIME: NONE • WF GF DF V

This dessert is super-quick and super-simple – sort of a deconstructed Bellini. If you're feeling fancy, why not go the full Melba and toss in a few raspberries?

> 4 ripe **nectarines**, peeled, stoned and cut into cubes
> the juice of ½ a **lemon**
> 1–2 tablespoons **icing sugar** (or to taste)
> 250ml **prosecco**
> **raspberries**, to serve (optional)

1. Put the nectarines, lemon juice and sugar into a clean bowl, toss together and leave to stand for 5 minutes.

2. Then divide them between 4 coupes and pour prosecco over each one. Top with fresh raspberries if you like. Make sure the fruit is at room temperature and that the wine is nice and cold.

Cheese, Pears & Honey

SERVES 2 • PREPARATION TIME: 10 MINUTES • COOKING TIME: NONE • WF GF V

This is not so much a recipe as a jolly good idea. And it's not one of ours. When Kay went on her honeymoon, she and Fred arrived at their hotel in Rome rather late on a Sunday. There was no food. Until the kindly barman returned with two plates of cheese, honey and pears, to be washed down with Sardinian *mirto*. Perfect.

It stands to reason that you want to buy the best pears you can find, and tip-top cheese.

> 2 **pears**
> 80g **Taleggio**
> 80g aged **Pecorino**
> 80g **Gorgonzola**
> 2 tablespoons **honey**

1. Place the pears on a board plate beside the cheeses. You can slice them if you like.

2. Spoon the honey into 2 small dishes, and pop them on the plates too. Serve with some good bread, and a knife to cut and smear.

TIPS

* Do vary the cheeses to your liking: ricotta is wonderful, especially with a grating of orange zest.

* You know at Christmas, when you're left with hordes of panettone? No? Well, we do. Thinly sliced and toasted, panettone is heaven on a plate with cheese, pears and honey.

Roasted Figs with Triple Sec

SERVES 4 • PREPARATION TIME: 10 MINUTES • COOKING TIME: 15–20 MINUTES
(BUT DO CHECK ON THEM, AS SOME FIGS COLLAPSE MORE QUICKLY) • WF V

Simple roasted figs, with a splash of liqueur.

> 8–12 ripe **black figs**
> 25g **butter**
> the grated zest of ½ an **orange**
> 4 tablespoons **triple sec**
> 2 tablespoons **honey**
> a pinch of **salt**

1. Heat the oven to 180°C/350°F/gas mark 4.

2. With a sharp knife, make a cross in the pointy end of each fig, cutting them about halfway through. Then squeeze the fat bottoms gently so that each fig opens up like a flower. Lay the figs in a roasting tray or ovenproof dish, and dot each one with a little butter.

3. Mix the orange zest and liqueur together in a bowl, and pour evenly over the figs. Drizzle over the honey and season with a pinch of salt. Pop them into the oven for 15–20 minutes. Serve hot, with some of the sauce spooned over them and some good ice cream or yoghurt.

TIPS

* Triple Sec is made from orange peel, and crops up most frequently in cocktails. If you don't want to use the alcohol, replace it with orange juice and serve the figs accompanied by some good vanilla ice cream.

* These are delicious with the Spiced Honey & Orange Cake on page 96.

Hot Chocolate 5 Ways

Warming and reassuring, it's a hug in a mug. Here are our top five:

① The Building Block Choc

MAKES 1 • PREPARATION TIME: 2 MINUTES • COOKING TIME: 10 MINUTES • V

The basic hot chocolate from which all the others (in this book) descend.

> 1 mug of **milk**
> 25–30g **good-quality dark chocolate**, grated

1. Heat the milk gently in a small saucepan. As soon as it reaches scalding point but before it boils, whisk in the grated chocolate until it has all melted thoroughly into the milk. (This has the added bonus of frothing everything up a bit.)

2. Pour out into your mug and serve.

② Mexican Hot Chocolate

Add a stick of **cinnamon**, a good grating of **orange zest** and a pinch of **chilli powder** to give your chocolate a South of the Border feel. Arriba!

③ Swedish Hot Chocolate

Adults Only ... well, you know what we mean ... add a good slug of **vodka** and pop an Abba track on the stereo.

④ Natasha & Eleanor's Hot Chocolate

Top the Building Block Choc with a good sprinkling of **mini marshmallows** and plenty of **whipped cream**.

⑤ Jamaican Hot Chocolate

Stir it up with a good pinch of freshly **ground allspice** and a slug of **Jamaican rum**. Now we be chillin'.

TIPS

* We're using a good dark chocolate here so we can avoid all the added sugar, etc. you'll find in powdered drinking chocolate.

* All recipes these days bang on about 'good-quality chocolate'. They'll then go on to specify a minimum of cocoa solids in the chocolate, and so on. In this case, the flavour of the dark chocolate *absolutely* determines the flavour of your hot chocolate, so buy the brand you like. We love Original Beans – for their flavour, of course, but also for their fantastic work in the conservation of threatened rainforests and sustainable farming practices.

TOMORROW

Who says it never comes? Here it is. Tomorrow. The bit of our book that is about things happening in a few days time, or weeks time, that are worth a little planning. For a few friends. For a larger family feast.

We cannot promise to eradicate completely the slight nervousness that comes when the doorbell goes and everything isn't perfect like in the movies, or like you had in mind, but we hope these recipes allow for a happy ending.

FOOD ON THE MOVE

These are edible messages of love. You send your kids, husband, wife or grandchild off to school or work with a package, to be opened up hours later as a reminder of home and of how great you think they are.

So that's why a Kit-Kat and a packet of crisps doesn't quite do it for me.

At Chase Side primary school in Enfield, you were either a school dinners kid or a packed lunch kid. I was a packed lunch kid and can remember very clearly where our table was and who sat there, and I can taste right now the ham and coleslaw sandwiches my mum used to make me. They used to set me up nicely for kiss chase, football or a fight with Matthew Skordis.

JOHN

Rachel McCormack's Tortilla Española

SERVES 2–4 • PREPARATION TIME: 15 MINUTES • COOKING TIME: 30 MINUTES • ✓ ♥ WF GF V

This is the basic recipe for a classic Spanish potato omelette. Rachel says the secret of a great tortilla lies in practice and a very good non-stick pan.

125ml **olive oil**
100g **onions**, finely sliced
375g **potatoes**, peeled and cut into small even pieces
4 **eggs**
a good pinch of **salt**

1. Heat the olive oil in a non-stick omelette pan or small frying pan over a medium low heat. Add the onions and then add the potatoes to the pan and let them poach in the oil for about 10–15 minutes. You're not deep-frying them here – you don't want either of them to get crunchy, you want them to remain soft.

2. Meanwhile, beat the eggs in a large bowl.

3. Once the potatoes and onions are soft and cooked, strain off the oil into a heat-resistant bowl and set aside. Allow the potatoes and onions to cool a little, then stir them into the beaten eggs and season with salt.

4. Return the pan to a medium-high heat. Add a tablespoon of the potato/onion oil and, when it's hot, pour in the egg mixture. Cook, shaking occasionally to see if the bottom is cooked properly, for about 5–10 minutes. (If the tortilla mix is very thick, turn the heat down a bit to make sure the middle cooks.) Use a palette knife or a saucer to round off the omelette in the pan.

5. Now, if you want to be traditional, Rachel says you should turn the omelette by taking a dinner plate, putting it on top of the frying pan, then flipping it over. Slide the omelette back into the pan, using the palette knife or saucer to make sure it keeps a nice round shape as it goes back in. Cook for about 5 more minutes, then turn out on to a plate.

6. However, if you find that daunting, you could finish the omelette off in the oven, preheated to 180°C/350°F/gas mark 4, for 5–10 minutes. Just make sure you are using a pan with a metal or ovenproof handle.

7. Turn out on to a plate and serve hot or cold with a salad, bread, tomato sauce, mayonnaise… anything you like.

Rachel is a woman obsessed. To hear her talk about Catalan cooking is a joy to behold. She's a great teacher, a damn fine cook and great company.

Rachel says: 'The best Spanish omelettes I ever had were made by Paquita, who ran a small bar with her husband below my flat on Carrer Bruniquer when I lived in Barcelona. They would have on the counter at least four huge round heavenly visions of yellow. All of them contained potato, the rest of the ingredients limited only by season and Paquita's imagination.'

RACHEL, PUERTO POLLENÇA, MALLORCA, 1981

Diamond Jubilee Chicken Sarnie

SERVES 4 • PREPARATION TIME: 15 MINUTES • COOKING TIME: NONE • ♥

This is based on a classic: Rosemary Hume and Constance Spry's world famous Coronation Chicken, created in 1953 for the Coronation of Queen Elizabeth II.

This is our updated Leon version, still using the same building blocks but, as an homage to the wonderful multicultural Caribbean, tweaked to make it a lighter, spikier sandwich.

2 tablespoons **thick yoghurt**
1 tablespoon good **mayonnaise**
2 teaspoons **curry powder**
300g cold **roast chicken**
4 slices from **your favourite bread**
salt and **freshly ground black pepper**

For the mango salsa:
2 ripe **mangoes**, peeled, stoned and cubed
a good squeeze of **fresh lime juice**
¼ of a **Scotch bonnet chilli**, deseeded and chopped
½ a **red onion**, finely diced
a good handful of **fresh coriander**, finely chopped
salt and **freshly ground black pepper**

1. Gently mix the yoghurt, mayonnaise, curry powder, salt and pepper together in a large bowl. Taste. Add more seasoning if needed.

2. Stir in the shredded roast chicken and coat well. Pop into a Tupperware container for travel.

3. To make the salsa, just mix all the ingredients together, taste for seasoning and place in a separate Tupperware or jar.

4. To put the Jubilee Sandwich together, first put celebratory crowns on heads.

5. Pile the curried chicken mixture on to your slices of bread.

6. Top with the mango salsa.

7. Salute the Queen and toast her heath with glass of bubbly. Huzzah!

TIPS

* We use Bolst's medium curry powder, but use whatever is your favourite.

* Homemade mayonnaise would be amazing in this.

'Rubies in the Sand' Salad

SERVES 4 • PREPARATION TIME: 25 MINUTES • COOKING TIME: 25 MINUTES • ✓ ♥ WF GF DF V

Quinoa is one of our great favourites. It contains no gluten and is a complete protein – ideal for vegetarians.

200g **dried quinoa**
300g **mixed peppers** (yellow, orange, red),
   deseeded and halved
2–3 sprigs of **fresh thyme**
2 **cloves** of **garlic**, unpeeled, crushed
1 tablespoon **olive oil**
a good handful of **fresh coriander**, chopped
100g **pomegranate seeds**

For the dressing:
2 tablespoons **extra virgin olive oil**
the juice of 1 **lime** or ½ **lemon**
2 teaspoons **ras al hanout**
salt and **freshly ground black pepper**

1. Wash the quinoa thoroughly, then cook it as per the instructions on the packet. Some bought quinoa is pre-soaked, some not, so you need to check. Once the quinoa is cooked, drain and set aside to cool.

2. Meanwhile, heat the oven to 180°C/350°F/gas mark 4.

3. Pop the peppers on to a roasting tray with the thyme, garlic and olive oil. Roast in the oven for about 20–25 minutes, or until al dente. Remove from the oven, discard the garlic and thyme, then set aside to cool. Chop the peppers into 2cm squares.

4. Mix the cooled quinoa with the mixed peppers, the chopped coriander and the pomegranate seeds.

5. Mix all the dressing ingredients together thoroughly. Stir into the quinoa mix. Taste and season with salt and pepper if needed.

TIPS

* Ras al hanout is a mixed spice quite readily available in most supermarkets. It's Moroccan in origin and contains cardamom, cloves, chilli, cumin and cinnamon, among other spices.

* Try this with about 100g of gently fried crispy chorizo scattered on top.

Benny's Scotch Eggs

SERVES 6 • PREPARATION TIME: 30 MINUTES PLUS COOLING • COOKING TIME: 20 MINUTES • ✓ WF GF

Benny Peverelli was a key part of the Leon team for eight years, a lot of that time as Executive Head Chef or Chief Foodie Personage. We love him. And we love his Scotch eggs.

> 7 medium **free-range eggs**, at room temperature
> 4–5 **rice cakes**
> **rapeseed oil** for deep frying (we reckon you'll need about a litre)
> 125g **rice flour**
> 2 tablespoons **milk**
> 6 **wheat-free**, **gluten-free pork sausages**

1. Ensure your eggs are at room temperature, then bring a medium pan of water to the boil. Gently lower 6 of the eggs into the boiling water and cook them for 6 minutes for soft centres, or 9 minutes for hard yolks.

2. Once the eggs are cooked, run them under cold water for 10 minutes to cool them down.

3. Gently tap the eggs all over to crack the shell, then peel them carefully as they will be soft. (Every time you take a bit of peel off, you should dip your fingers back into the water otherwise they may become tacky and you could break the egg.)

4. To make the crumb, break the rice cakes into small pieces, then pop them into a food processor and whizz for a minute or so.

5. Heat the rapeseed oil to 180°C in a deep-fat fryer. (You can do this in a heavy-based saucepan over a medium heat, but be very VERY careful. You do so at your own risk.)

6. While the oil is heating up, prepare your crumbing station: take 3 large-ish bowls and place your flour in one, your crumbed rice cakes in another, then break your final egg into the third bowl and whisk in the milk.

7. Cut out 2 large squares of clingfilm. Place one on your work surface and leave the other for later.

8. Now take a sharp knife and run it down the length of one of the sausages. Squeeze the contents of the sausage into your hand and squash together to form a ball. Repeat with the remaining sausages. Then place each sausage ball on the clingfilm. Put the other piece of clingfilm over the top and squash down until you have 6 sausage ovals, about 0.5cm thick.

9. Next dry your boiled eggs with a little kitchen paper and place one into the flour, coating it all over (this will help the sausagemeat stick). Peel a sausagemeat disc off the clingfilm and lay it over the egg. Gently fold the sausagemeat around the egg and press the join together. Put to one side. Repeat with the other eggs.

10. Now take a small bowl of water and dampen your hands. Use your damp hands to smooth the sausage-coated eggs and turn them into smooth egg shapes.

11. Take an egg shape and gently roll it all over in the flour. Then place it in the egg and milk mixture and coat fully. Now place it in the rice cakes crumbs and cover all over, patting the egg to make sure it all sticks. Repeat this for each egg.

12. Check your oil is hot enough by dropping a small piece of bread into the oil – if it gently bubbles and fries, it's the right temperature. Using a slotted spoon, gently lower your egg into the oil, making sure you keep splashing oil over it if it's not fully covered. Fry for 10 minutes (or 5 on each side if your egg is not fully covered), cooking up to 3 eggs at a time.

13. Once they're cooked, place the eggs on kitchen paper to drain.

14. Leave for 10 minutes to cool, then tuck in with some brown sauce.

SONNY AND HIS DOG COOPER

As soon as Sonny could stand, he had a place cooking with his daddy and he soon became the best potato-peeling three-year-old you have ever laid eyes on. Wherever Sonny went you could guarantee Cooper would be right there by his side, enjoying the spoils of Sonny's riches.

Sadly Cooper said goodbye in January 2012, but he will never be out of our thoughts, a true family dog and the perfect cooking companion.
R.I.P. COOPER

Ploughman's in a Box

SERVES 2 • PREPARATION TIME: 15 MINUTES • COOKING TIME: NONE • ✓

That great British pub staple – a perfect portable feast.

    250g **Cheddar cheese**
    4 fat slices of good **ham**
    2 large **pickled onions**
    2 **crisp apples** (we love Cox's)
    2 slices of your favourite **bread**
    50g **unsalted butter**
    2 sticks of **celery**, trimmed
    a splodge of **Branston pickle**, or homemade **chutney** of your choice
    salt and **freshly ground black pepper**
    a pint of **shandy** (optional)

1. Find a lovely box – something vintage would be great, but Tupperware or brown cardboard is just as good. Arrange everything, except the shandy, snugly inside. Tie up with string.

2. Chill the shandy.

3. Picnic.

TIPS

* Feel free to replace the Cheddar with your favourite cheese: we are fans of Stilton or Wensleydale.

* Add some spring onions if you like, and some wedges of crisp lettuce or endive.

WEEKEND BLOW-OUTS

I love get-togethers. With our extra time on the weekend, we can gather up friends, family, extended family for some old-style social networking. And I love to get everyone involved too. Back at my gran's house in Lewisham, she ruled her kitchen, but we all had our little jobs to help out while she knocked up epic Sunday lunches on a grand scale.

I can see the whole layout of her house right now: the wartime utility cabinets on the wall, painted a buttery yellow; a door that opened on to the garden path leading to the outside loo (my favourite – instead of a light, it had a torch hanging on the back of the door on a piece of string, which I thought was marvellous!); the serving hatch into the dining room. Those times around her table, with that old Tretchikoff print of the Chinese girl looking down on us from the dining room wall, make up some of my favourite memories.

Weekend blow-outs don't have to be fancy. But wine should be poured. Kids should race around. Board games should be played. This is about fun. And love and generosity. And making memories.

KAY

Oven-fried Chicken with Collard Greens

SERVES 6 • MARINATING TIME: 2 HOURS–OVERNIGHT • PREPARATION TIME: 20 MINUTES
COOKING TIME: 1 HOUR 20 MINUTES • ✓ ♥

Fried chicken: what else is there to say, other than that this is finger-lickin' good.

280ml **buttermilk**
½ tablespoon **English mustard**
½ tablespoon smooth **Dijon mustard**
1 clove of **garlic**, crushed
1 **bay leaf**
2 teaspoons **sea salt**
3 dashes of **Tabasco**

1 **chicken**, jointed into 8 pieces
100g **buckwheat flour**, sifted
100g **cornmeal** or **polenta**
1 tablespoon **Kay's Cajun Magic**
  (see page 57)
50ml **vegetable oil**, for frying
salt and **freshly ground black pepper**

1. Put the buttermilk and the mustards into a bowl and add the garlic, bay leaf, sea salt and the Tabasco. Coat the chicken liberally with the mixture and leave to marinate for at least an hour or two, but preferably overnight.

2. When you're ready to cook, heat the oven to 180°C/350°F/gas mark 4.

3. Mix together the sieved buckwheat flour, the cornmeal and Kay's Cajun Magic with a little salt and a good few grindings of black pepper.

4. Remove the chicken from the marinade and shake off any excess. Thoroughly coat each piece in the seasoned flour and cornmeal.

5. Heat the oil in a large non-stick frying pan until it's HOT. Fry the chicken – 3 or 4 pieces at a time, until golden. When its ready, place each piece on a rack in a roasting tray. Put the roasting tray into the oven and bake for about 40 minutes, until cooked through. Serve with mashed potatoes and collard greens (see below).

Quick & Easy Collard Greens

SERVES 6 • PREPARATION TIME: 15 MINUTES • COOKING TIME: 8 MINUTES • ✓ WF GF

70g **lardons**
vegetable oil (optional)
2 cloves of **garlic**, peeled and sliced
400g **baby spring greens**,
  sliced, with stems renoved

salt and **freshly ground**
  black pepper
a few dashes of **hot sauce** (optional)

1. In a dry sauté pan with a lid, cook the lardons over a low heat until golden and crispy. They should throw about a tablespoon of fat, but if the pan's looking a little dry, add a dash of vegetable oil. Then add the garlic, and sauté until golden.

2. Turn up the heat, add the greens and toss them with the lardons and garlic. Season with salt and pepper and the hot sauce, if using, then put the lid on, shake the pan to mix everything together, and cook for 3–4 minutes. Serve at once.

Henry's Sunday Lunch

(ROAST PORK BELLY & BUTTER BEANS)

SERVES 8 • PREPARATION TIME: 20 MINUTES • COOKING TIME: 3 HOURS 30 MINUTES • ✓ WF GF DF

This is a simple Sunday lunch that can largely be prepared beforehand, leaving you time to enjoy the day (see picture on page 196–7). The chilli lemon kale (opposite) makes a great contrast to the rich pork. This fast, slow, fast method of cooking the pork is the key to perfect crackling every time.

> 2kg **pork belly**, skin scored in thin lines
> a little **olive** or **sunflower oil**
> 2 x 400g **tins of butter beans**
> 4 large **carrots**
> 3 **leeks**
> 1 tablespoon **coriander seed**
> a large bunch of **fresh thyme**
> 1 bottle of **white wine** (see tips below)
> **sea salt** and **freshly ground black pepper**

1. Heat the oven to 220°C/425°F/gas mark 7.

2. Place the pork belly in a large roasting tray and smear it all over with the oil, salt and pepper, making sure to get a good amount of salt rubbed into the skin. Then put it into the oven.

3. Drain and rinse the beans. Chop the carrots and leeks into uneven smallish pieces, then, in a bowl, mix the beans and vegetables with the rest of the ingredients.

4. After the pork has been in the oven for 25 minutes, if any fat's come out, baste it once. After a further 20 minutes remove the roasting tray from the oven. The pork skin should be going a little brown and bubbly.

5. Take the pork out of the roasting tray and pour out the fat. Then tip in the beans, vegetables and wine. Place the pork belly on top and cover tightly with foil. Turn the oven down to 160°C/325°F/gas mark 3 and cook for another 2 hours.

6. When the time's up, remove the foil. If the vegetables at the bottom of the pan are drying out, add a touch of water. Turn the oven up to 200°C/400°F/ gas mark 6 and roast the pork for another 15 minutes, or until it is fully crisped. Depending on your piece of pork, this could take a further 30 minutes.

7. Transfer the meat to a board and carve at the table, and serve the vegetables and beans in a dish.

TIPS

* Play with the spices and herbs in the vegetables under the pork: the aniseeds (bulb fennel and fennel seed) work well.

* You can use pretty much any tinned beans (or soak and cook your own).

* If you are being frugal, use 100ml of white wine or cider vinegar and 650ml of stock instead of the wine.

* Any leftover veg can be used for Frank's Bubble & Squeak (see page 261).

Chilli Lemon Kale

SERVES 8 • PREPARATION TIME: 20 MINUTES • COOKING TIME: 30 MINUTES • ✓ ♥ WF GF DF V

700g **kale**, thick stalks removed
2 tablespoons **olive oil**
2 cloves of **garlic**, sliced
1 long **red chilli**, deseeded and sliced
the juice of ½ a **lemon**
salt and **freshly ground black pepper**

1. Prepare the kale by peeling off the big stalks and tearing any really big bits of leaf into smaller pieces. Blanch in salted boiling water for about 5 minutes – it should still have a good bite to it, as everything else in the dish will be soft. Drain really well and set aside – you can do this the day before, and keep it in the fridge until the next day if you like.

2. In a sauté pan, gently heat the oil over a low to medium heat and add the garlic and chilli. When it is letting off a nice aroma – but hasn't browned at all – add the kale and warm through gently. Season with salt and pepper, then add the lemon juice. Toss everything together off the heat, and serve.

JOSEPH, LIZA, HENRY AND EDMUND, 1977

There are very few businesses or ventures that are the work of one person. Partly because one needs complementary skills and approaches, partly because like wrestlers one needs a tag team partner. Henry is mine and mine is Henry. We dream, argue, inspire each other, rescue each other, and eat together. Henry is a Viking (no, really). A Winston Churchill-esque bulldog who will not give up that bone. That dogged commitment, love and knowledge of food, love for hard work, his intelligence, his determination to build an excellent organisation based on attention to detail and planning, his ability to build consensus, and his ability to not give up until a job is done would have not been out of place in the Cabinet War Rooms.

JOHN

Butt Chicken with Cajun Spices

SERVES 6 • PREPARATION TIME: 20 MINUTES • COOKING TIME: 1½ HOURS • ✓ WF GF

This is chicken. With a can of beer up its butt. We're not kidding.

1 x 1.5kg **chicken**
1 x 440ml **can of beer** or **lager**
3 **bay leaves**
a large sprig or two of **fresh thyme**
1 **spring onion**
3 cloves of **garlic**, lightly crushed
½ a **red jalapeño chilli**

2 tablespoons **light olive oil**
1 tablespoon **Kay's Cajun Magic** (see page 57)
½ teaspoon **ground cumin**
25g **unsalted butter**
salt and **freshly ground black pepper**

1. Heat the oven to 200°C/400°F/gas mark 6.

2. Season the chicken cavity with salt and pepper. Open the beer can and take a sip. Then shove the bay leaves, thyme, spring onion, garlic and jalapeño into the can. Stand it in a roasting tray, then push the chicken down on to the can. You should be able to fit most of it into the chicken and use the legs to help it balance.

3. Mix together the olive oil, Kay's Cajun Magic and cumin. Brush it all over the chicken. Roast in the oven for about 1 hour and 15 minutes, basting two or three times with the olive oil mixture. The steam from the beer will cook the chicken faster than a usual roast. Be very careful not spill the hot beer on yourself when you take it in and out of the oven.

4. When cooked, remove the chicken from the can and set aside. Tip the contents of the can into the roasting tray and cook over a high heat until the beer has reduced by two-thirds, then stir in the butter. Joint the chicken into 6–8 pieces and serve with a good splash of gravy and Almost-Philippe's Coleslaw.

Almost-Philippe's Coleslaw

SERVES 6 • PREPARATION TIME: 20 MINUTES PLUS STANDING • COOKING TIME: NONE • ✓ WF GF V

Philippe's is one of our favourite places in Los Angeles. It's been open since 1908. This is our version of their delicious coleslaw.

60ml **buttermilk**
2 tablespoons **sour cream**
2 tablespoons **mayonnaise**
a good squeeze of **lemon juice**

1 tablespoon **celery seed**
½ a **pointed spring cabbage**, shredded
salt and **freshly ground black pepper**

1. Put the buttermilk, sour cream and mayonnaise into a small bowl. Stir in the lemon juice. Season with salt, pepper, and the celery seed.

2. Put the cabbage into a large bowl, pour over the dressing and toss it all together. Leave to stand for at least 30 minutes, then serve.

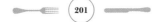

Roast Topside

SERVES 6 • PREPARATION TIME: 5 MINUTES • COOKING TIME: I HOUR • RESTING TIME: 30 MINUTES • ✓ WF DF

Topside roasts surprisingly well for such a lean cut of meat, as long as you keep it rare. So we'll say it now, up front: if you prefer your meat more towards the medium or well-done side of things, this dish is not for you. Make sure you get a piece with a nice layer of fat on the top – it'll throw some fantastic dripping and it will keep the joint deliciously moist.

> 1.5 kg piece of **topside of beef**
> 1 tablespoon **olive oil**
> **salt** and **freshly ground black pepper**

1. Heat the oven to 220°C/425°F/gas mark 7.

2. Rub the beef with the olive oil, then stand it in a roasting tray, fat side up, and season the fat well with salt and pepper. Put it into the oven for 25 minutes.

3. When the 25 minutes are up, baste the beef, then turn down the heat to 150°C/300°F/gas mark 2 and roast for a further 30 minutes or so, basting once. (If you have a larger piece of meat, you might want to give it 30 minutes for its initial blast of heat, then figure on cooking it for 10 minutes per 500g).

4. When it's cooked, remove it from the oven and allow it to rest for a good 30 minutes before carving. Make the gravy according to the recipe for Cheat's Demi-glace and serve with Celeriac Dauphinoise (see opposite).

Cheat's Demi-glace

PREPARATION TIME: 10 MINUTES • COOKING TIME: 30 MINUTES • ✓ WF GF

This doesn't have an awful lot to do with a formal demi-glace, but it makes a great base for a gravy.

> 1 tablespoon **olive oil**
> 1 **banana shallot**, finely chopped
> 1 **beef stock cube**
> 275ml **red wine**
> 1 **bay leaf**
> **salt** and **freshly ground black pepper**

1. Put the olive oil into a small pan over a low to medium heat, then add the shallot and cook until soft and just taking a hint of colour. Add 100ml water, then crumble in the stock cube. Stir everything together, add the wine and the bay leaf and simmer until the sauce has reduced by at least half. Set aside to cool.

2. To make the gravy, pour off the fat from the roast. Put the roasting tray on a medium heat and strain in the reduced sauce, discarding the shallot and bay leaf. Bubble it up, scraping up any bits from the bottom of the pan. Taste and season.

Celeriac Dauphinoise

SERVES 6 • PREPARATION TIME: 15 MINUTES • COOKING TIME: 45–60 MINUTES • ✓ ♥ V

This Dauphinoise tastes so luxurious that it seems as though it must have taken forever to make. But actually, it's a doddle, and its rich creaminess makes it the perfect foil for beef or game.

> 25g **butter**, plus extra for greasing
> 600g **celeriac**, peeled and very thinly sliced
> 50g **Gruyère cheese**, grated
> a good grating of **nutmeg**
> 100ml **milk**
> 150ml **double cream**
> 1 clove of **garlic**, peeled and finely chopped
> **salt** and **freshly ground black pepper**

1. Heat the oven to 180°C/350°F/gas mark 4.

2. Grease a baking tin, 29 x 18cm, and fill it with layers of sliced celeriac. Season each layer with cheese, nutmeg, salt and pepper as you go, until all the celeriac's used up.

3. Melt the butter, then in a jug combine it with the milk, cream and garlic. Stir, and pour it over the celeriac. Season the top layer with a final touch of cheese, nutmeg, salt and pepper, then bake in the oven for 1 hour. Check it after 45 minutes – when it's done, the celeriac should have a nice 'give' to it and the sauce should be silky and rich.

Mum's Chicken Curry
(MURG KORMA)

SERVES 4 • PREPARATION TIME: 20 MINUTES • COOKING TIME: 40 MINUTES • ✓ ♥ WF GF DF

Our friend Mamta Gupta makes many different curries. This is the one her daughters request most often. It's always known at their house as Mum's Chicken Curry. It's a typical northern Indian-style dish, and is the one on which Leon's Mamta's Curry is based.

2 tablespoons **vegetable oil**
½ teaspoon **cumin seeds**
1 large **onion**, chopped – about 250g
a 2cm piece of **fresh ginger**, peeled and chopped
2–3 cloves of **garlic**, chopped
2–3 **tomatoes**, chopped, or
   2–3 tablespoons **tomato purée**
2 tablespoons **dried fenugreek**
   or **methi leaves** (optional)
500g **chicken thighs on the bone**, skinned
½ teaspoon **homemade garam masala**
   (see page 207)
a handful of **fresh coriander leaves**, chopped
salt, to taste

The whole spices (see tip below):
1 **bay leaf**
1–2 pieces of **cinnamon stick** or
   cassia bark
2 large **cardamom pods**
3–4 small **green cardamom pods**
5–6 **black peppercorns**
4–5 **cloves**

The ground spices:
1 teaspoon **ground turmeric**
2 teaspoons **ground coriander**
1 teaspoon **paprika** (optional)
½ teaspoon **chilli powder,**
   or to taste

1. Heat the oil in a heavy-bottomed wok or sauté pan, and add the cumin seeds and the whole spices. Cook until the cumin seeds begin to sputter, being careful not to let them burn. Add the onion, ginger and garlic, and fry until browned and almost caramelized, stirring frequently so nothing sticks. Now stir in the ground spices, and cook for a few seconds to bring out their flavour.

2. Add the tomato and the fenugreek or methi leaves, if using, and cook, stirring frequently, until the oil separates. Finally, add the chicken, and cook over a medium to high heat, stirring frequently, until the chicken is well coated and sealed.

3. Cover the pan, and cook over a low to medium heat for about 15–20 minutes, or until tender. When the chicken is cooked, if the sauce looks a little thick, add some water to loosen. Turn off the heat, and stir in the garam masala and half of the coriander. Season with salt, to taste.

4. Finally, garnish with the remaining coriander leaves and serve with rice, naan, roti or chapati.

TIPS

* If you are short of one or more of the whole spices, leave them ALL out; use with 1½ teaspoons of homemade garam masala (see page 207) instead.

* Mamta says chilli powders can vary greatly in strength, so get to know yours and use accordingly.

* Mamta says you can make this curry a day ahead of time, then reheat, garnish and serve. This allows the flavours to mingle nicely.

Aubergine Pickle-style Bhaji

(BAINGAN (BRINJAL) AACHARI)

SERVES 4 · PREPARATION TIME: 10 MINUTES · COOKING TIME: 20 MINUTES · ✓ ♥ WF GF DF V

Mamta says that, in the UK, the word 'bhaji' is often used to refer to battered and deep-fried vegetables, which northern Indians call pakoras. Dry vegetable dishes are usually referred to as 'sabji' or 'bhaji', both words simply meaning 'vegetable'. This dish is called a pickle style bhaji because the whole panch pooran spices and mustard oil are often used in pickling.

2–3 tablespoons **mustard oil**
1½ tablespoons **panch pooran** (see tips below)
a pinch of **asafoetida**
1 whole **dried chilli**, broken up
300g small, thin **aubergines**, cut in half lengthways with stalks left on
1 tablespoon **fresh ginger**, peeled and grated or chopped
½ teaspoon **ground turmeric**
½ level teaspoon **chilli powder**, or to taste
1 teaspoon **salt**, or to taste
the juice of ½ a **lemon**
a small handful of **fresh coriander**, leaves chopped

1. Heat the oil in a wok and, when it's hot, add the panch pooran and asafoetida. When the seeds start to sputter, add the dried chilli and stir for 10 seconds. Then stir in the aubergines, ginger and all of the spices.

2. Season with salt and cook, covered, over a low to medium heat until the aubergines are tender, about 5–10 minutes. If you use a lower heat, you won't need to add any additional water.

3. Add the lemon juice, turn up the heat and stir gently, until all the liquid has been absorbed and the aubergines are shiny. They should not be mashed. Garnish with the chopped coriander leaves and serve hot with chapatis or daal.

TIPS

* Panch pooran is a mix of five spices from the Bengal and Bihar regions of India and Bangladesh. To make it, mix together 1 teaspoon each of cumin seeds, black mustard seeds, fennel seeds, nigella seeds and fenugreek seeds. Store them in an airtight jar. To use them in a recipe, heat some oil and add the spice mix – when the seeds sputter, add the onions or vegetables as your recipe requires.

* If you can't find small, thin aubergines, use large ones – just cut them into thick batons or fingers. With the smaller ones, Mamta prefers to leave the stalks on when she halves them because it helps them keep their shape.

FOOD FACT

ASAFOETIDA

Asafoetida is also known as the devil's dung because it doesn't smell so good when it's raw. But when it's cooked it takes on a flavour a little like cooked leeks. It's often used as an aid to digestion in India and Thailand, or as an anti-flatulent! And it's known in traditional medicine for its antimicrobial properties. Best of all, according to a report from the Kaohsiung Medical University in Taiwan, its roots may produce an antiviral compound that kills the H1N1 flu virus, confirming an idea floating around since asafoetida was used to combat the Spanish flu epidemic of 1918. So there.

Garam Masala

MAKES 50G • PREPARATION TIME: 2–5 MINUTES • COOKING TIME: NONE • ✓ ♥ WF GF DF V

Garam means hot, and masala means spice mix. Since many store-bought versions are padded out with extra cumin or coriander, Mamta suggests you make your own for that proper punch.

> 1 tablespoon **black peppercorns**
> 1 teaspoon **cloves**
> 4–5 **brown cardamom pods**
> 4–5 **dried bay leaves**
> a 6cm piece of **cinnamon stick** or **cassia bark**
> 4–5 **green cardamom pods** (optional)
> ½ a **nutmeg**, freshly grated (optional)
> 1–2 tablespoons **cumin seeds** (optional)

1. Grind all the ingredients together finely in an electric coffee grinder or in a pestle and mortar. Then sieve to remove any husks or fibres.

2. Store in an airtight container.

TIPS

* Mamta does not recommend toasting the spices before you make your garam masala. Toasting releases the flavours, so they will be lost if you store the spices for any length of time. 'Raw' ground spices will last much longer.

MAMTA WITH KAVITA, 1972

MAMTA WITH HER PARENTS, YASHODA
AND SURESH, LONDON, 1972

Mamta's daughter Kavita says, 'Though Mum's Indian dishes are definitely our comfort food, my sister and I never learned to cook Indian food in any meaningful way – we didn't pick up the techniques, the instinctive use of spices and wide repertoire of dishes that our cousins in India grew up with.

'When we left home, we missed Mum's Indian cooking the most and we'd frequently phone home for advice on making keema peas or chicken curry. We begged Mum to write her recipes down for us and so began the laborious process of handwriting a family cookbook.

'It wasn't long before the idea of a website version surfaced and Mum, my husband Pete and I created Mamta's Kitchen (www.mamtaskitchen.com) back in 2001. We don't believe in secret family recipes. Today we receive 2 million hits a year to our 1,500 recipes, discussion forum, menu tips and festival page. Mum's recipes are at the core, but we also love sharing contributions from family, friends and readers who want to be part of our family cookbook on the web.'

Rob Elliott Smith's Prawn Creole

SERVES 4–6 • PREPARATION TIME: 25–30 MINUTES • COOKING TIME: 45 MINUTES • ✓ ♥ WF GF DF

Our American friend Rob makes a mean prawn creole: spicy, sweet and moreish. He would generally make a roux to thicken this, but here we have a lighter, just-as-delicious version.

2 **red peppers**, finely chopped
2 **onions**, finely chopped
4 sticks of **celery**, finely chopped
1 clove of **garlic**, peeled and chopped
2–6 **medium-hot red chillies**, deseeded and chopped
3 tablespoons finely chopped **flat-leaf parsley**
1.25kg **prawns**, peeled reserving the heads and shells
2–3 slices of **lemon**
2 tablespoons **vegetable oil**
6 **ripe tomatoes**, peeled and chopped
2 tablespoons **tomato purée**
3–4 sprigs of **fresh thyme** (optional)
salt and **freshly ground black pepper**

1. Heat the oven to 200°C/400°F/gas mark 6.

2. Put the chopped peppers, onions, celery, garlic, chillies and parsley into a bowl and mix together thoroughly. Set aside.

3. Put the prawn heads, legs, and shells into a pan. Pour in just enough water to cover, add the lemon slices and season with salt and pepper. Place the pan on a medium to high heat and boil for 3–5 minutes, skimming off any scum that rises, to make a rich prawn stock. Strain the stock and set aside.

4. Heat the oil in a large, wide frying pan. Add the vegetable mixture and cook until softened but still retaining a little bite. Transfer to a large ovenproof casserole.

5. Add the tomatoes, 500ml of the prawn stock and bring to the boil. Cook over a medium heat until the tomatoes break down and release all their juices. Stir in the tomato purée and add the sprigs of thyme if using. Season to taste with salt and pepper.

6. Remove from the heat, add the raw prawns, then put the casserole into the oven and bake for 25 minutes.

7. Serve on white rice, with cornbread (see page 210) and additional hot sauces for the brave.

TIPS

* If you can't buy prawns with their clothes on, don't worry. Just buy 1kg of peeled prawns and make 500ml of fish stock with a good brand of cube or powder.

Cornbread

SERVES 8 • PREPARATION TIME: 10 MINUTES • COOKING TIME: 25 MINUTES • WF GF V

A Southern staple in the good old US of A. As well as making the perfect foil for Rob's Prawn Creole (see page 209), you could also serve it with the Oven-fried Chicken on page 195. And it's a great alternative to bread with soup or salad.

ROB WITH TWO BOOTLEGGERS,
ALABAMA, 1968

a little **butter** or **bacon fat**, for greasing
125g **cornmeal** or **polenta**
110g **buckwheat flour**
50g **sugar**
½ teaspoon **sea salt**
1 tablespoon **gluten-free baking powder**
65ml **vegetable oil**
100ml **milk**
100ml **buttermilk**
1 large **egg**, lightly beaten

1. Heat the oven to 200°C/400°F/gas mark 6. Grease a 20cm square baking tin with butter or – better yet – bacon fat!

2. Combine the dry goods in a bowl. Then add the wet goods. Mix together thoroughly and pour into the prepared tin.

3. Bake in the oven for about 25 minutes, or until golden. To test that it's cooked, jab it in its thickest part with a toothpick. If it comes out clean, it's done. Serve warm with Prawn Creole.

TIPS

* Kay has a vintage cast-iron mould which makes cornbread shaped like corn cobs. Occasionally they pop up for sale on American eBay, and they're brilliant kitchenalia.

* To ring the changes, you could add a chopped, deseeded jalapeño, or 100g of fresh or tinned sweetcorn, or 100g of cubed Cheddar or Gruyère, or some fresh chopped sage, to the batter. Rob, being a Southern gentleman of integrity, feels these additions are just plain wrong, but we love them.

* For a sweeter, more muffin-like cornbread, you can add an extra 100g of sugar with the dry ingredients.

Rob was born in Birmingham, Alabama. See the picture above? That's his grandpa taking him to visit the bootlegger … which reminds me: why not make a nice Mint Julep to sip while you're making this? Crush the leaves from a sprig of mint into a teaspoon of sugar. Pour over 50ml of bourbon. Stir together. Top up the glass with crushed ice. Most refreshing.

Rob's Prawn Creole on page 209 is a version of his Daddy's traditional shrimp creole. Rob says: 'Back home shrimp creole is a special meal, reserved for large family gatherings, probably in the summer. Something more intimate and traditional would be squirrel and dumplings. My great-grandmother – 'Mom' – would prepare a batch of squirrels we'd shot; pan-fry them in a bit of flour, salt and pepper, and stew with thick flour-and-lard dumplings. She'd serve the whole, ginormous bowl just for me. I'd always ask if she'd like some herself, but she invariably replied, 'I'll just gnaw on these,' presenting a plate of squirrel heads, deep-fried. Most people I meet prefer to stick with the creole.'

Gardener John's Roasted Vegetables

SERVES 4 • PREPARATION TIME: 10 MINUTES • COOKING TIME: 50–60 MINUTES • WF GF DF V

John and Katie know a gardener called … John. He has been a gardener for a long time, and he leaves them gifts in the form of root vegetables. The trouble is he forgets to tell them when he's left them. So he will pop round and say, 'Did you cook those sweet potatoes I left at the end of the garden for you?' 'Er, no, sorry, we didn't know they were there.' Fortunately root vegetables are hardy and so most of the time they are in good nick still.

Roasting vegetables is easy – the trick is to learn which vegetables take longer to cook. As a general rule, if the vegetable's harder (like a parsnip), it will take longer to cook than a softer vegetable, say, a sweet potato or tomato. You can somewhat level the playing field by slicing the harder vegetables more thinly. Or, if you want to, you can experiment by adding the softer vegetables later on during the roasting.

That's all very nice, but the icing on the cake, sort of, is the tangy dressing you add at the end. Try the Salsa Verde on page 170, a balsamic dressing, or a mustard and honey vinaigrette. (Or cheat with a bottle of salad dressing. As long as you keep an eye on the ingredients in the bottle, you can do much worse.)

> 3–6 **parsnips**, cut into medium to thin strips
> 3–4 **onions**, red if you have them, cut thickly
>   (as these will cook quickly and can burn)
> 2–3 **sweet potatoes**
> **any other vegetables** you have in your arsenal that day
>   (**squash**, **aubergine**, etc.)
> lots of **garlic** (to go posh you can cut a whole head in half)
> a good handful of **fresh rosemary** and **fresh thyme**
> enough **olive oil** to make all the vegetables oily (maybe
>   6 tablespoons, maybe ½ a mug)
> the **tangy dressing** of your choice
> **salt** and **freshly ground black pepper**

1. Heat the oven to 200°C/400°F/gas mark 6.

2. Put the chopped vegetables and the garlic and herbs into a roasting tray. Season with salt and pepper, then pour on the olive oil and tumble the vegetables through it.

3. Put the tray of vegetables into the oven and roast for 50–60 minutes, taking it out halfway through for a little shake.

4. Once cooked, add your tangy dressing.

TIPS

* For meat-eaters who want to turn this into a feast, you can add chicken. Just sauté some sliced chicken in olive oil with a few herbs or spices, and add it to the veg.

Lamb Boulangère

SERVES 6 • PREPARATION TIME: 25 MINUTES • COOKING TIME: 1 HOUR 20–30 MINUTES • ✓ WF GF

A great piece of saltmarsh lamb, a glut of King Edwards and a cool wind blowing the leaves in September: this is a classic, traditionally cooked in a baker's oven. We love it.

1 **leg of lamb** (weighing roughly 1.5–2kg), bone in or part boned
2 large sprigs of **fresh rosemary**, broken into small shards
4 cloves of **garlic**, cut into slivers
2 tablespoons **olive oil**
25g **unsalted butter**
1kg **potatoes**, peeled and thinly sliced
2 **onions**, thinly sliced
2 sprigs of **fresh lavender**, roughly torn
200ml **lamb stock**
100ml **white wine**
1 x 400g tin of **flageolet beans**, drained and rinsed (optional)
a glass of **wine** or 100ml **lamb stock** or **water**
an extra knob of cold **butter**
salt and **freshly ground black pepper**

1. Heat the oven to 200°C/400°F/gas mark 6.

2. Pat the lamb dry with kitchen paper and make small incisions all over the lamb with the tip of a knife. Insert the shards of rosemary and the slivers of garlic into the incisions. Rub 1 tablespoon of the olive oil over the lamb and season generously with salt and pepper.

3. Put the lamb into a large roasting tray and pop it into the oven for 30 minutes.

4. Meanwhile, put the potatoes and onions into a bowl with the remaining tablespoon of olive oil, salt and pepper, lavender and any bits of leftover garlic and rosemary.

5. After 30 minutes remove the lamb from the oven and place it on a plate. Put the potato and onion mixture into the roasting tray and add the stock and wine. Dot the butter evenly over the surface of the potato, then put the tray back into the oven. Place the leg of lamb directly on the rack above the spuds – the drip, drip effect will give you glorious potatoes.

6. Roast for a further 40–50 minutes. Then remove the lamb from the oven and set aside on a plate or board to rest for 15–20 minutes. If the spuds need a bit more browning, leave them in the oven. When they are ready, remove them to a serving dish with a slotted spoon, keeping as much goo in the tray as possible.

7. Once you have removed the potatoes, place the roasting pan over a low heat and deglaze the tray with a glass of wine and let it bubble away, scraping down the sides until it's looking thick and smelling good. Add the (optional) flageolet beans and the knob of cold butter and heat through. Carve the lamb into slices and serve with a generous portion of the potatoes and a good dollop of gravy (and beans if using).

Momma's Apple Pie

SERVES 6 • PREPARATION TIME: 20 MINUTES • COOKING TIME: 1 HOUR • V

'As American as Mom and Apple Pie,' as the saying goes … This double-crust, rather old-fashioned pie reminds us of the pies we grew up seeing in the movies.

Serve it with cream, if you like. But to be really authentic, you should really have it *à la mode* with a scoop of excellent vanilla ice cream. God Bless America.

500g **plain flour**
250g **unsalted butter**, straight from the fridge
a large pinch of **sea salt**
2 tablespoons **caster sugar**, plus an extra
  tablespoon for the top
1 small glass of **iced water**
1 **egg**, beaten, to glaze

For the filling:
900g **apples**, peeled, cored and sliced – we use
  a mixture of Braeburn, Bramley and Cox's
100g **caster sugar**
the juice of 1 **lemon**
½ teaspoon **ground cinnamon**
a good grating of **nutmeg**

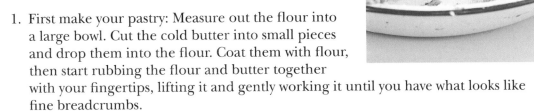

1. First make your pastry: Measure out the flour into a large bowl. Cut the cold butter into small pieces and drop them into the flour. Coat them with flour, then start rubbing the flour and butter together with your fingertips, lifting it and gently working it until you have what looks like fine breadcrumbs.

2. Add the salt. Then the sugar. Mix well. Now add the iced water a teaspoonful at a time, working everything together with your hands until the pastry just comes together. Don't add too much water, or you'll get a hard pastry. Roll it into 2 loose balls, cover with clingfilm and refrigerate for at least 30 minutes.

3. Heat the oven to 180°C/350°F/gas mark 4 and grease a 23cm pie dish.

4. Put the sliced apples into a large bowl. Sprinkle over the sugar, lemon juice, cinnamon and nutmeg and mix well.

5. Take the pastry balls out of the fridge and roll them out, one at a time, into circles the size of your pie dish. Line the bottom of the dish with one circle. Tip in the filling, then cover with the other circle and crimp the bottom and top together.

6. Bake the pie in the oven for 20 minutes. Then remove it from the oven and brush the top with the beaten egg. Sprinkle over the extra caster sugar and bake for another 40–50 minutes, or until golden brown and cooked through. Serve with vanilla ice cream.

Anna Hansen's Pumpkin & Miso Cheesecake

SERVES 8–12 • PREPARATION TIME: 1 HOUR • COOKING TIME: 1 HOUR 15 MINUTES
COOLING TIME: MINIMUM 4 HOURS • V

Anna is an extraordinary chef. At her restaurant, the Modern Pantry in Clerkenwell, London, she marries flavours that most of us would never dream of. As Kay has often said, Anna's palate is her playground. She designed this dessert just for us.

500g **cream cheese**
180g **caster sugar**
2 tablespoons **icing sugar**
60g **miso paste**
the seeds of 1 **vanilla pod**
500g **roast pumpkin purée** (see tip)
5 whole **eggs** and 2 **egg yolks**

For the base:
140g **gingernut biscuits**
120g **digestive biscuits**
1 tablespoon **muscovado** or **soft brown sugar**
120g **butter**, plus extra for greasing
300ml **double cream**, whipped, to serve

TIPS

* Pumpkin purée is very easy to make yourself, and the superior flavour of your cheesecake will be your reward. Simply roast 750g of pumpkin, skin on, in chunks, covered in foil, in a preheated oven, 200°C/400°F/ gas mark 6, for about 40 minutes to 1 hour – the length of time will depend on your pumpkin. When it's cooked, allow it to cool for a little while, then peel off the skin and blitz the flesh in a food processor. However, if you're feeling lazy, you can simply buy it in a tin!

* Sometimes cheesecakes will 'crack' when cooked – it depends on your oven. Don't worry if this happens – it won't affect the flavour of the finished product.

1. Heat your oven to 160°C/325°F/gas mark 3. Line the base of a 23cm spring-form cake tin with baking parchment and thoroughly grease the sides.

2. Start by making the base: blitz all the biscuits and the sugar to a medium fine crumb in a food processor. Melt the butter, add to the biscuit crumbs and pulse until just mixed. Tip the mixture into the lined cake tin, then press it evenly into the bottom of the tin. Bake for 10 minutes, then remove from the oven and leave to cool.

3. Turn the oven up to 180°C/350°F/gas mark 4. Wipe out the bowl of the processor, then tip in the cream cheese, sugars, miso paste and vanilla seeds. Blend for a minute or so until smooth, scraping down the sides of the bowl. Add the pumpkin purée, eggs and yolks and blend again until smooth, making sure you scrape down the sides of the bowl once more.

4. Tip the mixture into the cake tin and bake for 15 minutes, then reduce the heat to 110°C/225°F/gas mark ¼ and bake for a further 50 minutes to 1 hour and 10 minutes. It's ready when set around the edges and still slightly wobbly in the centre.

5. Remove from the oven and leave the cheesecake to cool in its tin on a wire rack for an hour or so. Then run a knife around the edges of the tin, carefully remove the ring and slide the cheesecake on to a plate. Leave to cool completely before serving – at least 4 hours, if not overnight in the fridge.

6. Serve with whipped cream.

ANNA WITH HER FRIENDS, NGATEA, NEW ZEALAND, 1975

Banana & Flake Ice Cream Surprise

SERVES 8 • PREPARATION TIME: 5 MINUTES PLUS FREEZING • COOKING TIME: NONE • V

Katie says: 'Like so many of us, I'm keen to please and yet have precious little time for faffing around. This dessert, which comes from an idea from my friend Julia Parker, falls into the winning category of being (a) popular with all ages, (b) phenomenally straightforward and cheap, and yet (c) looks really rather snazzy.'

> a tub of inexpensive **vanilla ice cream**
> 2 **bananas**
> 2 **chocolate flakes**

1. Empty the tub of ice cream into a bowl that you can put into the freezer. Let it warm up just a little so that you can work with it and mix it around a bit. Mash the bananas and stir them into the ice cream. Smooth it all over.

2. Bash up the chocolate flakes and sprinkle them generously on top. Put in the freezer until you're ready to serve. (We told you it was easy.)

TIPS

* We've yet to meet a kid (or adult, for that matter) who doesn't love this. We're sure you can think of a whole host of additional surprises to mix into the ice cream (crumbled biscuits, perhaps? Raspberries?). Katie tends to hand the whole affair over to the kids who are going to eat it, and lets them get on with it.

Eleanor's Eating Mess

SERVES 6 • PREPARATION TIME: 10 MINUTES • COOKING TIME (MAKING THE MERINGUES): 2 HOURS
COOKING TIME (BUYING THE MERINGUES): NONE • WF GF V

Eleanor, John and Katie's daughter, age six, came to the (mistaken) conclusion that Eton Mess is actually called Eating Mess. So in their house it has become such. (Hayward's Heath also inadvertently became Famous Thief.) Eleanor has become really quite a special cook and likes to make this simple but rather calorific concoction as a variation on the classic.

500ml **double cream**, whipped
450g **strawberries**, hulled and halved

For the meringue:
3 **egg whites**
150g **caster sugar**

1. First make your meringues: Heat the oven to 120°C/250°F/gas mark ½. Whisk the egg whites into stiff peaks. Then beat in a tablespoon of sugar, until the mixture looks like satin. Wait for about a minute, then fold in the remaining sugar in 2 batches.

2. Line a baking sheet with greaseproof paper, scoop the egg white onto it and, with a spoon, spread it into a 14–16cm disc. Pop it into the oven for about 1½ hours, until the meringue is golden on the outside and slightly gooey in the middle. Remove from the oven and leave to cool on a wire rack.

3. To make the mess, break up the cooled meringue into a bowl. Add the cream, and then the strawberries. Stir all the ingredients gently together. It should look as though a pavlova has slid off the parcel-shelf in the back of the car and splatted on to the windscreen. Serve at room temperature.

TIPS

* Egg whites freeze brilliantly. So you can use the two you'll have left over from Anna Hansen's Pumpkin & Miso Cheesecake on page 216.

* If you don't have time to make your own meringues you can always buy them. We won't tell on you. You'll need 6 meringue nests for this recipe.

Giancarlo Caldesi and his wife Katie run Caffè Caldesi and
La Cucina Caldesi, London's only Italian cookery school.
Giancarlo is an amazing cook with an infectious passion
for his native Tuscany.

GIANCARLO CALDESI'S
PIZZA & PASTA MAKING CLASS

We asked Giancarlo Caldesi to show a bunch of Leon-flavoured nippers how to make pizza and pasta. These recipes are not dumbed down for children. They're the real deal and great fun to make.

Impasto per la Pizza
(PIZZA DOUGH)

MAKES 4 PIZZAS • PREPARATION TIME: 25 MINUTES PLUS PROVING • COOKING TIME: 4–7 MINUTES • V

500g **'00' white flour**
   or half **plain** and half **strong white flour**
2 teaspoons **salt**
10g **fresh yeast**
325ml tepid **water**

1. Place the flour and the salt into a large bowl. In a separate small bowl add the yeast to the tepid water and mix until thoroughly combined. Add the yeast mixture to the flour and salt and mix together to make a dough.

2. Place the dough on to a lightly floured surface and knead for 8–10 minutes, until smooth and elastic. Cut into four and shape into balls. Cover each ball with a little oil to stop them forming a crust and leave to rest on a floured surface. Cover the balls with an upturned bowl or a tea towel and leave to rise until they have doubled in size.

3. Meanwhile, heat the oven to its maximum temperature.

4. On a lightly floured surface, roll out each ball until you have a disc of pizza dough about 1cm in thickness.

5. Now pop two inverted baking trays into the oven to heat through – these will be your substitutes for a pizza stone.

6. Top the pizza dough with whatever you fancy (we used tomato-based sauce (see pages 40–1), cheese, salami and olives) and transfer to the oven straight away before it goes soggy, using a floured board or a paddle to shunt it onto your heated baking trays. Bake for 4–7 minutes, or until crispy around the edges and hot and bubbling on top.

Pasta Fresca

(FRESH PASTA)

MAKES ENOUGH PASTA FOR 4 AS A MAIN COURSE OR 6 FOR A STARTER
PREPARATION TIME: I HOUR • COOKING TIME: 2 MINUTES • V

This is the general guide to pasta – 1 egg to 100g of '00' flour. However, as egg sizes differ, a little bending of the rules is sometimes necessary. Ideally pasta is made on a wooden surface, as the tiny particles of wood that project from the surface add texture, helping the pasta to absorb the sauce that eventually coats it. Many Italians use a tablecloth for the same purpose.

The surface of pasta rolled on a metal surface, or a work surface, or through a pasta machine is completely smooth and not so absorbent. This means that dried pasta, which is normally made through metal rollers, has a smooth, harder exterior better designed for liquid sauces such as seafood or tomato. Its lack of absorbency prevents it from becoming soggy.

200g **'00' flour,** plus a little extra for dusting
2 medium **free-range eggs**, preferably corn-fed for colour

1. Tip the flour into a bowl and make a well in the middle. The walls around the edge of the mound of flour should be high enough to contain the eggs. Crack the eggs into the well.

2. Using a table knife, mix the egg and flour together. Keep mixing the until they form a thick paste, using the fingertips of one hand to incorporate the rest of the flour.

3. The dough should form a soft, but firm flexible ball. If it still sticks to the palm of your hand, add a little more flour, but be cautious and stop adding flour as soon as it stops feeling sticky. If it's really dry and starts to crack, add a tablespoon of water.

4. Remove the dough to a lightly floured surface and knead it for 5–10 minutes, or until it springs back to the touch. Don't overwork it, or the result will be tough pasta. If you cut the ball of dough open at this stage it should be full of small air bubbles – this means you have kneaded it for long enough.

5. Lightly dust the dough with flour and wrap it in clingfilm to prevent it from drying out, then let it rest at room temperature for 20 minutes. Meanwhile, clean your work surface.

6. Lightly flour your work surface, flatten out your pasta dough and, following the instructions on your pasta machine, start feeding the dough through it, rolling it thinner each time. DON'T ROLL IT THROUGH MORE THAN 6 TIMES – this will be the difference between a silky pasta and one with the texture of leather. Add the cutting attachment of your choice, depending on what shape pasta you want, then roll it through the machine a final time to cut.

7. Bring a large pan of salted water to a rolling boil. Add your pasta and boil for 2 minutes. Remove the pasta from the pan with a slotted spoon and place on to a warmed plate or tray. Serve immediately with a sauce of your choice (see pages 40–1 for some ideas).

BIRTHDAYS

OK, I'll admit it.

I LOVE birthdays.

I LOVE gifts.

I LOVE sausages on sticks.

Birthdays should be celebrated. I don't care how old you are. All this nonsense about not wanting to share your age with the world is piffle! Every day is an achievement.

HAPPY BIRTHDAY!

KAY

The Spritz

SERVES 2 • PREPARATION TIME: 2 MINUTES • COOKING TIME: NONE • WF GF V

The Venetian drink of choice. It's cool, bittersweet and colourful – just what you need for a party.

> a dash of **Aperol** or **Campari** per glass
> 250–300ml **prosecco** (or white wine and sparkling water)
> a small bowl of **ice**
> 2 chunks of **orange** (preferably sanguinella or blood orange)
> 2 **green olives** in brine, rinsed

1. Pour a dash of Aperol or Campari into each glass.

2. Top up to about half full with the prosecco or white wine and sparkling water. Pop a cube of ice in.

3. Skewer an orange chunk and an olive on each of 2 long cocktail sticks and place one in each glass. Serve with the bowl of ice on the side.

Vince Jung's Margarita

MAKES 1 • PREPARATION TIME: 2 MINUTES • COOKING TIME: NONE • WF GF V

Kay's friend Vince is the third-generation owner of the landmark Hollywood bar, the Formosa Café, which has been serving everyone from movie stars to hoodlums since... well... it depends on who you talk to, but no one's really sure. Vince's margaritas are the business.

> 60ml **silver tequila**
> 30ml **Cointreau**
> the juice from 1½ **limes**
> 45ml **simple syrup** (see opposite)

FORMOSA CAFÉ, 1956

1. Fill a metal cocktail shaker with ice and add all the ingredients. Shake briskly. Serve on the rocks or straight up in a salt-rimmed glass, and garnish with a wedge of lime.

If you ask Vince about the Formosa's past, most likely he'll ask you if you want the clean or dirty version. You definitely want the dirty version. Vince's grandfather's business partner Jimmy Bernstein won the restaurant in a bet. Before that, it had supposedly been owned by the mob. Vince says: 'This place was a one-stop shop. Back in the day, you could come in here, cash a check, get a drink, place a bet, have your lunch and get a date.' Vince has been in charge since 1993 and, while there aren't any mobsters any more, it's one of the few places in town with that old Hollywood vibe where you can still rub shoulders with a movie star on their day off.

VINCE, LOS ANGELES, 1966

The Rude Boi

MAKES 1 • PREPARATION TIME: 2 MINUTES • COOKING TIME: NONE • WF GF V

Here's a tropical-inspired non-alcoholic cocktail for the kids, which we invented for Kay's nephews Alex and Alastair when they were younger. The high point in its genesis was the time Alastair discovered the cocktail shaker, and that fizzy drinks don't respond well to shaking, all in the same afternoon.

ice
shop-bought mango and passion fruit smoothie
ginger beer

1. Fill a Collins glass with ice. Pour in 1 measure of the mango and passion fruit smoothie. Top up with ginger beer. Stir to blend and serve at once.

ALEX & ALASTAIR, GOZO, 2002

TIPS

* You can substitute the ginger beer for sparkling pineapple and grapefruit drink if you prefer.

Simple Syrup

A cocktail staple, this is super-easy to make and will see you through countless margaritas and other cocktails.

100g caster sugar
100ml water

1. Over a low to medium heat, mix the sugar and water together in a pan until the sugar is completely dissolved. Don't allow to boil.

2. Once it's all dissolved, set the pan aside to cool, then decant the syrup into a jam jar or bottle with a good fitting lid and store until you need it.

TIPS

* Be sure to sterilize your jam jar or bottle first.

* Simple syrup is also now available to buy in bottles at most supermarkets.

LEFT TO RIGHT: THE RUDE BOI; THE SPRITZ; VINCE JUNG'S MARGARITA

Devilish Chicken Drumsticks

MAKES 12 • PREPARATION TIME: 15 MINUTES PLUS MARINATING • COOKING TIME: 40 MINUTES • ✓ ♥

Chicken drumsticks are a party food staple. It's not just that they taste great. They're also really good for waving around when you're a bit tiddly and in the middle of an anecdote. These ones are 'devilish' because they're based on a *pollo alla diavolo*, so they're proper fiery.

1 teaspoon crushed **dried chilli**
½ tablespoon **black peppercorns**, cracked
½ tablespoon **white peppercorns**, cracked
2 tablespoons **olive oil**
1 tablespoon **English mustard**
the leaves from 1 sprig of **fresh rosemary**
the juice of 1 **lemon**
a good pinch of **sea salt**
12 **chicken drumsticks**

1. In a large bowl, mix the chilli and peppercorns with the oil, mustard, rosemary and lemon juice.

2. Clean and dry the chicken drumsticks and cut some slashes into the meat. Add them to the bowl with a good pinch of salt and mix together well. Leave to marinate for at least an hour.

3. Heat the oven to 200°C/400°F/gas mark 6. Lay the drumsticks in a roasting tray, making sure not to overcrowd the pan, and roast them for 40 minutes, or until crispy and cooked through.

4. Serve with something cool to put out the fire.

TIPS

* These are terrific on the barbecue. Just grill over medium coals until they're done. For an extra twist, soak the sticks from some old rosemary prunings in cold water for a few hours and throw them on to the coals before you put on the chicken. The rosemary smoke will add a super flavour.

POPPY, MADDIE, JAMES, SARAH & DAISY, 2012

Annette's Sweet & Sour Chicken Drumsticks

MAKES 12 • PREPARATION TIME: 15 MINUTES PLUS MARINATING • COOKING TIME: 40 MINUTES • ✓ ♥

We first had this at Margaret Morris's place in Jamaica, then promptly lost the notebook with the recipe in it. So it's very much a re-creation. But it's a great dish for a party, especially one where everyone's expected to eat with their hands.

1 chicken **stock cube**
1 tablespoon **vegetable oil**
1 tablespoon **light soy sauce**
2 tablespoons good **mango chutney**,
   plus an extra 1½ tablespoons for a final glaze
1 clove of **garlic**, crushed
the zest and juice of ½ a **lemon**
1 tablespoon picked **thyme leaves**
12 **chicken drumsticks**
salt and **freshly ground black pepper**

1. Put the stock cube and the oil into a bowl and crush together into a paste. Add the soy sauce, chutney, garlic, lemon zest and thyme, and stir everything together well.

2. Clean and dry the chicken drumsticks, then cut shallow slashes into the meat. Add them to the marinade, season with salt and pepper, and mix everything thoroughly, working the marinade into the cuts in the chicken legs. Leave to stand for a good hour.

3. Heat the oven to 200°C/400°F/gas mark 6.

4. Lay the chicken drumsticks in a roasting tray, making sure not to crowd them too closely together. Roast them in the oven for 40 minutes, or until the chicken's cooked through and the marinade has become like sticky-sweet trousers on the drumsticks.

5. In the last 5 minutes, stir in the final 1½ tablespoons of mango chutney to complete the glaze.

6. Sprinkle a little lemon juice over the top and serve piping hot.

TIPS

* For an extra Jamaican kick, why not add a tablespoon of Pickapeppa Sauce to the marinade?

THINGS ON STICKS!

The Italian Job
✓ ♥ WF GF V

Have a bowl of ripe **cherry tomatoes** at the ready. Oh, and a bowl of **baby mozzarella** (*bocconcini*) or just regular mozzarella chopped into bite-sized pieces, and bathed in some **extra virgin olive oil**, **salt** and **pepper**, and a crushed clove of **garlic**. Some nice **fresh basil** leaves, too. And a small bowl of mixed sea salt and freshly ground black pepper. Some sticks. You do the maths.

Henley Regatta Smoked Trout & Cucumber Club

Toast as many pieces of **white AND brown bread** as you like. Lightly butter each piece. Peel and slice a **cucumber** very thinly.

Lay liberal slices of **smoked trout** on a piece of brown toast. Season with **lemon juice** and **freshly ground black pepper**. Top with a piece of white toast. Liberally layer that with slices of cucumber. Season with **salt** and pepper. Lay another slice of brown toast on and again layer with smoked trout. Season with a dash more lemon juice and some black pepper. Finish off with a slice of white toast.

Cut into squares and skewer.

Porchetta on a Stick
✓ WF GF DF

Cube some **pork leg steaks**. Crush some **toasted fennel seeds** and some stripped **rosemary leaves** together. Mix with a good amount of **olive oil**. Marinate the pork for as long as you can. Season with **salt** and **pepper**. Then pan-fry for 7–10 minutes, or until cooked. Just before you take the pork out of the pan, add a crushed clove of **garlic** and stir it around – you want it to stick to the meat, but not to burn. Skewer. Be careful not to burn your fingers.

TIPS

* If you are making BIG STICKS and popping them on the grill, remember to soak the sticks in water first.

What's a party without things on sticks? Our friend Zack says: 'There's no foodstuff that can't be improved by putting it on a stick.' We quite agree with you, Zack. Here are a few of our favourites:

Samurai on Horseback

✓ WF GF

You've heard of Devils on Horseback. You've heard of Angels on Horseback. Now, new and exclusive to Leon we give you Samurai on Horseback!!

Stretch some **streaky bacon** rashers with the back of a blunt knife. Cut them in two. Open a tin of **water chestnuts** and drain them. Wrap each water chestnut in half a bacon rasher and secure with a stick.

Pop them on a baking tray, and into the oven at 200°C/400°F/gas mark 6 for about 20–25 minutes, or until the bacon is crisp.

Remove from the oven and serve. But be careful – the water chestnuts retain a furious heat! Serve with a bowl of spicy **Sriracha Sauce** or some good **mango chutney**.

Cold Roast Beef, Blue Cheese & Grapes

✓ WF GF

Stack a thin slice of **rare roast beef** on top of a chunk of **blue cheese** and a **grape**. Spike it. Eat it and weep.

Grilled Cheese

V

Spread 2 slices of **white bread** with **butter** on one side. Place a dry frying pan over a medium heat.

Slice some **cheese**. Have some **ham** if you like.

Place the first slice of bread, butter-side-down in the pan. Immediately place the cheese slice(s) on top. (Pop the ham in if you like.) Slap the second piece of bread on top, butter side UP. Press down gently with a spatula. Flip the sandwich. The underside should be golden brown. Cook the other side until it is just as golden brown, and the cheese is melt-y.

Remove from the pan. Cut into 4 squares. Stab with sticks. Serve **mustard** to dip. And some sharp **pickles** on the side.

Honey Mustard Sausages

✓

An oldie, but a goodie! Buy some **good-quality (preferably gluten-free) cocktail sausages**. Pop them in a roasting tray and into the oven at 200°C/400°F/gas mark 6 for about 20 minutes. Meanwhile, mix together 1–2 tablespoons of **runny honey** and 1–2 tablespoons of **grainy Dijon mustard** – depending on how many sausages you have! Take the sausages out of the oven and baste them liberally with the honey/mustard mixture.

Return them to the oven for about 5–10 minutes, or until sticky and golden brown.

Stab them with cocktail sticks.

Chorizo & Halloumi Skewers

✓

Cube some **halloumi cheese** and marinate it in **olive oil** with a crushed clove of **garlic** and some fresh or dried **oregano**.

Cook an ample amount of sliced **chorizo** in a pan until just oozing red oil and slightly cooked. Skewer the chorizo and halloumi together. Griddle over a medium heat for about 5 minutes. Serve at once, before the halloumi turns to rubber.

KAY, BANGKOK, 1968

Fig or Pear & Cheese

✓ WF GF V

Chunk up a ripe **pear** in the winter, or a ripe **fig** in the summer. Skewer it together with your favourite **cheese**: blue cheeses go particularly well. So does a gooey Taleggio.

Vickie Sponge Squares

V

Who says all stick-y snacks have to be savoury? Make a classic **Victoria Sponge** — we like the recipe in *LEON Book 3: Baking & Puddings*. Fill with the **jam** of your choice (we love a little rose petal jam and some Greek yogurt or the classic combination of strawberry jam and whipped cream). Cut into small squares or wedges, dust with icing sugar and SPIKE.

Cake Pop

V

Really? Our gorgeous friend Bumble guiltily admits she loves these… it's simply your favourite cake… on a stick.

Make your absolute favourite **cake**. Maybe the gluten-free Flatplanet Brownies on page 80? Or any cake you like. Cut up and stick on a stick.Now the naughty bit. DUNK it in:

- **Creamy butter icing**: double the weight of butter to sugar, with an added vanilla or chocolate or caramel hit. And a splash of liquid. Milk or booze. Your call.

- **Whipped cream**. Yes. Whipped cream. It is a birthday after all

- **Low-fat yoghurt, honey and toasted linseed** – because you are GOOD.

- **Strawberries** or **raspberries** whooshed with a dash of **lemon juice** and a dash of **icing sugar**. And for the grown-ups – a dash of **kirsch** or **Cointreau**.

Natasha's Buttered Toffee Apple Ice Cream

SERVES: 6–8 • PREPARATION TIME: 1 HOUR PLUS FREEZING • COOKING TIME: NONE • WF GF V

John's daughter Natasha loves apples and she loves ice cream. So Kay made this up for her.

400ml **milk**
4 **egg yolks**
200g **caster sugar**
85g **unsalted butter**, softened
the zest and juice of ½ a **lemon**
1 teaspoon **sea salt**
900g **apples** (about 8 apples), peeled, cored
    and chopped – we like to use Cox's
400ml **double cream**

1. Bring the milk up to the boil but DO NOT let it boil. Then take the pan off the heat and set aside.

2. In a large bowl, using an electric whisk beat the egg yolks with 50g of the sugar.

3. Add the milk to the egg yolks and stir to combine. Pour the mixture back into the pan and put back on the stove to heat gently, stirring all the time. DO NOT let it boil. When you have a nice coating of custard forming over your spoon, remove from the heat. Set aside and leave to cool.

4. Meanwhile, spread the butter in the bottom of a smallish pan or sauté pan about 20–24cm in diameter. Squish it down evenly with your fingers. Mix the rest of the sugar, the lemon zest and the salt together and sprinkle it over the butter. Pop the apple pieces into the pan and try to keep them all in one layer. Pour over the lemon juice. Then put the pan over a low heat and melt the butter and sugar slowly.

5. Once it has melted, start gently flicking and spooning the mixture over the apples, making sure you shake the pan to move things around so that nothing burns or sticks to the bottom. Keep gently turning the apple pieces in the hot buttered toffee for about 20 minutes, or until the apples are soft and the mixture has a beautiful golden amber colour. Remove from the heat and let the apple mixture cool completely.

6. When it's cold, mash the toffee-d apple mixture and stir it into the custard. Don't worry if it's not smooth – the chunky bits go nice and chewy once they're frozen.

7. Stir in the double cream. Then pour into your ice cream maker, and churn as per its instructions. Serve.

TIPS

* Make a quick batch of crumble topping with 100g of plain flour, 50g of unsalted butter, 50g of demerara sugar and a pinch of salt. Heat the oven to 190°C/375°F/ gas mark 5. Rub the butter and flour together until it resembles breadcrumbs. Stir in the sugar and salt. Tip on to a lightly greased baking tray and pop into the oven for 15–20 minutes, until nice and crunchy. Serve sprinkled on to the ice cream.

* Homemade ice cream has a different texture to store-bought. If it seems a little soft, just put it into a lidded container and freeze for a bit. And remember, if it has been in the freezer for more than a few hours, you may have to soften it by popping it into the fridge for 30 minutes or so before serving.

Saffron, Honey & Orange Blossom Ice Cream

SERVES 4 • PREPARATION TIME: 10 MINUTES PLUS FREEZING • COOKING TIME: 15 MINUTES • ✓ WF GF V

This really is sunshine-chilled-on-a-plate – one of our favourite summer creations. Serve with a slab of the clementine polenta cake from *Leon book 3: Baking & Puddings*, and with a hunk of honeycomb sliding down the side …

> 1 teaspoon **orange flower water**
> a large pinch of **saffron**
> 285ml **milk**
> 4 **egg yolks**
> 4 tablespoons good **runny honey**
> 285ml **double cream**

1. Infuse the orange flower water with the saffron and set aside.

2. Bring the milk up to the boil but DO NOT let it boil. Take it off the heat, add the saffron and orange flower water, and set aside for 30 minutes.

3. In a large bowl, beat the egg yolks with the honey until combined and creamy. Add the milk mixture to the egg yolks and stir.

4. Pour the mixture back into the pan and heat gently, stirring. Again, DO NOT let it boil. When it coats the back of your spoon remove from the heat. Leave to cool.

5. When it's cold, stir in the double cream. Pour into your ice cream maker, and churn as per its instructions.

Apple's Easy Chocolate Birthday Cake

SERVES: 6–8 • PREPARATION TIME: 15–20 MINUTES PLUS COOLING • COOKING TIME: 50 MINUTES • V

Let's face it, you cannot have a proper birthday without cake. We think that, for birthdays, the cake's got to be chocolate. This one, from Katie's cousin's wife Apple, a perennial Leon favourite cook, never fails with kids and adults alike.

For the cake:
100g **unsalted butter**
250g **light brown sugar**
50ml **sunflower oil**
25g **cocoa powder**
2 teaspoons **vanilla extract**
4 **eggs**
80ml **milk**
100ml **double cream**
300g **plain flour**
3 teaspoons **baking powder**

For the frosting:
50g **unsalted butter**
300g **icing sugar**
50ml **double cream**
25g **cocoa powder**

1. Preheat the oven to 180°C/350°F/gas mark 4 and grease a 22cm cake tin.

2. Over a low heat, melt the butter in a small pan. While it's on the hob, put the sugar, oil, cocoa powder and vanilla extract into a bowl. Then, when the butter has melted, add it to the bowl and beat the mixture together until it's smooth.

3. Add the eggs, milk and cream and mix until smooth. Sift the flour and baking powder together, and beat them into the chocolate mixture.

4. Pour the cake batter into the greased cake tin, cover it with foil, and bake it in the oven for 30 minutes. Then remove the foil and bake for a further 20 minutes, or until it's cooked. You can test it by stabbing the thickest part of the cake with a skewer. When it's done, the skewer will come out clean.

5. Let the cake cool in its tin for about 10 minutes or so. Then remove, and set it aside on a wire rack to cool completely.

6. When the cake is cold, you can ice it as follows: melt the butter over a low heat. Then pour it into a bowl with the icing sugar, cream and cocoa, and beat until smooth. If it's looking too thick, add a little water to loosen. Smear it liberally over the cake, then decorate to suit its lucky recipient.

CHRISTMAS & BOXING DAY

Christmases in Bangkok as a child were quite something. It would be 33°C in the shade, but we still insisted on having the full roast turkey and all the trimmings, with the caveat that we had the air conditioning turned up to max, and plenty of fake snow sprayed on the windows. Outside, it was sweltering. Inside, it was a winter wonderland, complete with fir-cone-people skiing down fibreglass slopes on the sideboard!

Our regular treat was a frozen turkey imported from the US which, much to my fascination, had a thermometer that popped out of the bird when it was done. What technology!

Christmas remains my favourite time of the year. While the food is a key component, it's more important to enjoy it. Really, you're just making a bumper-big Sunday lunch. So don't stress. It'll all come together just fine. Merry Christmas to you all!

KAY

Roast Turkey with Scarborough Fair Butter

PREPARATION TIME: 30 MINUTES PLUS RESTING • COOKING TIME: SEE CHART • ✓ ♥ WF GF

Christmas lunch, Christmas dinner: we don't mind when you eat it. But when it comes down to it, we're turkey people. A great turkey, cooked just right, is a joy to behold. A proper feast. Of course, this requires a good turkey. We work hard to source meat from the best farms we can. And when it comes to turkeys, we're huge fans of the Kellys' KellyBronze.

The Kellys have been farming turkeys since the 70s, and they're utterly dedicated to the flavour of their free-range birds. They also supply poults (or baby turkeys) to certified farmers across the UK, who are expected to keep to their standards. The cooking times in this recipe are based on their recommendations. Guideline timings (for **unstuffed turkeys**):

OVEN READY ROASTING WEIGHT	TIME (WITHOUT STUFFING)	SERVES	OVEN READY ROASTING WEIGHT	TIME (WITHOUT STUFFING)	SERVES
4 KG	2 HOURS	8–9	8 KG	3 HOURS	16–17
5 KG	2¼ HOURS	10–11	9 KG	3¼ HOURS	18–19
6 KG	2½ HOURS	12–13	10 KG	3½ HOURS	20–22
7 KG	2¾ HOURS	14–15	11 KG	3¾ HOURS	23–25

In case you think these timings seem short, don't worry, they work. The important bit is to ensure your bird is a) properly thawed if frozen, and b) at room temperature – get it out of the fridge a good 2 hours before you want to cook it. Let's go:

1 **KellyBronze turkey**
1 large **onion**, roughly chopped
1 sprig of **fresh thyme**
1 **bay leaf**
salt and **freshly ground black pepper**

For the Scarborough Fair butter
(makes enough to stuff up to a 7kg bird – double it if you are going bigger):
125g **unsalted butter**, softened
2–3 tablespoons chopped **fresh parsley**
3 big leaves of **fresh sage**
the leaves from 1 good sprig of **fresh rosemary**
the leaves from 4 sprigs of **fresh thyme**
the zest of ½ a **lemon**

For the gravy:
the **turkey giblets**
1 **onion**, roughly chopped
1 sprig of **fresh thyme**
1 sprig of **fresh parsley**
1 **bay leaf**
1 litre **water**
350ml **Madeira**
25–50g **unsalted butter**

TIPS

* We recommend using a meat thermometer if you are unsure about your turkey's 'doneness'. Remember, each turkey and each oven is different.

1. Heat the oven to 180°C/350°F/gas mark 4.

2. First, make the Scarborough Fair butter to push up under the turkey's skin before roasting. It adds moisture and gives the skin a lovely St Tropez tan… Put all the ingredients into a blender or food processor and whizz them together.

3. Now – CAREFULLY – slip your hand (or the smallest family member's hand) up and under the turkey skin, gently prying it away from the flesh (there is a fine membrane holding them together). Try not to rip the skin. Gently push your way through (you can even, if your hands are small enough, loosen the skin that encloses the dark thigh meat, which really adds juiciness to these somewhat drier parts), and push the butter up and under the 'glove' you've created, pushing and smoothing as gently as possible until you have worked the butter as far in as you can. Rub any excess butter over the bird, paying particular attention to the legs and thighs.

4. Season the cavity of the bird with salt and pepper, and put the roughly chopped onion and the herbs inside.

5. Roast the turkey in the oven breast side down for all but 30 minutes of its cooking time. The turkey's fat lies in its thighs and back. So it will trickle gently down basting the meat throughout the cooking time.

6. Half an hour before the end of cooking turn the bird on to its back. Baste the breast and return it to the oven for the last half hour.

7. When the time's up check it's cooked by stabbing a skewer into the thickest part of the thigh. The juices should run clear. If not, baste it again and roast a little longer until they do.

8. Leave the turkey to rest for 30–60 minutes before carving. This is really important. It gives the juices time to spread back through the meat, and gives you the time to finish preparing the rest of the meal.

9. While the turkey's in the oven make a giblet stock. Reserve the liver and put the rest of the giblets into a saucepan with the roughly chopped onion, the herbs and the water, and bring it to the boil. As it bubbles up it will throw a greyish scum to the surface. Skim this off and reduce the liquid by half. Season with salt and pepper and set aside to cool. Chop the liver into 1cm cubes.

10. When the turkey's resting pour all the cooking juices into a heatproof bowl. Pour 2 tablespoons of the turkey fat (from the top of the cooking juices) back into the roasting pan. Then skim off the rest of the fat.

11. Heat the 2 tablespoons of fat in the roasting pan and sauté the turkey liver until it's nicely sealed on all sides. It should take no more than a couple of minutes. Deglaze the pan with the Madeira. Bubble it up hard to cook out the alcohol, then add the giblet stock and the skimmed roasting juices. Stir it all together and reduce by between a third and a half. Taste and adjust the seasoning, then whisk in the butter to enrich it.

12. Carve the turkey and serve with all the yummy trimmings.

Three Ways to Get Stuffed

We love stuffing … but we prefer to cook it OUTSIDE the bird – the texture is better, it creates a nice crunchy top, and the turkey takes much less time to cook. Here are three options.

Sausage & Wild Rice Stuffing

SERVES 6–8 • PREPARATION TIME: 25 MINUTES • COOKING TIME: 1 HOUR 10 MINUTES • ✓ WF GF

150g **wild rice**
1 tablespoon **olive oil**
400g **gluten-free sausagemeat**
1 **onion**, peeled and chopped
½ a **red pepper**, chopped
½ a **green pepper**, chopped
1 clove of **garlic**, peeled and chopped

2 sticks of **celery**, chopped
2–3 sprigs of **fresh thyme**, leaves picked
a small handful of **fresh parsley**, chopped
2 teaspoons **Kay's Cajun Magic** (see page 57)
125ml **white wine** or **stock**
salt and **freshly ground black pepper**

1. Bring 1 litre of salted water to the boil. Add the wild rice and bring back to the boil. Turn down the heat, cover, and simmer for 40 minutes, or until the rice grains split open. Strain the rice, then run it under the cold tap to stop it cooking. Set aside.

2. Heat the olive oil in a frying pan and fry the sausagemeat until it is cooked through. Remove with a slotted spoon and set aside. If there is too much liquid or oil remaining in the pan, drain some off. You may need to drain it all and add about a tablespoonful of olive oil – it will depend on how much liquid has been thrown by your sausagemeat.

3. Add the onion, peppers, garlic and celery to the pan and cook over a low heat for 4–5 minute, or until just softened. Stir in the thyme and parsley. Tip into a clean bowl and mix with the sausagemeat and the cooked wild rice. Add the Kay's Cajun Magic and mix in well. Season with salt and pepper, then taste and adjust the seasoning. Add the wine or stock and mix again. Spoon into a greased ovenproof dish and cook in a preheated oven at 190°C/375°F/gas mark 5 for 30–35 minutes, or until crisp on top and fragrant.

Herby Sausage & Apple Stuffing

SERVES 6–8 • PREPARATION TIME: 25 MINUTES • COOKING TIME: 55 MINUTES • ✓ ♥ WF GF

1 tablespoon **olive oil**
400g **gluten-free sausagemeat**
the **turkey liver**, chopped (optional)
1 **onion**, chopped
2 **apples**, peeled, cored and chopped
125g **cooked chestnuts**,
　　roughly chopped

125g **gluten-free breadcrumbs**
8 small leaves of **fresh sage**, chopped
8 sprigs of **fresh thyme**, leaves picked
a pinch of **ground allspice**
125ml good **cider**
50ml **water**
salt and **freshly ground black pepper**

1. Heat the olive oil in a pan and fry the sausagemeat until cooked. Remove with a slotted spoon and set aside. If there is a lot of fat left in the pan, drain some off.

2. If using, add the turkey liver to the pan and fry until cooked. Remove and set aside. Add the onions and apple to the pan and fry until slightly soft.

3. Put everything into a large bowl and mix together thoroughly, adding the cider and water. Drink the rest of the cider while greasing an ovenproof dish. Spoon the stuffing into the dish and pop into a preheated oven at 190°C/375°F/ gas mark 5 for 30–35 minutes, or until crispy on top.

Polenta Stuffing

SERVES 4–6 • PREPARATION TIME: 20 MINUTES • COOKING TIME: 1 HOUR 5 MINUTES • WF GF V

200g **polenta**
a good grating of **nutmeg**
1 tablespoon **olive oil**
85g **golden raisins**
40g **pine nuts**, toasted
1 teaspoon **dried sage**

1 **egg**, lightly beaten
2 tablespoons **Marsala**
100ml **vegetable stock**
50g **butter** (optional)
salt and **freshly ground black pepper**

1. First make the polenta according to the packet instructions, adding a knob of butter, a grating of nutmeg and salt and pepper to taste. You should end up with 400–500g of made polenta.

2. Pour the polenta into a greased roasting tray and let it cool completely. You can do this any time on Christmas Eve if you like, just to make things easier.

3. Slice the polenta into fat strips. Brush the olive oil all over the strips of polenta to coat, then grill for about 5–8 minutes, turning once, until they're crisp and golden. Remove from the heat and set aside on kitchen paper to cool slightly.

4. When cool enough to handle, roughly crumble the polenta into a bowl. Add the remaining ingredients, except the optional butter, and mix well, without breaking the polenta up TOO much more. Pop it all into a greased ovenproof dish, and if you like finish with a few dots of butter on the top. Bake in a preheated oven at 190°C/375°F/gas mark 5 for 35–45 minutes, or until golden and crispy on top.

Perfect Roast Potatoes

Crisp on the outside, fluffy within, this is just the best way to roast a potato. (And who says they're just for Christmas? These tatties will brighten up any day you like!)

> as many **floury potatoes** as you need (we use King Edward)
> 3 tablespoons **goose** or **duck fat** per tin
> **sea salt**

1. Peel the potatoes and cut them into about 5cm pieces. Pop them into salted water and parboil them for 10–15 minutes, or until soft but not completely cooked through. Drain them in a colander. If they don't look fluffed up on the outside, pour them back and forth between the colander and the pan a few times, just to break up the outside. Allow them to dry and cool. (You can do this step quite a way in advance, if you like.)

2. When you're ready to cook them, heat the oven to 200°C/400°F/gas mark 6.

3. Heat the fat in a large roasting tin. When it's hot, carefully put in the potatoes. Make sure not to overcrowd the tin – if you're feeding a lot of people, do 2 tins and baste the potatoes with the hot fat. Season with salt, then pop them into the oven. Roast the potatoes for 1 hour, turning them every 20 minutes or so, until they're crispy and golden brown.

TIPS

* Generally speaking, roast potatoes like a hot oven (up to 220°C/425°F/gas mark 7). But if you've only got one oven and the turkey's in it, you have to make do initially with the temperature the turkey needs. Don't worry. Pop them in anyway, then turn up the heat to 200°C or 220°C (depending on what you need for your stuffings) when you pull out the turkey to let it rest.

* To get the proper crispiness, you must use a floury variety of tatty such as King Edward, maris piper or desirée. Otherwise you're doomed to disappointment.

Spiced Red Cabbage with Dates

SERVES 6-8 • PREPARATION TIME: 15 MINUTES • COOKING TIME: 40 MINUTES • WF GF V

Rather than those long slow braises this is a quicker way of cooking red cabbage, and thanks to the dates there's no added sugar.

25g **unsalted butter**
1 **onion**, finely sliced
1 **small red cabbage** (about 750–800g),
  halved, cored and finely sliced
1 **apple** or **pear**, peeled, cored and sliced
2 tablespoons **Somerset Pomona** or **apple liqueur**
100ml **red wine vinegar**
100ml **water**
20 **dates**, pitted and chopped
10 **cardamom pods**, gently crushed
a large pinch of freshly ground **Jamaican allspice**
salt and **freshly ground black pepper**

1. Melt the butter in a large solid pan or casserole – one that has a good lid. Add the onion and sauté until just soft. Add the red cabbage and the apple or pear, and mix together well.

2. Add the Somerset Pomona, red wine vinegar, water, dates and spices. Bring to the boil. Then turn the heat right down, cover and simmer gently for about 30 minutes.

3. Season with salt and pepper, then serve.

TIPS

* You can make this the day before – even two days before. Keep it refrigerated and just heat it up when you need it. You may need to add a couple of tablespoons of water when you reheat.

* Add a handful or two of sultanas or raisins too, if you like.

* If you can't find the Somerset Pomona, you can substitute a mix of cider and Marsala or amontillado sherry.

FOOD FACT

Somerset Pomona is made by the brilliant Somerset Distillery, whose apple brandies are extraordinary. It's an aged blend of apple juice and cider brandy – sort of a fortified apple juice, if you will. It's delicious with cheese and great to cook with.

Brussels Sprouts Three Ways

Brussels sprouts are a force for good … promise! Here are three sure-fire sprout recipes which have, so far, never failed to convert the doubters.

Sautéd Brussels Sprouts
WITH CANDIED WALNUTS

SERVES 4–6 • PREPARATION TIME: 10 MINUTES • COOKING TIME: 25 MINUTES • ✓ WF GF V

Thanks to Kay's lovely friend Sue McNamara for introducing us to these delicious walnuts.

400g **Brussels sprouts**, trimmed and halved
25g **butter**
1 tablespoon **olive oil**
salt and **freshly ground black pepper**

For the candied walnuts:
60g **walnut halves**
2 tablespoons **brown sugar**
a good pinch of **salt**
a pinch of **chilli powder** or **cayenne pepper**
a dash of **olive oil** or **walnut oil**

1. To make the candied walnuts, put all the ingredients into a wide frying pan over a medium heat. Keep stirring the nuts and sugar in the oil so that nothing gets too stuck together as the sugar begins to caramelize and coat the nuts. This should take about 3–5 minutes. Keep your eye on them, as they can burn quite easily. Tip them out on to some baking parchment and set aside until needed.

2. To cook the sprouts, bring a large pan of salted water to the boil. Plunge the sprouts in for a minute or two, just to blanch them. Drain them, then plunge them into a bowl of cold water to stop them cooking. You want them a little tender, but still with some bite to them. Dry them well.

3. Now heat the butter and olive oil in a wide frying pan or casserole dish. Pop in the sprouts and sauté them until they are catching and browning on some bits – about 5–7 minutes. (You may need to do this in two batches – you don't want to overcrowd the pan.) Season them with salt and pepper.

4. To assemble the dish, transfer the sprouts to a serving bowl and gently stir in the candied walnuts, saving some to scatter over the top.

Puréed Brussels Sprouts

WITH ALLSPICE

SERVES 6–8 • PREPARATION TIME: 25 MINUTES • COOKING TIME: 15 MINUTES • WF GF V

This is heavenly, but very rich – a little goes a long way!

400g **Brussels sprouts**, trimmed
100ml **crème fraîche** or **double cream**
25g **unsalted butter**
a pinch of **ground allspice**
salt and **freshly ground black pepper**
a good grating of **nutmeg**, to serve

1. Bring a large pan of salted water to the boil. Toss in the Brussels sprouts and cook until just tender.

2. Drain the sprouts and pop them into a food processor or blender. Add the crème fraîche or cream, the butter, allspice, salt and pepper, and whiz until you have a gorgeous creamy green purée.

3. Serve sprinkled with a grating of nutmeg.

Shredded Brussels Sprouts

WITH CHESTNUTS, CHILLI & PANCETTA

SERVES 6–8 • PREPARATION TIME: 20 MINUTES • COOKING TIME: 10 MINUTES • ✓ WF GF

2 tablespoons **olive oil**
70g **pancetta cubes**
2 cloves of **garlic**, sliced
1 **red serrano** or other **medium-hot chilli**, deseeded and sliced
75g **cooked chestnuts***, chopped
400g **Brussels sprouts**, trimmed, shredded and washed
salt and **freshly ground black pepper**

1. Heat 1 tablespoon of the olive oil and fry the pancetta over a low to medium heat until it's crispy.

2. Now add the remaining oil, followed by the garlic and chilli, and sauté until the garlic turns translucent, but hasn't quite begun to colour. Add the chestnuts, and sauté for another minute or so.

3. Turn up the heat and add the Brussels sprouts. If they're still damp from washing, so much the better. If not, you may need to add a dash of water, just to get that steam into the pan to help them along. Sauté the sprouts for about 3–4 minutes. Season with salt and a few grinds of black pepper, and serve.

* YOU CAN BUY THESE VACUUM-SEALED. WE THINK THEY HAVE A TERRIFIC FLAVOUR, AND THEY CRUMBLE WELL INTO THE PAN.

Bryn Williams's Bread Sauce

SERVES 6–8 • PREPARATION TIME: 10 MINUTES • COOKING TIME: 15 MINUTES • V

Kay was never a huge fan of bread sauce until she worked with Bryn Williams on his book *Bryn's Kitchen: 5 Brilliant Ways To Cook 20 Great Ingredients*. This is his version, based on his gran's recipe.

6 thick slices of **white bread**
1 **onion**, cut in half
1 **bay leaf**
1 **clove**
500ml **milk**
50g **butter**
a pinch of grated **nutmeg**
sea salt and **freshly ground black pepper**

1. Cut the crusts off the bread and discard. Then cut the slices into 2cm squares.

2. Chop one half of the onion as finely as you can and leave the other half intact. Place the half onion, the bay leaf and the clove in a small pan with the milk and bring to the boil. Simmer gently for about 2 minutes. Take off the heat and set aside to cool.

3. In a heavy-based pan, melt the butter and sauté the chopped onion. Cook gently until the onion is soft, but not coloured – about 2 minutes.

4. Strain the milk through a sieve and pour on to the chopped onions and butter. Now bring to the boil. Once it reaches boiling point, remove from the heat and add the diced bread. Stir the mixture until combined and slightly softened – you still want some texture.

5. Season to taste with salt, pepper and nutmeg. Cover the pan with a lid and keep the sauce warm until needed.

Cranberry Sauce

SERVES 6–8 • PREPARATION TIME: 5 MINUTES • COOKING TIME: 10 MINUTES • ♥ WF GF DF V

Of all the sauces you can serve with a turkey, nothing goes better than a tart cranberry sauce. This one's so simple to make. Best of all, you get to control the amount of sugar that goes into it.

300g **fresh cranberries**
1–2 tablespoons **sugar**, to taste
the juice and zest of 1 **orange**
100ml **water**
1 stick of **cinnamon**, broken in half

1. Place all the ingredients in a small pan and bring to the boil over a medium heat. Turn down the heat and simmer until the berries start to burst. This should take about 8–10 minutes.

2. Remove from the heat, spoon into another container and allow to cool to room temperature. Done. (We prefer the berries to retain a little bite so we cook this for as little time as possible, just until everything's combined.)

TIPS

* Kay prefers her cranberry sauce to be very tart. Feel free to add an extra tablespoon of sugar if you prefer.

* For an extra kick, add a little grated fresh ginger just before you take it off the heat.

* You can also add a plethora of other, festive ingredients – throw in some currants or raisins, or add a grating or two of nutmeg. We've had blueberries in it before now.

* For a more adult sauce, why not add a slug of Grand Marnier or kirsch?

Spiced Cranberry & Apple Crumble

SERVES 4–6 • PREPARATION TIME: 30 MINUTES • COOKING TIME: 35 MINUTES • V

Apple crumble with a seasonal twist: the only decision is cream, ice cream or custard...?

175g **plain flour**
110g **unsalted butter**, chilled
50g **demerara sugar**, plus an
    extra 2–3 tablespoons
a pinch of **salt**
750g **Bramley apples** or other
    sharp cooking apples
175g **fresh** or **frozen cranberries**
the juice and zest of 1 **orange**
½ teaspoon **ground cinnamon**
½ teaspoon **ground allspice**
a good grating of **nutmeg**

1. Heat the oven to 200°C/400°F/gas mark 6.

2. Sieve the flour and put it into a bowl. Cut in the butter, and using the tips of your fingers rub it together with the flour, lifting it high out of the bowl every now and again, until you have what looks like coarse breadcrumbs. The coarser the crumb, the crumblier the crumble.

3. Mix in 50g of the demerara sugar and a pinch of salt with your hands, then set aside.

4. Peel, core and slice the apples, and pop the pieces into another bowl. Add the cranberries, orange zest and juice, the spices and the remaining demerara sugar. Mix together well and place in a lightly buttered ovenproof dish.

5. Cover with the crumble mixture and cook in the oven for 35 minutes. Serve crisp and bubblin'.

TIPS

* You could use a Magimix or blender to make your crumble. Kay prefers the texture and feel of the fingertip method.

Steamed Spiced Marmalade Pudding

WITH CRÈME JAMAIQUE

SERVES: 6–8 • PREPARATION TIME: 20 MINUTES • COOKING TIME: 2 HOURS • V

This is a great alternative to a traditional Christmas pudding. It still has all those festive spices, but none of the heavy fruit.

8 tablespoons good **marmalade**
175g **unsalted butter**, softened
175g **caster sugar**
2 teaspoons **ground ginger**
a really good grating of **nutmeg**
½ teaspoon **vanilla extract**
the zest of 1 **orange**
a pinch of **salt**
6–8 grinds of **black pepper**
175g **self-raising flour**
1 teaspoon **gluten-free baking powder**
1 tablespoon **orange juice**
3 **eggs**

1. First grease a pudding basin with a little butter, then spoon the marmalade into the bottom of it.

2. Now cream the butter and sugar together thoroughly. Add the ground ginger, nutmeg, vanilla, orange zest, salt and black pepper, and mix them in well.

3. Sieve the flour and baking powder together. Add a spoonful of the flour into the butter and sugar. Add one egg, then the orange juice. Then add the remaining eggs one at a time and fold in the rest of the flour until you have a smooth batter. Pour the batter on to the marmalade. Your basin should now be about three-quarters full.

4. Cover the basin with greaseproof paper into which you've folded a pleat and tie it on securely with string.

5. Steam in a tiered steamer for about 2 hours, or until the pudding has risen and it's light and airy. (To test it's cooked, remove the greaseproof paper and stab the pudding with a skewer, right to its middle. If it comes out clean, the pudding's cooked. Just so you know, though: if it's not cooked, you'll need to re-paper it and carry on steaming. So if in doubt, let it go a little longer. Unlike a cake, it's not going to burn, and these puddings re-steam well. So an extra 15 minutes isn't going to hurt.)

6. Turn the cooked pudding out on to a serving plate. Spoon any marmalade that's stayed in the bowl over the top, and serve with Crème Jamaique (see opposite).

TIPS

* If you want more marmalade, don't put any more into the pudding bowl. It's best to melt a little in a saucepan and then pour it over the pudding once it's cooked.

Crème Jamaique

SERVES 6–8 • PREPARATION TIME: 5 MINUTES • COOKING TIME: 20 MINUTES • WF GF V

This is an allspice-and-rum-infused take on a classic crème Anglaise that'll put sunshine into the most wintry dessert.

> 1 tablespoon **allspice berries**
> 250ml **whole milk**
> 4 **egg yolks**
> 50g **caster sugar**
> 1 tablespoon good **rum** – we prefer Appleton's
>   for that proper Jamaican flavour

1. Bring a pan of water to the boil on the back of your stove.

2. In a dry non-stick pan, toast the allspice berries over a medium heat for about a minute, just to bring out their flavour. Crack them open in a pestle and mortar or with the back of a knife, then put them into a heavy-based pan with the milk.

3. Put the pan of milk and allspice on a low heat. While the milk comes up to scalding point, beat the egg yolks, sugar and rum together in a bowl big enough to sit over your pan of boiling water.

4. When the milk reaches scalding point strain through a seive on to the egg yolks, whisking them together. Heat the mixture in its bowl over the boiling water making sure the bottom of the bowl doesn't touch the water below, stirring all the time until it reaches your preferred thickness. (We don't think you want it too thick, just nicely glossy and silky.)

Glögg

SERVES 10–12 • STEEPING TIME: 2–4 HOURS • HEATING TIME: 20 MINUTES • V

Kay got this recipe from her mum and dad, who in turn got it from Scandinavian friends in Bangkok back in the day … It will certainly make a Christmas party go with a swing!

> 1 bottle of **vodka**
> 1 bottle of **red wine**
> 5 **cardamom pods**, cracked open
> 5 **cloves**
> 1 stick of **cinnamon**
>
> 1 piece of **orange rind**
> 1 piece of **fresh ginger**
> 200–300g **sugar** (or to taste)
> **peeled almonds** and **raisins** – a big
>   handful of each (to serve)

1. Mix all the ingredients and leave for 2–4 hours.

2. Heat the Glögg slowly. Do not boil.

3. Add the almonds and raisins just before serving.

BOXING DAY

Whilst Christmas Day is pretty much formulaic for most families, it seems to me that each family use Boxing Day as a day to freestyle, while at the same time establishing quite strict traditions.

Katie's family has a Boxing Day routine that is very established and also very dear to them. At the heart of that is Pop Derham's potato cakes with redcurrant jelly. Miggy, aka Liz, Katie's sister, is very particular about having her redcurrant jelly, and they are all very particular about their ham. Boxing Day lunch is always a full, plated affair with crackers and hats again, and often a chance to do Christmas Day lunch again, maybe without the argument about how to cut and serve the Turkey.

JOHN

Rulle Pulse

SERVES: 6–8 • PREPARATION TIME: 25 MINUTES • COOKING TIME: 2 HOURS 30 MINUTES • ✓ WF GF

John says: 'We have a friend called Christina. She is one of the best adverts for Denmark one can imagine. She is the reason why many dads like taking their kids to school for the drop-off. Toby is good at darts. But I guess there must be more to why he ended up with such a lovely wife. This is Christina's mum's creation, and much cooked by her daughter. It's good Viking food, which makes something a little bit special from a cheap cut of meat. In Danish, its name means "rolled sausage", but it's so much more. You can serve it thinly sliced as an hors d'oeuvre; it's good for a starter served with a little salsa or salad; or simply eat it on an open sandwich as the perfect lunch meat.'

> about 750–800g **lean lamb** or **pork belly** or **breast**
>   (which can be bought from supermarkets pre-rolled and tied)
> a generous bunch of **fresh dill** and **parsley**, chopped
> 2 cloves of **garlic**, crushed
> 8 **whole anchovies** in pure olive oil (can be bought in small glass jars)
> 250ml **stock** of your choice
> **salt** and **freshly ground black pepper** or **chilli pepper**
>
> * You will also need a clean brick, wrapped in kitchen foil, to act as a compress

1. Heat the oven to 120°C/250°F/gas mark ½.

2. Remove the ties from the meat (if elastic, keep them to one side as they'll be useful to re-tie the joint). Unravel, remove any excess fat, and partially lift open the layers of meat. Sandwich in the rest of the ingredients, apart from the stock, laying the anchovies flat. Ensure that all the surface area is covered with the herbs, especially the side that you will start rolling up the joint from, so that you will see a complete spiral of green when you come to cut the finished pulse. Roll up the breast as tightly as possible, then re-tie.

3. Put a large sheet of extra strong foil in a 23 x 13cm loaf tin. Place the pulse on top so it pushes the foil into the tin, then pour the stock around it before wrapping it up in the foil. Place it in the oven for 2½ hours.

4. Remove from the oven and put the foil-wrapped brick compress on top. Once cool, place in the fridge for at least 24 hours. When you are ready to serve, remove the foil and cut into thin, even slices.

TIPS

* This keeps and travels well, so it's ideal picnic, hiking or camping food – which would be accompanied by a healthy shot of Gammel Dansk to warm you up.

CHRISTINA WITH HER MUM, HENRY AND FLORENCE, 2006

John Derham's Potato Cakes

(BOLINHOS DE BATATA)

MAKES 21 CAKES • PREPARATION TIME: 15–20 MINUTES • COOKING TIME: 10 MINUTES PER CAKE • V

John Derham aka 'Pop' is Katie's dad. On Boxing Day, at supper/dinner time, he puts on his apron, requests people make some space for him by the stove, and embarks on a dish that all the family would be bereft without.

Serve with redcurrant sauce. (If you don't, Katie's sister Miggy will have something to say about it.)

1.3kg **potatoes**, peeled and chopped
1 **onion**, chopped finely
100g **cheddar**, grated
1 **egg**
60g **breadcrumbs**
a large handful of **fresh parsley**, chopped
plain flour, for dusting
vegetable or **groundnut oil**
salt and **freshly ground black pepper**

JOHN AND BROTHER TONY, TRUNKS, BUCKETS AND SPADES, C.1960

1. First boil the potatoes – don't let them get so boiled that they fall apart, or they'll be too wet. Then drain and mash them dry.

2. Fry the onion in a little butter until it's soft and translucent. Set aside.

3. While the mashed potatoes are still warm, mix in the cheese, egg, breadcrumbs, cooked onion and parsley, and season well with salt and pepper. Set aside to cool.

4. Now form the cakes: in your hands, shape the cakes into large croquettes, about 5cm long and 2cm in diameter, then dust them in the flour. Heat 2 tablespoons of oil in a clean frying pan, and fry the first batch of potato cakes on both sides until crispy and golden brown. You will find that they take up some of the oil as they fry, so you will probably need to add more as you work your way through the cooking. It's not an exact science. Just keep an eye on things, and keep adding oil between batches as you see fit. And make sure the oil's hot enough before you add the next few cakes. Serve, piping hot.

Frank Plunkett's Bubble & Squeak

SERVES: DEPENDS ON YOUR LEFTOVERS • PREPARATION TIME: 8 MINUTES • COOKING TIME: 25 MINUTES

Kay says: 'Dad's bubble and squeak is a family tradition. And it's only with much cajoling that I've managed to pry his closely guarded recipe away from him. Well, I say much cajoling. All it took was a Christmas jumper and a hug (thanks, Dad). He's been making it in one form or another since he was twelve years old. With both his mum and dad at work, it was often his turn to make the dinner, and this was a Monday night regular, using up the leftovers from their Sunday roast.'

leftover potatoes, and any other **leftover vegetables** from Christmas dinner, enough to make a 2cm layer in your biggest frying pan
1 teaspoon **chicken stock powder**
1 teaspoon **anchovy sauce** (optional)
1 teaspoon **light soy sauce**
1 teaspoon **Worcestershire sauce**
1 teaspoon **oyster sauce**
50g **butter**
salt and **freshly ground black pepper**

FRANK PLUNKETT, EGYPT, 1952

1. Make sure all your vegetables and potatoes are at room temperature. Chop them all up – not too finely – and put them into a bowl with the stock powder and the sauces. Mix everything together well. (You could use a masher, but you want some texture.)

2. Melt the butter in a nice wide frying pan – the wider the better. When the butter's foamy and hot, pop all the vegetables into the pan and start moving them around, breaking them up, keeping things going on a medium flame. You want the outside of the bubble and squeak to crisp up and the inside to heat through properly. The best way to do it is to keep it moving around to cook everything, then to leave it on the heat to crisp up. Serve piping hot on its own or topped with a fried egg.

My dad, Frank Plunkett, has led an extraordinary life. Born just off the Old Kent Road, he's a Londoner through and through. An evacuee during the war, he served as a paratrooper in Suez, before joining Ford at Dagenham after demob. After becoming an overseas Ford service representative, he left the company to join the Ford dealership in Thailand, and over the years he worked his way up to chairman of the company until he retired. Every so often, when I was a girl, I'd be lucky enough to accompany him up-country, and he knew all the best food stalls from Ayutthaya to Yasothorn. So thanks, Dad, for a brilliant food education!

IF YOU'RE GOING TO CATCH ANYTHING, CATCH FISH.

10 THINGS YOU SHOULD KNOW HOW TO COOK BEFORE YOU LEAVE HOME

The thing about leaving home is that you suddenly realize just how expensive takeaways are. So we've pulled together a short collection of recipes to keep you going.

Mum's Roast Chicken

AND HOW TO USE THE LEFTOVERS

SERVES: DEPENDS ON YOUR LEFTOVERS. THE CHICKEN ON ITS OWN WILL FEED 4
PREPARATION TIME: 10 MINUTES • COOKING TIME: 1 HOUR 30 MINUTES • ✓ ♥ WF GF DF

Roast chicken is one of those dishes that everyone loves because it's a taste of home. Kay says: 'My mum always used to make it whenever I came home to Thailand from school. And even now, it's the first meal I cook when I have been away.'

> 1 x 1.5kg **chicken**
> 1 small **onion**, peeled
> a small bunch of **fresh herbs**
> 1 **lemon**, left whole, but stabbed a few times with a sharp knife
> 1 tablespoon **olive oil**
> **salt** and **freshly ground black pepper**

1. Heat the oven to 200°C/400°F/gas mark 6.

2. Pat the chicken dry and season the cavity with salt and pepper. Then shove in the onion, herbs and lemon. Pour the oil over the top of the chicken, then season with salt and pepper.

3. If you like, you can now sprinkle the chicken with the dried herb or spice of your choice – sometimes we throw on a pinch of thyme, oregano, za'atar, Kay's Cajun Magic (see page 57) – something to give it a little extra zing. (Sometimes, Kay adds a knob of butter into the creases between the thighs and the body of the bird.)

4. Then slam it in the oven until it's done – about 1 hour 30 minutes in all – basting every 20 minutes or so.

5. Since a chicken must be properly cooked through, the best test is simply to stab it with a knife in the thickest part of the thigh and make sure the juices run clear. If they don't, just pop it back in the oven for another 5 minutes or so.

TIPS

* You can't beat a jug of gravy with a good roast chicken. We tend to skim off the excess fat in the roasting tray, then bung in about 250ml of wine or chicken stock and bubble it up, scraping up all the yummy sticky roasty bits. Our design guru Anita's mum used to stir in a Boursin cheese too.

THE DAY AFTER
Homemade Chicken Stock

1. Strip the chicken meat off the bones. Then put the carcass into a big pan with 1 roughly chopped **onion**, 1 roughly chopped **carrot**, a **bay leaf**, a few **peppercorns** and a pinch of **salt**.

2. Cover with water, bring to the boil, then simmer for an hour to an hour and a half.

3. Leave to cool, then strain through a sieve for a simple, clean chicken stock you can use for soup on pages 34–9 or any of the risotti on pages 102–5.

CHEAP CHEAP

Quick Cheap Student's Risotto
(FOR 1)

1. Finely chop a small **onion**.

2. Bring your **homemade chicken stock** (see page 265) to a simmer on the back of the stove.

3. Melt 1 tablespoon of **olive oil** in a small pan and cook the onion until soft.

4. Add 100g of **arborio rice** and make your risotto following the basic method on page 103.

5. Finish the dish with **salt**, **pepper**, the zest of ½ **lemon** zest, the chopped leaves from a sprig of **fresh rosemary**, and a good grating of **Parmesan**.

Chicken Curry
(FOR 2 IF NOT 4)

1. In a frying pan, soften a finely chopped **onion** in 1 tablespoon of **vegetable oil** for about 3 minutes.

2. Add 2 chopped cloves of **garlic** and cook for 1 minute or so. Add 1 tablespoon of the **curry powder** of your choice, and cook it in the oil and garlic until fragrant.

3. Add 300–400g of the **chicken**, toss it through the onions and add 350ml **stock**.

4. Now add some **tomatoes** (canned if you like), maybe some **okra** or some **potatoes**. Simmer for 20 minutes, or until the sauce has reduced.

5. If you have it, add a little **coconut milk**. Stir it through the sauce. Then bung in a handful of chopped **fresh coriander** and serve with **rice**.

Chicken Pot Pie
(FOR 2–4)

1. Chop an **onion**, a **carrot** and a stick of **celery** and soften them in 1–2 tablespoons of **olive oil** for about 5 minutes or so.

2. Add 300g **chicken**, some sliced **potatoes** (leftover ones are fine), some **dried herbs** – maybe thyme and oregano, 100g **frozen peas** and 400ml **stock** (including any **leftover gravy**). Mix it all up together and season with **salt** and **pepper**.

3. Now you can either cook it right now or leave it to cool and cook it later. Either way, when you're ready to cook it, pop it all into a large ovenproof dish. Then brush the rim of the dish with some **beaten egg**.

4. Roll out some **shortcrust pastry** (shop bought is fine) and place it over the top. Pinch the pastry rim to seal. Brush the top with the rest of the egg. Cut a couple of holes in the top and bake it in a preheated oven, 200°C/400°F/gas mark 6, for 35 minutes, or until golden brown on top. Serve piping hot.

Quick Cornerstore Curry

SERVES 2-4 • PREPARATION TIME: 10 MINUTES • COOKING TIME: 30 MINUTES • ✓ ♥ WF GF DF

There's almost always a bag of spinach or chard lurking in the local late-night shop. Maybe some spuds or sweet potatoes. Some shallots and some garlic, too. A tin of chickpeas. Or lentils. Or black beans. Or kidney beans. Or anything you find in your cupboards.

1 tablespoon **vegetable oil**
2 **shallots** or **small onions**, chopped
2 cloves of **garlic**, chopped
1 teaspoon **ground cumin**
1 teaspoon **ground coriander**
4 **cardamom pods**, lightly crushed
250ml **vegetable stock**
1 teaspoon **chilli powder**
1 large **potato/sweet potato**, chopped
2 x 400g **tins of pulses/beans**, drained and rinsed
400g **spinach** or **chard**, washed and roughly torn, any tough stalks removed
a handful of **fresh coriander**, chopped
salt and **freshly ground black pepper**

1. Heat the oil in a frying pan over a medium heat, and cook the shallots or onions until they're soft and translucent. Add the garlic, cumin, coriander and cardamom, and cook until fragrant, a minute or two. Then add the stock.

2. Bring to a simmer, add the chilli powder, potato and pulses, and cook over a low heat until the potato's soft.

3. Now add the spinach or chard and let it wilt into the curry. Season with salt and pepper. Serve with rice, and garnish with the chopped coriander.

John's Cheat's Chicken

SERVES 2–4 • PREPARATION TIME: 10 MINUTES • COOKING TIME: 30 MINUTES • ✓ ♥ WF GF DF

This isn't chicken for people who are unfaithful. Rather, it is chicken that is far lovelier than the effort that goes into it. Efficient. Good use of natural and human resources. It goes like this:

1. Put some **olive oil** in a frying pan. Add a chopped **onion**. Or two. Add a few shakes of **curry powder**.

2. Fry 2 **chicken thighs** per person in the sizzling oil and onion. Add a bit more oil or curry powder if you think it is a good idea. Season with **salt** and **freshly ground black pepper**. Ta-daaaaa.

TIPS

* Try adding sultanas. Or flaked almonds. Or minty yoghurt. Any other top tips? Write to me. Or add them at www. leonrestaurants.co.uk

Bumper Beef Stew with Dumplings

SERVES 8 • PREPARATION TIME: 30 MINUTES • COOKING TIME: 3 HOURS 20 MINUTES

A rich, warming stew that goes a long way. Feel free to replace the plain flour with buckwheat flour – the dumplings will be a little chewier, but in a good way.

1–2 tablespoons **plain flour**
1kg **stewing beef**, cubed
4 tablespoons **olive oil**
1 large **onion**, chopped
3 **carrots**, chunkily sliced
1–2 cloves of **garlic**, chopped
a small handful of **fresh parsley**
a few sprigs of **fresh thyme**
2 **bay leave**
several good dashes of
   Worcestershire sauce

2–3 teaspoons **tomato purée**
2 **beef stock cubes**
salt and **freshly ground black pepper**

For the dumplings:
4 tablespoons **suet**
8 tablespoons **plain** or **buckwheat flour**
2 teaspoon **dried thyme** or **marjoram**
salt and **freshly ground black pepper**

1. Heat the oven to 200°C/400°F/gas mark 6.

2. Put the flour into a large freezer bag and season it with salt and pepper. Add the stewing beef, hold the bag closed, and shake until the meat is well coated. Remove it from the bag, shaking off any excess flour, and set aside.

3. Put 1 tablespoon of the oil into a frying pan over a medium heat. Add the onion and soften until it's translucent, about 5 minutes or so. While it's cooking, put the carrots, garlic, herbs, Worcestershire sauce and tomato purée into a large casserole, and crumble in the stock cubes. When the onions are done, add them.

4. Turn up the heat under the frying pan and add 2 more tablespoons of oil. When it's hot, brown the floured pieces of meat in batches – don't overcrowd the pan – until they're nicely caramelized, then add them to the casserole.

5. Keep the frying pan on the heat and pour in a small glass of water. Bubble it up, scraping up the cooking residues on the bottom of the pan, then pour it all into the casserole. Stir all the ingredients together, add enough water to just cover the meat. Put the lid on and pop it into the oven for 30 minutes.

6. Turn the oven down to 180°C/350°F/gas mark 4, and leave it for a further 2 hours.

7. When the 2 hours are up, it's time to make the dumplings. In a dry bowl, mix the flour and suet together with the herbs, a good pinch of salt and plenty of pepper. Gradually add a little water and mix until you have a sticky dough. Too little water, and the flour won't combine with the suet; too much, and it will be too wet. You're looking for a claggy mess.

8. Take out the stew, turn the oven back up to 200°C/400°F/gas mark 6, then divide the dumpling dough into 8 even chunks with a spoon, and add them to the casserole. Baste them with the gravy, then put the casserole back into the oven, uncovered, for another 35 minutes. Serve with mashed potatoes and green vegetables.

Tagliatelle Aglio, Olio e Peperoncino

SERVES 2 • PREPARATION TIME: 5 MINUTES • COOKING TIME: 10-12 MINUTES

This is one of the world's simplest dishes to make, and one of the most satisfying, too.

200g **tagliatelle**
2 tablespoons **olive oil**
1–2 cloves of **garlic**, peeled and sliced
1 teaspoon **dried chilli flakes** or
  1 **fresh red chilli**, sliced
1 tablespoon **fresh flat-leaf parsley**,
  finely chopped (optional)
salt and **freshly ground black pepper**
freshly grated **Parmesan**, to taste

1. Bring a large pan of salted water to a rolling boil and cook the pasta according to the packet instructions.

2. Put the olive oil into a heavy-based sauté pan over a low–medium heat and add the garlic and the chilli. Cook until the garlic turns a deep golden brown.

3. When the pasta's done, use a pair of tongs to scoop it into the garlic, chilli and oil. You want a little residual cooking water to go with it. Stir everything together, season with salt, pepper and the parsley, if using, and serve at once with a good sprinkling of freshly grated Parmesan.

TIPS

* You can make this with most of the longer pastas, spaghetti, linguine, capellini… we wouldn't go for one that's much fatter than tagliatelle, and as for pasta shapes, well, there really isn't enough sauce here to get deliciously caught in their crenellations, so what's the point?

Simple Thai Pad Pak Ruam Mit

WITH JASMINE RICE

SERVES 2 • PREPARATION TIME: 10 MINUTES • COOKING TIME: 10 MINUTES • ✓ ♥ WF GF DF V

Pad pak ruam mit means stir-fried mixed vegetables. This is a really easy way to serve some of your five a day.

> 1 tablespoon **vegetable oil**
> 2–4 cloves of **garlic**, finely chopped, depending on size
>   (and how much you like garlic)
> 100g **baby corn**, cut in half
> 100g **mangetout** or **sugarsnap peas**
> 1 tablespoon **nam pla** (fish sauce)
> 1 teaspoon **sugar**
> 1 head of **pak choi**, sliced (about 150g in total)

1. Heat the oil in a wok. Add the garlic and cook until fragrant, but don't let it colour. Add the baby corn, then, after a moment, the peas.

2. Add a dash of water for the steam, then the *nam pla* and sugar. After a couple of minutes, add the pak choi, and another tiny dash of water if you like. Keep stir-frying until the vegetables are cooked, about another 3 minutes. Serve piping hot, with jasmine rice (see below).

TIPS

* As a general rule, Thai mixed vegetable stir-fries don't feature chilli. If you'd like to punch up the heat, add 1 sliced bird's-eye chilli at the same time as the garlic.

Jasmine Rice

SERVES 2 • PREPARATION TIME: 2 MINUTES • COOKING TIME: 12–15 MINUTES • WF GF V

140g **jasmine rice**
170ml **cold water**

1. Rinse the rice: pop it into a sieve and splash it under the cold tap, swishing it about with your hands until some of the starch has run off. Rinse until the water runs clear.

2. Put the rice and the water into a pan or casserole that has a tight-fitting lid. Place on the heat and bring to the boil. As soon as it's boiling pop the lid on, and turn the heat right down to a simmer. Cook for about 8–12 minutes.

3. When the time's up, taste it. If it's not quite cooked, add a dash more water and cook for a little longer. You should be able to smell when it's done – its wonderful perfume fills the kitchen.

4. Turn off the heat and let it rest for at least 5–10 minutes, so that each individual grain of rice can puff up to its perfect glory. It will happily sit and keep warm for up to 30 minutes.

Four Cheat's Desserts

Affogato Arabesque

SERVES 4 • PREPARATION TIME: 10 MINUTES • COOKING TIME: NONE • ♥ WF GF V

A Lebanese twist on an Italian classic.

1. Make your fresh coffee in your usual way, adding 2 cracked-open cardamom pods and their seeds to the grounds (we find one of those Italian, hob-top espresso pots the best for this).

2. Place a scoop of a good vanilla ice cream into each of 4 bowls. Serve with a shot of espresso on the side. Then pour the espresso over the ice cream, and enjoy!

Cheat's Chocolate Trifle

SERVES 4 • PREPARATION TIME: 5 MINUTES • COOKING TIME: NONE

2–4 **Flatplanet Brownies** (see page 80)
1 shot of **espresso**
1–2 shots of **rum** (optional)
1 batch of **Fred's Chocolate Mousse** (see opposite)
300ml **double cream**, whipped
20g **dark chocolate**, grated

1. Lay the brownies in the bottom of a serving dish and pour over the coffee (and the rum, if you're using it). Smooth the chocolate mousse over the top of the brownies.

2. Top with the whipped cream and sprinkle with the grated chocolate. If you're feeling *really* naughty, you could also whip some rum into the cream!

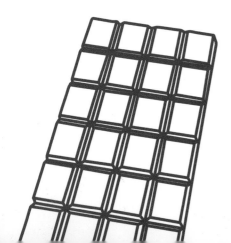

TIPS

* Get retro and channel the 70s by sprinkling some bottled morello cherries between the cake and the mousse. And don't forget to balance one of the cherries artfully on top of the cream for a groovy Black Forest trifle. Serve wearing a medallion.

Fred's Chocolate Mousse

SERVES 4 • PREPARATION TIME: 25 MINUTES PLUS CHILLING • COOKING TIME: NONE • V

Fred says: 'I first learnt to make a chocolate mousse from my sister's copy of the *My Learn to Cook Book* which featured a red cat and a blue dog guiding you through some simple recipes. Honestly, I think my chocolate mousse recipe has barely changed over the years, though it's probably included progressively less sugar.'

> 75g **dark chocolate**, with at least 70% cocoa solids
> 2 **eggs**
> 2 teaspoons **caster sugar**
> 70ml **double cream** (optional)

1. Bring a pan of water to the boil. To melt the chocolate, break it up, put it into a large bowl and sit it on top of the pan, making sure the bottom of the bowl does not touch the boiling water.

2. While the chocolate is melting, separate the eggs into two bowls. Whisk the whites into stiff peaks and fold in the sugar. Gently beat the egg yolks in the separate bowl.

3. When the chocolate has melted, take off the heat and mix the egg yolks into it and add the cream, if using. Fold the egg whites gently into the chocolate mixture, taking care not to knock too much of the air out of them – the lighter your touch, the lighter the mousse. Pour into individual ramekins, and leave to set in the fridge for at least an hour.

FRED, FAWLEY, 1975

TIPS

* If you don't like your chocolate mousse too sweet, you can halve the amount of sugar.
* This is a great dessert to make up to a day before you want to serve it.

Henry's Salted Caramel Bananas

SERVES 4 • PREPARATION TIME: 1 MINUTE • COOKING TIME: 15 MINUTES • WF GF V

> 4 **bananas**, peeled
> 25g **butter**
> 100g **caster sugar**
> a good pinch of **sea salt**
> 25ml **brandy** (optional)

1. Slice the bananas in half lengthways. Heat the butter in a pan and fry the bananas until they're a little brown.

2. Sprinkle on the caster sugar and the sea salt, and cook until the caster sugar has caramelized. Then, if you like, flame it with the brandy (not necessary, but fun).

3. Serve with vanilla ice cream.

DANCE WITH ME

YESTERDAY

This is a little bonus section. It is a collection of memories. Things we cooked on our first dates.

Technicolour memories from our childhood. The wisdom of grandmas. And recipes from our extended Leon families and friends.

Please share your memories with us at www.leonrestaurants.co.uk

MEMORY LANE

We could get all Proust about this, and bang on about madeleines. But let's face it, he was a genius nineteenth-century French novelist, and we're just food writers. Suffice to say that the relationship between food and memory is well known. Something to do with the relationship between the olfactory bulb and the amygdala, where the brain processes emotion. So they say. I would argue it's a little less cerebral and a lot more emotional.

So here we have some recipes and memories from both Kay and John, as well as from some of the rest of our Leon family.

Marion's Bacon & Egg Pie

SERVES 4 • PREPARATION TIME: 40 MINUTES • COOKING TIME: 50 MINUTES • ✓

John says: 'Between the ages of one and late teens, I spent most spring and summer weekends on and in the marshes of the Thames estuary, in a place called Tollesbury, near Maldon. It wasn't really a gourmet experience. In fact, I seem to remember that I ate a lot of crisps, and when not drinking coke I drank a synthesized non-alcoholic version of rum and coke … for kids. And what's not to like about scampi or chicken in a basket? In *Leon Book 2: Naturally Fast Food* I included my Mum Marion's Scotch egg recipe, which she would make in London and which we would eat once we'd arrived. This recipe is for the bacon and egg pie we used to eat with it. You know, if I had to tell you which I enjoyed more, I am not sure I could. I hope you enjoy it, too.'

110g **unsmoked streaky bacon**
3 **eggs**
275ml **single cream**
75g **Gruyère cheese**
freshly grated **nutmeg**
salt and **freshly ground black pepper**

For the pastry:
175g **plain flour**, plus extra for dusting
a pinch of **salt**
50g firm **butter**, cut into 1cm pieces
50g **lard**, cut into 1cm pieces

1. First make the pastry: Sift the flour and salt into a mixing bowl. Add the butter and lard, and rub lightly into the flour with the tips of the fingers until the mixture resembles breadcrumbs. Add enough cold water to bind the mixture and make a firm dough, handling the pastry as little as possible.

2. Place the dough on a lightly floured board and gather it into a ball. Wrap the dough in a polythene bag and put into the fridge for about 30 minutes.

3. Now heat the oven to 200°C/400°F/gas mark 6.

4. Sprinkle a small amount of flour on the board and roll the pastry as lightly as possible, lifting the rolling pin between strokes. Line a 20cm flan ring with a removable base (fluted if possible) with the thinly rolled pastry, pressing it well into the base of the flan ring. Trim the edges and prick the base with a fork. Line the base with greaseproof paper and put baking beans on top.

5. Bake in the oven for 10 minutes, then remove the beans and allow the pastry to cool. Pre-cooking the pastry stops it becoming soggy when the filling is added.

6. To make the filling, cut the bacon into 2cm strips and cook them in a non-stick frying pan until the fat starts to run, then place them in the pie case.

7. Beat the eggs lightly, stir in the cream, cheese and seasonings, and pour over the bacon in the flan. Immediately transfer the pie to the oven and cook for 30–40 minutes. When cooked, the bacon and egg pie should be golden brown.

TIPS

* You can leave out the bacon if you prefer.
* Add a good pinch of dry mustard (¼ teaspoon) to the mixture and omit the grated nutmeg.

Betty's Mah Jong Lunches

Who knows what Mah Jong is? Hands up? It's a Chinese game. And my mum and her gang played it back in the day. No, I don't know how to play it. I just remember the laughter, the clickety-clack of the Mah Jong tiles as they tumbled on the green baize card table, the shouts of 'NORTH WIND; SOUTH WIND,' the 'serious' matchstick gambling, and the smell of compact powder and waxy rose-scented lipsticks.

Most of all I remember the food. The ladies would sometimes have sandwiches. Cakes always. Noodle soups from time to time. But the one dish that trumped them all was Som Tam. Here's my version of Mum's favourite.

KAY

Som Tam Thai

SERVES 1–2 • PREPARATION TIME: 20 MINUTES • COOKING TIME: NONE • WF GF DF

This is pretty much the dish Mum used to love – spicy, tart and refreshing.

1 **bird's-eye chilli**
1 tablespoon **tiny dried shrimp**
1 **clove of garlic**
1 **large tomato**, sliced
a small handful of **green beans**, chopped
the juice of 1 **lime**
1 tablespoon **palm sugar**
1 tablespoon **nam pla** (fish sauce)
2 large handfuls of **grated green papaya**
a handful of **toasted peanuts**, to serve

1. Pound the bird's-eye chilli in a pestle and mortar. Add the dried shrimp and pound again. Then add the garlic and pound it just enough to break it open and release its oils – we're not making a paste here.

2. Put the tomato and the green beans in a bowl and stir in all the other ingredients, lifting and pushing back down with a spoon. Add the lime juice, palm sugar and nam pla, stir, then add the green papaya. Mix everything together well, stirring and pounding to bruise the papaya.

3. Taste and adjust for balance, then turn out on to a plate. Top with the peanuts, and serve.

John's Chicken Ce Soir

SERVES 2 • PREPARATION TIME: 10 MINUTES • COOKING TIME: 30 MINUTES • ✓ WF GF

When Katie and I were first dating, I announced to her that I was going to cook. Now, I am from the 1980s. Well, from the 70s too, but I grew up with two types of food. Traditional shepherd's pie, and liver and bacon on the one hand, and packaged goods like Smash on the other: dry goods that we could stash away when sailing across to Holland. So I really, really thought that buying a jar of Chicken Tonight and putting it on to some grilled chicken constituted cooking. I turned up at Katie's flat in Notting Hill one evening and when I whipped it out (that jar of mushroom and cream sauce), I sensed a little surprise. I am good with body language. Especially when people are laughing and pointing. So here it is, my Chicken Ce Soir, my attempt to make two things:

(1) An authentic version of that night's dinner.

(2) Amends.

1 tablespoon **olive oil**
2 **chicken breasts**, cut into chunks
20g **butter**
1 **clove** of **garlic**, crushed
150g **chestnut mushrooms**, trimmed and sliced
125ml **white wine**
150ml **double cream**
1 tablespoon **fresh parsley**, finely chopped
salt and **freshly ground black pepper**

1. Heat the oil in a heavy-based sauté pan and fry the chicken pieces until they're golden and cooked through. Remove from the pan and set aside.

2. Now melt the butter in the pan and when it starts to foam, add the garlic. Cook, stirring for a couple of minutes, until you can really smell it, then add the mushrooms. Sauté for about 5 minutes, until you've cooked out their moisture, then remove them from the pan and set aside.

3. Now deglaze the pan with the wine, bubbling it hard and scraping up any cooking bits from the bottom of the pan with a wooden spoon. Then add the cream, stirring it into the sauce, and let bubble and thicken.

KATIE AND JOHN, EARLY DAYS 1995

284

Leon's Poker Night Chilli

SERVES 4 • PREPARATION TIME: 15 MINUTES • COOKING TIME: 10-15 MINUTES • ✓

Leon is John's dad. John's dad is Leon. We thought it was a nice name for our good fast food chain. And here we are. In the 1970s, Leon played poker. Every Monday evening. Well, for most of the night. Each week, a different wife would have the delight of catering for their husband's friends. (In a nice way.) Smoke would fill the house. And someone would walk away richer. But a little tired for work. Mostly the food would consist of sandwiches and pies, except on so-called 'gala nights', when there was a more 'exotic' offering like chilli con carne. This is how it went …

2 tablespoons **vegetable oil**
1 **onion**, finely chopped
1 clove of **garlic**, finely chopped
500g **minced beef**
½ a **beef stock cube**
125ml **water**
1 tablespoon **tomato purée**
1 x 400g **tin of tomatoes**
1 x 400g **tin of red kidney beans**, drained and rinsed
2 teaspoons **dried oregano**
1 teaspoon **ground cumin**
½ teaspoon **ground cinnamon**
½–1 teaspoon **chilli powder**, to taste
salt and **freshly ground black pepper**

1. Heat the oil in a large saucepan over a medium heat, and gently fry the onion until it's soft and translucent.

2. Add the garlic and cook until fragrant, just for a couple of minutes, then add the minced beef. Brown the meat thoroughly.

3. Crumble in the stock cube and add the water. Stir everything together well, bubbling it all up, then add the tomatoes, tomato purée the beans, and the herbs and spices.

4. Season with salt and pepper, then simmer over a low heat for 30–40 minutes, until it has reduced to a thick, fragrant, spicy chilli.

5. For that final 70s touch, serve with rice or crackers and a good grating of Cheddar cheese.

LEON, EASTERN MEDITERRANEAN, 1957

Kay's Coq au Vin

SERVES 4-6 • PREPARATION TIME: 15 MINUTES • COOKING TIME: 2 HOURS • ✓

This is the first meal that Fred cooked for me (or wooed me with, depending on how you look at it) on our second date. (The first one consisting mainly of martinis…) Suffice to say, I rushed back for a third … and we have been fighting over kitchen counter space ever since.

50g **unsalted butter**
a dash of **olive oil**
100g **bacon lardons**
1 small **onion**, chopped
1 x 1.5kg **chicken**, jointed into 8 pieces
70ml **brandy**
750ml **red wine**
450ml **chicken stock**
a bouquet garni of thyme, bay and parsley
1 tablespoon **tomato purée**
2 **carrots**, chopped
2 **cloves** of **garlic**, finely chopped
250g **pearl onions**, peeled
250g **mushrooms**, trimmed
25g **flour**
salt and **freshly ground black pepper**

1. Heat the oven to 200°C/400°F/gas mark 6.

2. In a heavy-based frying pan, melt 25g of the butter and a little olive oil (to stop it burning). Add the bacon and onion and fry until lightly browned. Scoop them out and transfer to a heavy casserole.

3. Add the chicken pieces to the pan and brown thoroughly on all sides, in batches, removing them to a separate plate as you go. You may need to add a little more oil from time to time.

4. When all the chicken pieces have been browned, return them to the pan. (Now for the fun bit!) Pour in the brandy and, standing at arm's reach, set fire to the lip of the pan. Gently shake the pan back and forth until the flames subside. Then transfer the chicken to the casserole.

5. You should be left with a rich brown juice in the frying pan. Add about a glass of the red wine. Bubble it up fiercely as you scrape up the cooking residues from the pan, and reduce it by at least half. Add the stock, stirring it together with the reduced wine over the heat, then pour all of this into the casserole.

6. Now add the herbs, salt and pepper, tomato purée, carrots and garlic to the casserole, mix it all together, and pour in enough red wine to just cover the chicken. Cover the casserole and place in the oven for 30 minutes, then turn down the temperature to about 160°C/325°F/gas mark 3, and cook for another hour or so.

7. While the chicken is cooking, sauté first the pearl onions and then the mushrooms in about a tablespoon of olive oil. The mushrooms will throw quite a lot of liquid in the pan: make sure you cook all of it out. Set the onions and mushrooms aside separately when they're done.

8. When the chicken is ready remove it from the sauce and keep warm on the side. Skim off any excess fat on the surface. Check the seasoning, and if needed, add a little more salt and pepper.

9. Boil the sauce rapidly to reduce by at least a quarter. Then remove the bay leaf.

10. While the sauce is reducing, blend the remaining 25g of butter with the flour to make a smooth paste (this is called a *beurre manié*). When you've reduced the sauce, vigorously whisk the paste into it to thicken it. Once the paste is all absorbed, you should end up with a sauce thick enough to coat a spoon lightly. Now return the chicken to the sauce with the onions and mushrooms and serve.

FRED AND KAY, GOZO, 2000

TIPS

* It's best to use a whole chicken when you make this because it adds a greater depth of flavour (keep the spine, and shove that in too). But if you're in a hurry, a couple of packs of chicken thighs will work just as well.

* You can leave out the onion and the mushroom step, but don't miss out the *beurre manié.* – it's a vital part of the sauce's silky mouth-feel, and it's worth taking a little time over.

Mary's Victorian Diable

SERVES 4 • PREPARATION TIME: 10 MINUTES • COOKING TIME: 40 MINUTES • ✓ ♥

Anita is our Leon design guru. She makes everything look good. She says: 'My mum, Mary, was a great cook and was always trying out new recipes. One staple was a very posh sounding "Victorian Diable", which my brother, sister and I giggled at initially. Then it just became part of our vocabulary. Mum would often make this on a Monday using the leftovers from the Sunday roast, mostly lamb or beef. I particularly remember the capers, as we three would leave them on our plates at the end.

'Now I'm a mother, I have to bite my tongue when my kids leave the "green bits or the black bits" that they don't want. They'll come round, eventually.'

This is based on a *Reader's Digest* recipe from the 1970s.

4 tablespoons **gluten-free breadcrumbs**
1 tablespoon **olive oil**
2 **onions**, finely chopped
1 **clove** of **garlic**, crushed
1 tablespoon **gram flour**
1 tablespoon **Dijon mustard**
1 tablespoon **white wine vinegar**
220ml **beef stock**
2 level teaspoons **soft brown sugar**
½ teaspoon **Worcestershire sauce**
1 teaspoon chopped **capers**
1 **bay leaf**
8–10 slices **cooked meat** or **poultry**
25g **unsalted butter**, melted,
    plus a little extra to toast the breadcrumbs
salt and **freshly ground black pepper**

MARY WITH STEPHEN, LISA AND ANITA, MALLORCA, 1974

1. Melt a little butter in a heavy-based saucepan. Pop in the breadcrumbs and stir, moving the crumbs around until golden and crunchy. Remove with a slotted spoon and set aside on a plate lined with kitchen paper.

2. Heat the oil in a large frying pan over a medium heat, and cook the onions and garlic until golden brown.

3. Add the flour and stir to blend. Add the mustard and vinegar and gradually stir in the stock. Bring this sauce to boiling point and stir until thick and smooth. Add the sugar, Worcestershire sauce, capers and bay leaf, and season with salt and pepper. Simmer for 5–10 minutes, stirring frequently.

4. Meanwhile, heat the oven to190°C/375°F/gas mark 5.

5. Put the sliced meat into a buttered ovenproof dish. Pour over the sauce (remove the bay leaf), sprinkle with the breadcrumbs and pour the melted butter over.

6. Bake in the centre of the oven for about 20 minutes, or until golden brown. Serve hot, with buttered rice.

Stella Matthews's Cawl

SERVES 8–10 • PREPARATION TIME: 230 MINUTES • COOKING TIME: 3 HOURS • ✓ WF GF

In Wales, this old recipe is made whenever anybody is coming down with cold or flu symptoms. It banishes them! Or at least lessens them. It's the Welsh echinacea

600g **beef shin**
2 **onions**, peeled and sliced
1.5 litres **water**
1 **small swede**, diced
3 **parsnips**, diced
3 **large carrots**, diced
3 **leeks**, sliced into rings
4 **large potatoes**, quartered
a small handful of **chopped fresh parsley** (optional)
salt and **freshly ground black pepper**

1. Put the beef shin and onions into a large saucepan. Pour over the water, bring it to the boil, then reduce the heat and simmer for about 2 hours, or until the meat is tender.

2. Take off the heat and allow to cool completely. Skim off all the fat from the surface, then shred the meat into small pieces and return it to the saucepan.

3. Add about 500ml of the beef stock to the meat. Then add the swede, parsnips, carrots and leeks. You may need to add a little more water to make sure everything's completely covered. Put back on the heat and cook until the vegetables are nearly done – about 15 minutes, then add the potatoes and cook until they're soft.

4. Serve in bowls, sprinkled with the chopped parsley, with crusty bread and strong Cheddar cheese.

TIPS

* You can buy shin of beef either cubed or in slices on or off the bone. If it's on the bone, make sure you use the marrow!

STELLA AND GRANDPA, ANDREW AND
JONATHAN, SOUTH WALES, 1979

Andrew Matthews-Owen is a classical pianist, a lover of fine food, and a great friend of Katie and John. His mum, Stella, grew up in the town of Llanberis, at the foot of Snowdon. Whenever her kids where coming down with the lurgy, she'd make a batch of this and it always kept illness at bay.

Pam Edwards's Date & Walnut Loaf

MAKES 8–10 SLICES • PREPARATION TIME: 15 MINUTES • COOKING TIME: 30 MINUTES • V

Glenn Edwards says: 'Mum used to bake this loaf for the holidays in the family caravan. Whilst Mum reckons its best the next day, Dad always preferred it buttered, still warm from the oven (in fact, I'm not sure it ever lasted until the next day?).'

225g **self-raising flour**
1 level teaspoon **salt**
1 level teaspoon **bicarbonate of soda**
250ml **milk**
85g **pitted dates**
55g **sultanas**
55g **walnut halves**
2 tablespoons **golden syrup**
85g **demerara sugar**

1. Heat the oven to 190°C/375°F/gas mark 5. Grease and line a 20 x 10cm loaf tin.

2. Sift the flour, salt and bicarbonate of soda into a bowl. Put the remaining ingredients into a food processor and blend for about 20–30 seconds. Stir into the dried ingredients and, when they're well combined, pour the mixture into the prepared loaf tin.

3. Bake in the oven for 30 minutes, then leave to cool on a wire rack.

4. It's at its best served the next day, sliced and buttered … if it lasts that long.

PAM AND GLENN, CUMBRIA, 1980

Glenn is a rather new member of the Leon team. He's very tall. You may find him at one of our shops dressed as a chef. Or 'test-eating'. Pam is his mum. Back in the 70s, she was a beauty queen. We think this cake's a beauty, too.

Crêpes Suzette

SERVES 6–8 • PREPARATION TIME: 15 MINUTES • COOKING TIME: 10-15 MINUTES • V

Surely this is the mother of all 70s dinner party classics. The 70s were when dinner parties were dinner parties. Half dinner, half party. And half Charlie's Angels-esque fashion show, if you can have three halves. Which you could back then. John remembers the tablecloth that used to be laid. The smell of cigarettes and perfume and alcohol. And the guests. Chaz and Jean. Paul and Rosemary. In fact, Rosemary used to make Crêpes Suzette at her dinner parties, too. It was a dish that got around.

110g **plain flour**
2 **eggs**
275ml **milk**
a pinch of **salt**
50g **butter**
the zest of 1 **orange**
1 tablespoon **caster sugar**

For the sauce:
40g **unsalted butter**
the juice of 2 **oranges**
the zest of 1 **orange**
1 tablespoon **caster sugar**
3 tablespoons **Grand Marnier**, plus extra for flambéing

1. Sift the flour into a bowl and make a well in the middle. Add the eggs and a dash of the milk. Whisk in the rest of the milk and the salt until all the lumps are gone. Melt half the butter and add to the mixture along with the orange zest and the sugar. Leave to rest while you sauce the sauce.

2. Meanwhile, to make the sauce, put the unsalted butter into a pan along with the orange juice, orange zest, caster sugar and Grand Marnier and heat gently until the butter has melted. Keep warm while you make the pancakes.

3. Melt the remaining 25g of butter in a frying pan and add a small amount of the batter. Cook for a few minutes on each side. Pile up the pancakes on a warmed serving plate covered with greaseproof paper. This amount of mixture should make 16 thin pancakes.

4. When they're all cooked, cover the folded pancakes with the orange sauce. If you want to flambé the Grand Marnier, warm a small amount of the alcohol in a small pan, light it with a match and pour over the pancakes and the sauce.

To celebrate *Leon Family & Friends* and its whole *raison d'être*, we asked our customers to send in their food memories and favourite family recipes. The winner would have their recipe printed in this book. We were overwhelmed with entries, all of them fantastic. So much so that we've found it hard to choose just one winner. So we've chosen two. Meet Lucie and Ayaz – we're think they're fab.

Chicken à la Grecque

FROM LUCIE FIALOVA

SERVES 4 • PREPARATION TIME: 35 MINUTES • COOKING TIME: 2 HOURS • ✓ ♥ DF

Lucie says: 'my mum's been making this recipe ever since I can remember. I'm not sure where the name comes from, as the combination of mustardy roast potatoes and root vegetables is probably as far as you can get from authentic Greek cuisine. But this dish has always had a special place on our Sunday table – and in our hearts.'

4 **chicken legs portions**
2 tablespoons **herbes de Provence**
2 tablespoons **olive oil**
1kg **potatoes**, peeled and chopped into 2cm pieces
3 tablespoons **Dijon mustard**
3–4 **lemons**
250g **carrots**, peeled and quartered
250g **parsnips**, peeled and quartered
1 small **celeriac**, peeled and cut into 2cm pieces
250g **mushrooms**, sliced
2 large **onions**, quartered
2 **apples**, cored and quartered
4 cloves of **garlic**, sliced
salt and **freshly ground black pepper**

LUCIE AND MARCELA, PRAGUE, 1987

TIPS

* If you can't fit everything in a single layer, put the vegetables on top of the chicken for the initial hour. Then, when you take the foil off, give it a good stir and move the chicken to the top, skin side up.

1. Heat the oven to 200°C/400°F/gas mark 6.

2. Season the chicken pieces well with salt, pepper and herbes de Provence. Heat the olive oil in a frying pan and brown the chicken over a medium heat.

3. While the chicken is in the pan, toss the potatoes in a bowl with the mustard and the juice of 2–3 lemons.

4. When the chicken's nicely browned, place it in a large shallow roasting tin with the potatoes, the rest of the vegetables, the apples and the garlic. (Lucie says: 'My mum has one that doubles as an oven shelf, if you've got one of those you're golden.') You want just a single layer of ingredients in the pan.

5. Squeeze the juice of the remaining lemon over everything and season with salt and pepper. Cover tightly with foil and bake in the oven for about an hour, until the potatoes are tender Remove the foil, and cook for a further 30 minutes or so until the chicken skin is crispy and the vegetables are sticky, soft and golden.

Nanabhai's Kulfi

FROM AYAZ HOSSAIN

MAKES 18–20 SMALL KULFI MOULDS • PREPARATION TIME: 10 MINUTES • COOKING TIME: 20 MINUTES • WF V

Ayaz says: 'I am a thirty-two-year-old British Indian Muslim who grew up in the sunny Lancashire Pennines. From ages four to eighteen, my mother and father would take my sister and me to India, more precisely Kolkata, more precisely the black hole of. Having been dragged from our home to the dirt, noise and over-populated former outreach of the British Empire which was actually its capital for over 100 years, my grandfather (or as we say Nanabhai) would attempt to cheer us up with his creation of "ice cream". It would take him the best part of the day, the excitement of a cold treat tantalized by frequent power cuts and water shortages that would mean freezing the end product became quite a challenge.

'Anyway, both my sister and I have now eaten kulfi at various restaurants but none bring back those memories of seeing my grandfather in his vest stirring away in the heat quite like the recipe below. One spoonful of this and I'm back in West Bengal. These days my mother (Nanni Ammi) has modified the recipe for the current generation of grandchildren, and is now a firm family favourite.'

a good pinch of **saffron**
1 litre **whole milk**
2 tablespoons **cornflour**
1 x 397g **tin of sweetened condensed milk**
6 **whole green cardamom pods**, finely powdered or the seeds, ground
25g **almonds** or **shelled pistachios**, soaked overnight, peeled and sliced

TIPS

* Ayaz uses his grandfather's stainless steel kulfi moulds. If you don't have any, you can use paper cups, half-filled, or small yogurt pots.

* To speed up the process, you can cool the mixture quickly by placing the pan into a large bowl of cold water.

1. Soak the saffron in a tablespoon of the whole milk and set aside.

2. In a separate small bowl, make a paste with the cornflour and 2 tablespoons of the whole milk.

3. Mix the rest of the milk and the condensed milk together in a pan and bring to the boil, stirring continuously. Reduce the heat and simmer for 10 minutes, stirring all the time.

4. Add the cornflour paste and continue stirring until the mixture thickens.

5. Remove from the heat, but keep stirring and allow to cool slightly.

6. Add the saffron in its milk and mix well. When completely cool, add the powdered cardamom and almonds *or* pistachios. Pour into kulfi moulds and freeze.

AYAZ AND NANABHAI, KOLKATA, 1983

RECIPE INDEX

Gluten free

INDEX

THANK YOU

FROM KAY

John Vincent - for giving me an amazing opportunity and for being a terrific partner in crime • Henry Dimbleby and the LEON team – for allowing me to play in their sandpit • Ottie Ise, for keeping JV on the straight and narrow • Anita – for designing a stunner of a book. King Size. • Georgia – amazing photography and giggles • Abi and Issy – the backbone of the whole Lymers operation • Willis, Arnold & Kimberly. You know why. • Alison Starling, Sybella Stephens, Jonathan Christie and all the fantastic team at Octopus • To my family – Dad, Kim and Nick, Alex and Alastair, The Kintbury Hogges: Gavin, Ann Marie, James and Sarah; Alice and Corinna, Joyce, Bramble and Philip for all being so supportive • My wonderful agent Felicity, and the redoubtable Becky • Jo Wander – TV beckons • Katie and the Vincent girls for allowing us to descend on their domestic idyll and, frankly, to trash the place • Wilcox and Hepburn, kitchen cats • And last but not least, Fred, without whom I couldn't have done any of this.

FROM JOHN

Big thanks to: Katie for being the most fiercely supportive wife a man can get • Natasha and Eleanor for caring very much about their Dad and what he does • Mum and Dad aka Marion and Leon for being positively brilliant • Henry D, a partner who becomes more wise each year, we have something special, so let's keep going day by day • Ottie for being committed beyond comprehension • Dave for great loyalty and friendship • Giancarlo and Katie Caldesi for hosting the kids cooking class with such flair • To all the friends and family I wrote about at the back of book 2 • To Migs and Will (and Wilf) for supporting the photoshoot with your presence. Special thanks to Hutch • To all of my Leon colleagues, past and present • To Brad Blum who is fast becoming a very special friend and collaborator. May your dream for 'Good Food for the Planet' come true • To Vivian and Jacques for support and friendship and patience • Georgia for the photo magic • Anita for designing this book with such grit and determination and character under tough time pressures • And of course to Kay for being formidable and for your love of exclamation marks(!)

CONTRIBUTORS

Many thanks to the following contributors for permission to use the recipes they have contributed to the book: Giancarlo Caldesi: Impasto per la Pizza, Pasta Fresca • Christina Coleman: Rulle Pulse • Katie Derham: Sprout & Caramelized Onion Soup, Tarteflette • Qing Derham: Auntie Qing's Sushi Roll • Henry Dimbleby: Meatballs with Herb Salad, Sunday Lunch • Lucie Fialova: Chicken à La Grecque • Anna Hansen: Pumpkin & Miso Cheesecake • Deb Henley: Chicken Enchiladas Verdes • Alice Hogge: Vegetarian Autumnal Pie • Fred Hogge: Classic Burger, Chocolate Mousse, Joyce Ann's Jamaican Curried Lamb Shanks, The Rude Boi, Ragù alla Toscana, The Wheel of Tomato-Based Pasta Sauce • Ayaz Hossain: Nanabhai's Kulfi • Vince Jung: Margarita • Jenny Linford: Sago Gula Melaka • Anita Mangan: Mary's Victorian Diable • Stella Matthews: Cawl • Rachel McCormack: Tortilla Española • Ralph Monthienvichienchai: Mango Lassi • Justin Ovenden: Mackerel Ceviche • Benny Peverelli: Scotch Eggs • Apple Pickard: Easy Chocolate Birthday Cake • Frank Plunkett: Bubble & Squeak • Kim Pusinelli: Spanish Style Chicken • Phillip Regan of KellyBronze Turkeys: turkey cooking times • Gill Siebert: Halloumi, Spinach & Chorizo Salad • Robert Elliott Smith: Prawn Creole • Susanna Usai: Almond Macaroons • Bryn Williams: Bread Sauce.

SUPPLIERS

Philip Regan at Kelly Turkeys for our amazing Leon Christmas bird; Dodie at The Cool Chilli Company for pure corn tortillas and Mexican magic, Chris Hughes at Parson's Nose Putney for being my super-top butcher who supplied all the meat I needed for this book with inimitable good humour, and Georgie at LDR London PR for the Appleton Estate Rum. Matilda Harrison and Bee Bedford for the generous loan of their lovely props. Thank you all.

THE LEON TEAM

Salvatore Bellavia • Meriem Benouguef • Nawal Boukhemma • Agne Bucmyte • Mara Casolari • Arsenji Cechonin • Justina Ciuksyte • Marc-Alexis Constance • Edes Dutra Torelli • Fabiano Gonilde • Talita Sahai Heshiimu • Francisco Javier Iglesias Mori • Peter Jablonski • Alejandro Garcia Jinorio • Natalia Koc • Egle Ozolaite • Sarah Rees • Lauren Roverts • Salvatore Scarpa • Anastasia Voronina • Olivier Aka-Kadjo • Matthew Alp • Steve Bage • Luch Buckingham • Holly Clare • Lysette Cook • Samuel James Field • Elisabeta Gjovani • Nora Ivette Goboly • Tom Green • Eszter Hajmal • Vadim Ivanov • May Kovacova • Jirina Kralova • Nicholas William Kraus • Robert Lorik • Kristel Maley • Tia Paige Marks • Joshua Martins • Ashley Kathleen Peters • Istvan Szep • Guenzit Reives Arthur Tanoh • Birgit Arumetsa • Bozena Bobowska • Oriana Catino • Simona Cijunskyte • John Paul Corrigan • Nicolle Dawkins • Alexandra Elzbieta Kralewska • Valentina Manea • Anna Miller • Amita Shrestha • Gytis Sirinskas • Jurgita Sirvinskiene • Andrius Venclovas • Maria Trinidad Anca Julian • Bernando Aragao • Pedro Barchin • Michaela Boor • Yok Ming Chung • Rute Cristina Coelho Da Rocha • Kristina Dabkeviciene • Claire Didier • Kimberley Frost • Meritxell Gabarra • Margarita Kvasaite • Yinghua Luo • Florent Magnoux • Carlos Martinez Munecas • Sini Marika Mulari • Elizabeta Pac • Roberta Rimkute • Alvaro Santamaria • Lydia Rachel Turner • Gwendoline Blandine Vinard • Simona Vysniaukaite • Christopher Ali • Matthew Ali • Vadims Belovs • Pawel Bojanowski • Remi Chmieliauskas • Mirela-Ana Hapsa • Vydmante Kalvynaite • Viktor Kanasz • Nicola Kibble • Maciej Marek • Rodrigo Menezes De Carvalho • Evijs Ozols • Anna Robero Carro • Marton Vandlik • Maria Alcolea Fernandez • Nina Amaniampong • Yeray Bautista Armas • Claudinei Da Silva • Anax Gregory Da Silva Jorge Matias • Karolina Driessen • Lucas Drotar • Reda El Guebli • Patricia Ferreira Martins • Ema Claudia Gomez Pinto • Ali Grossi • Thomas Anthony Holden • Anna Kireeva • Katre Aurika Kurosu • Bernardo La PortaDa Silva • Acacio Machado Oliveira • Edvinas Marma • Tamara Morero Ruiz • Julia Nauer • Tran Nguyen Hoang • Nadia O'Mara • Justas Pokvytis • Anu Rego • Renan Rodrigues Lozano • Fernandinho Roberto Santo Veronese • Navina Senivassen • Michal Mikolaj Tobiczyk • Daniel Trevor Benjamin • Ineta Bliudziute • Ursula Bowerman • JulianGomes • Katrina Hassan • Monika Jaworska • Mariana Kastrati • Menlin Kook • Taz Kucuk • Simon Marin Montoya • Hong Thi Ngo • Oxana Popa • Egle Rimaite • Anna Sobczak • Ayanetu Degefa Tollesa • Martyn Trigg • Ruth Zenaida Yuste Alonso • Kayan Ayob • Maija Bika • Alessandro Bonny • Jenna Brehme • Nilton Caboco • Alessia Cardace • Soozi Carter • Fabio De Micheli • Terhi Evakallio • Valentina Fiorio • Dean Leacey • Thomas Malley • Mary Catherine Mannion • Lauryna Massionyte • Emanuele Mazzocca • Rafael Mollfuelleda • James Norris • Nuria Olmedo Nieto • Justy Ovenden • Bernardas Rindokas • Jennifer Karen Shearman • Thiago Turibio Da Silva • Megan Bailey • Nickie Bartsch • Agnieszka Chmieliauskas • Vasilica Cirican • Tom Davies • Henry Dimbleby • Simon Drysdale • Glenn Edwards • Toph Ford • James-Lee French • Steve Superstar Oakley • Ben Oliver • Georgie Sanderson • Tom Ward • Renan Amorin • Pedro Candida • Maria Capuano • Olga Chwilowicz • Davide Dabala • Marta Goszczynska • Annie Elizabeth Grant • Marion Christiane • Jennie Helly • Malgorzata Herda • Marta Klosinska • Saga Levin • Rasa Raskeviciute • Deivid Santos Grigorio • Denszso Zrinszki • KadijaBegum • Zoheir Benalia • Steph Brown • Katrina Bulman • Oliver Thomas Callway • Lukas Cholewinski • Agata Cyminska Thomas • Micheline Essomba • Abdelhadi Fekier • Helen Susan Foan • Liliya Georgieva • Cecilia Julia Amanda Holmgren • Andrew Hyman • Ben Iredale • Zoe Langley-Brown • Tom Lee • Bruno Lupi • Hester Mary Alice • Macdonald Thomas • Robert Arthurt William Machin • Philippe Rui Mesquita • CarolineMikkelsen • Sandra Navaro • Olufunmilola Grace Opeyemi • Clara Magdalena Ostman • Isabela Santos • Francisco Luis Gomes Silva Ramos Barbosa • Kamila Webb • Matthias Abdel-Haiat • Anna Anuscenko • Fred Balbi Amatto • Amy Browne • Charles Casey • Joao Carlos Da Cruz Moreira • Alaric Benjamin Demmer • Natalia Joanna Farnaus • Fayomi Fashanu • Anderson Gomcalves • Kayleigh Goodger • Nerea Hoyos • Osiur Khan • Svetlana Kokotkina • Lacey Lawson • Nicolo Lenzi • Orlan Masilu • Mourad Moukhalis • Olumide Otti Otusajo • Alicja Maria Pawlitko • Mark Prove • Benoit Ratinaud • Dominic Sherington • Nora Szosznyak • Eimear White •

To the memory of my beautiful mum Betty, and to mums everywhere

KAY

To my mum, Marion, who is, I truly believe, the most positive person I will ever meet.
To my dad, Leon, whose principles, honesty and values are steadfast, and an inspiration.
Plus you are very funny. Thank you for all the adventures and laughing.

JOHN

BETTY, JON TIEM, 1962

JOHN AND LEON, 1981

First published in 2012 by Conran Octopus Limited,
a part of Octopus Publishing Group,
Endeavour House, 189 Shaftesbury Avenue,
London WC2H 8JY
www.octopusbooks.co.uk

An Hachette UK Company   www.hachette.co.uk

British Library Cataloguing-in-Publication Data.
A catalogue record for this book is available from
the British Library.

Publisher: Alison Starling

Senior Editor: Sybella Stephens

Project Co-ordinator: Fred Hogge

Design and Art Direction (for Leon): Anita Mangan

Art Director (for Conran Octopus): Jonathan Christie

Illustrations: Anita Mangan

Photography: Georgia Glynn Smith

Production Manager: Katherine Hockley

ISBN 978 1 84091 609 6

Printed in China

A note from the authors…
We have endeavoured to be as accurate as possible in all
the preparation and cooking times listing in the recipes
in this book. However they are an estimate based on our
own timings during recipe testing, and should be taken
as a guide only, not as the literal truth. We have also
tried to source all our food facts carefully, but we are
not scientists. So our food facts and nutrition advice are
not absolute. If you feel you require consultation with a
nutritionist, consult your GP for a recommendation.

DOES THE BULL LOOK GOOD IN THIS?

ABI AND ANITA DOING THEIR BEST DRAWING

THE THREE SISTERS

EEYORE MISSING ELEANOR

ISSY ON THE TABLE

CY WITH A PASTA FACE AT CALDESI'S

ABI GOING IN FOR THE MOULES SHOT

WHERE'S THE DISH?

ISSY GETTING INTO CHARACTER

KAY NOT WASTING THE PROSECCO

UNUSED PROP TRYING TO GET A LOOK IN

OUT ON DAY RELEASE